Healing Ourselves

HEALING OURSELVES

A book to serve as a companion
in time of illness and health

Based on the lectures and teaching of
NABORU MURAMOTO

Edited and supplemented by Michel Abehsera

A SWAN HOUSE BOOK PUBLISHED BY AVON

HEALING OURSELVES is published by Avon Books
in association with Swan House Publishing Company.

AVON BOOKS
A division of
The Hearst Corporation
959 Eighth Avenue
New York, New York 10019

First Avon Printing, September, 1973.
Sixth Printing

AVON TRADEMARK REG. U.S. PAT. OFF. AND
FOREIGN COUNTRIES, REGISTERED TRADEMARK—
MARCA REGISTRADA, HECHO EN U.S.A.

Printed in the U.S.A.

To every mother

father

and child

To all people

of good will

To you reader

life

full of health

and

goodness

CONTENTS

* *

HEALING OURSELVES *was produced thanks to the joint effort of Robert Jones, who wrote down Muramoto's lectures; Armand Abehsera, who sifted out errors in the notes; Michael Tilles, who contributed to the editing and arranging of the content; Susan Hatsell, our editor, who corrected the text and made the manuscript clear; Michael Muchnik, our exceptional illustrator, who gave of his time and skill to make this book as practical as it is beautiful; and Vail-Ballou Press, our diligent printer in Binghamton, with special thanks to George Mueller for planning the typography.*

* *

HOW THIS BOOK WAS BORN

IT WAS NECESSARY that a book of this kind be written about Oriental medicine. Such a project required a genuine expert with vast practical experience, not a "tourist" who would travel to Japan or China, collect some concepts and data, and incorporate them into a book. We took our time—two years—until the right man presented himself.

Naboru Muramoto has been studying Oriental medicine for nearly thirty years. From personal experience we knew him to be skilled at both practicing and teaching it. When he arrived on the West Coast to speak there, we invited him to come to Binghamton to give a series of lectures. He accepted, and a month later he was here.

For four weeks he talked every morning to a steady crowd. Every word he said was written down. Each afternoon one or two editors studied with him privately to clarify each point and give it its proper place in the total perspective. All his answers were promptly recorded. At the end of the month, Mr. Muramoto ceased teaching the large daily classes and worked with the editors, reviewing all that had been said and correcting any possible misinterpretations. The editors, being well aware of the incompleteness of their understanding of Oriental medicine, were very careful to obtain clear answers, hoping to anticipate any difficulties that the reader might encounter.

After Mr. Muramoto left, a team of writers and editors was formed and the book began to take shape. We soon found that we would have to write an introduction for each chapter in order to smooth out the lectures and make of them an open garden where the reader could be at ease. We also found it necessary to weave in additional material to expand and connect the various ideas for the reader who was not fortunate enough to have heard the lectures "live." In addition, several initial chapters had to be written to prepare the reader, since many of the Oriental concepts may be unfamiliar to him.

Once the book was written, we sent one of the editors to San Francisco, where Mr. Muramoto is living, to check for errors and gather whatever information was necessary to fill in and complete the text.

A sensitive and talented illustrator was needed also, one who would give the reader a feeling of ease and joy; for when pain strikes, warmth and understanding are needed to help heal it. As if by plan, we received a surprise visit from a young man who was eager to work for us. One look at a sample of his drawings and we were convinced that he was the right one for the job.

Once the work on the content was finished, there remained the choice between a classical textbook form and a looser construction. We chose the latter in order to make the book accessible to laymen. What we at Swan House hoped to produce was a book of live teachings of Oriental medicine, as open and accessible as possible and directed to the needs of the people of the United States.

Wherever you stand, whatever your beliefs and creed, you cannot fail to notice the dedication from which this book evolved. And if you come to see this, you are not far from believing in the practicality and efficacy of the content of this book.

THE HUMAN MEDICINE

We MUST LEARN to heal ourselves; it is our right. It is unnecessary to depend on others, however qualified, to do it for us. There are many ways to get rid of a cold besides simplistically taking pills which "work" for one day only. The cure must be complete. When we know how clogged our organs and arteries are, we have an insight into the extent of our freedom. If his body fluids do not run freely, how free can a man then be?

Perhaps the time is not too far off when most of us will be able to care for our health by ourselves, and do so simply, using what nature freely offers. It must be recognized that everyone is capable of curing himself. No miracles are involved. It is inspiring to realize that each of us can test how free he is by practicing his own medicine in a simple manner. Our present condition and mood, along with our inherited constitution, point out the proper cure.

This book is not meant to cause a rapid and revolutionary change in the field of medicine and in the treatment of disease. It has been written so that everyone, whatever his orientation, can learn a simple, useful principle for everyday life, so that he will not panic over minor illness and rush to offer his body to the nearest doctor.

Oriental medicine has always taught that food is the best medicine. That is probably why traditional Eastern doctors did not expect to be paid; they believed that nature was doing the job, not they. In fact, it is said that in the ancient Orient doctors' salaries were suspended if their patients became worse, the doctor himself being held responsible for all expenses. It was agreed that the doctor's job was to keep people well.

The *Shurai,* a three-thousand-year-old Chinese book, distinguishes five levels of doctors according to the type of medicine being practiced. The highest doctor is the Sage; he is followed by the food-doctor, the surgeon, the doctor of general medicine, and the animal doctor.

The most venerated doctor, the philosopher-doctor, teaches about the harmonious order of man and his world. The teachings of the food-doctor are classified as preventive medicine, which is known as the "medicine of longevity." The surgeon employs his special skills to remedy the effects of violent injuries, also using herbs and food to help extend his patients' lives. The doctor of general medicine uses herbs and employs the techniques of acupuncture, moxibation, and massage to cure specific ailments.

Oriental medicine operates on the principle of balancing Yin and Yang in all its remedies. This method based on subtlety and gradually changing balance is gentle, safe and long-lasting.

Modern medicine is preoccupied mainly with treating symptoms. Every year new sicknesses arise; every year a virus or a microbe makes the news. When a microbe is caught like a thief at the time of illness, it is immediately called "germ" and assumed to be the cause of the disease. The next step is to eliminate it with surgery or drugs.

The Oriental approach is totally different. Nothing is destroyed out of fear, since the elimination of symptoms not only fails to help, but actually weakens the organism. A person with a healthy way of thinking does not try to separate himself from the world of bacteria. He knows that microbes and viruses too have their purpose and are beneficial to man. They are not our enemies, they are contained in our very life—in the food we eat and in the water we drink. And they cannot harm a person in good health. It is an ancient Oriental belief that disease destroys only those who deserve it. Science's anti-microbe attitude has developed as a result of modern man's inability to make himself stronger in body and mind.

Modern medicine is highly analytical. Its practitioners usually tend to reduce the body to its component parts. They try to isolate the disease to a single area and then concentrate on healing that specific part of the body. Thus, if there is pain in the stomach, most modern doctors will conclude that the stomach alone is sick. Sometimes they will "cure" the diseased area by removing it, as in the case of gastric ulcers. Gastric ulcers result from overeating and poor digestion. Removing organs is too simplistic an approach. To destroy something is not to cure it. We cannot remove a part of our body without adversely affecting the whole.

Traditional Oriental medicine does not conceive of the body in parts; it considers the organ a part of the whole, and disease a deterioration of the entire body-system. Its highest practitioners reflect constantly upon the role of man in this world and the role of disease in this life. They know that our bodies are inseparable from the soil that feeds us. The earth, the plants it produces, the animals and mankind are all interrelated. Modern medicine says that the body consists of cells and that the cells themselves become diseased. This is a fine theory, but it remains for the Western doctor to realize that a disease in any part of the body always reflects a malfunctioning of the whole. Otherwise, too much time is spent in subdividing and classifying, a preoccupation which makes study unduly difficult. A Western doctor can spend eight years in medical school and emerge having mastered only the names of the parts of the body, the names of their diseases, and the names of the drugs to treat them. Based on its assumption that the body is an organic whole, Oriental medicine has names for only about one hundred types of diseases; the others simply fall into general categories. By realizing this unity, and by briefly studying the Yin-Yang principle, we can more easily learn the methods for healing ourselves.

There are several schools in Japan teaching traditional Oriental medicine. All recommend food as preventive medicine, but each has its own particular method of treating disease. We will not enumerate here the various forms of medicine being practiced in Japan and China today. While this would arouse the reader's wonder regarding the wide spectrum of healing techniques, it would leave him with little substance to work with, merely broadening his acquaintance with the world of medicine in a cursory and superficial way.

We thought we would best serve the reader's interest if we avoided directing his attention in too many directions at once. Therefore, instead of reviewing separately each of the diverse systems and techniques, we have chosen to unify them all in one simple method. This method incorporates all the basics: how diseases develop, how they can be prevented, and how they may be cured in the most practical way. The importance of food is stressed in this book precisely because food is so basic. No responsible doctor will ever prescribe a medicine before making sure his patient understands the importance of a healthy, balanced diet. We should not fool ourselves into thinking that disease is caused by an enemy from without. We are responsible for our diseases, for disease often results from mistakes in our choice of food. According to what we choose to eat and what we do with it—chewing it or not, digesting it well or not—we develop health or sickness. Cells must be nourished with this food's essence. If our organs fail to supply that essence from the food, our cells become weak, inviting all kinds of diseases to invade.

The true practice of medicine requires judgment. We must be able to select our own food and medicine, thereby declaring our freedom to grow as man was meant to grow. Oriental medicine is unique in that it can be applied by everyone. The medicine presented here does not involve complex rules which place it out of reach of all but the few; it speaks the language of Man.

This book includes much information that the reader will need in order to learn to prevent disease by the proper use of food. Through it the reader will come to understand the connection between Man and Nature as revealed in the Five Elements Theory. He will be able to diagnose various diseases and, after some experience, to determine the food, herbs or external treatments necessary to cure them. From his knowledge of physiology, gained with the help of the Yin-Yang principle, he will see that sickness arises when the change from Yin to Yang and from Yang to Yin is prevented from taking place.

Any human medicine should teach the elementary practice of a simple medicine, so that we as social beings can be freed from systematic reliance on another man's judgment, good or bad—a reliance which only obscures the goal toward which we all strive. Let us all make the effort to be free, lest our generation and the generation following us sink into a world of fear and dependency.

We could have included acupuncture here, but since our main goal was to make as practical a book as possible, we chose not to do so. Acupuncture is now in vogue, but to cover the subject completely would require a more in-depth study than we are prepared to make in this text. Nevertheless, some important pressure points are given here, which can be massaged without the use of needles. This technique may prove helpful for diagnosis or for relieving minor pains such as headache.

We could also have included pulse diagnosis, which is of the utmost importance in Chinese medicine. But whatever we might have written about it would have been insufficient. Twelve pulses are used—six on each wrist. A whole treatise would be required to do this technique justice. To understand and practice it properly, a long period of study and experience with the best teacher possible is necessary.

The approach described in this book is general and comprehensive. The techniques included here are easy enough for everyone to practice. This book does not dwell on the symptomatic removal of pain; it attempts to explain the importance of basic things like proper diet, as well as diagnosis and specific cures.

The reader who has experienced the unpleasant feeling of dependence on another man's techniques—and shortcomings—will perceive the importance of this book. May he find the beginning of freedom in a world in which machines are replacing the natural judgment of Man.

M.A.

YIN AND YANG

Even nature does not last long. . . .

How much less would human beings?

THE YIN-YANG PRINCIPLE is simple. Fundamental to it is the assumption that the elements of nature are ephemeral and that, once aware of this, we must conduct our lives accordingly. These two forces are always opposite and antagonistic, and yet at the same time they are complementary, for they are forever combining and cooperating, both within the body and without. Thus the principle of Yin and Yang developed in the Orient is one of "dualistic monism."

Yin

In the Far East, *Yin* is the name given to that force which produces expansion. Water, air, trees, flowers, etc. are all "expanding" elements in nature, since their essential tendency is to forever fill up the dimensions of space. Certain fruits grow quickly and yet are larger than others which take time to grow. The force within these fruits which makes them grow faster and larger than others, is Yin. Therefore, we consider as Yin anything that grows to a relatively great size in a relatively short time.

Something termed "Yin" is not labeled such solely because of its superior size. True, size is often the identifying attribute of Yin; however, this is only one of its qualities. Yin, as we have said, is that force which causes expansion. Drugs, for example, tend to make us expand in all ways, physiologically and mentally. Alcohol tends to produce the same effect. In other words, Yin dissipates. Elements which make us dizzy or "light-headed" when taken as food or medicine, are Yin.

It takes a great binding force (Yang) to balance the great expansion created by Yin (drugs, alcohol, sugar, etc.). It is due to this difficulty in maintaining equilibrium that all kinds of sicknesses arise.

In summary, the Yin force is the opposite of the binding force. Yin always tends to expand as contrasted with the Yang force, which tends to contract.

Yang

Now that we are somewhat acquainted with the idea of Yin, we can understand what Yang must be. Yang is that force which tends to make things contract, to be dense and heavy. It does not extend things spatially; on the contrary, its tendency is to cause elements to contract to the utmost of their potential. Any given element will continue to contract as long as the Yang force is still dominant. When that force is exhausted, the element then tends to expand, since there is no remaining force to keep it from expanding.

For example, salt is Yang. Pickling vegetables in salt is a Yang process which tends to shrink the vegetables. As long as there is salt around and inside the vegetables, they will continue to shrink. If too little salt is used with the vegetables, they will spoil and eventually rot. The Yang quality of the salt is what preserves them, and the longer they are pickled, the more Yang they will be. Time and salt, along with heat and pressure, are very strong Yang forces in nature.

Fruits generally are not dominated by the Yang force. Roots are mostly dominated by Yang. The fa-

8

mous ginseng, for example, is an extremely Yang root. Some roots are more Yang than others. Usually, the smaller the root, the more Yang it is. But that is not always the case. Some roots are large but, because they grow in a cold and mountainous region over a long period of time, they are still Yang.

Yang does not cause dizziness as Yin does. Salt, soya sauce, ginseng, etc. are rather effective in eliminating dizziness. However, they should not be taken in exaggerated amounts. Too much of anything will produce its opposite.

You can now see the fundamental difference between Yin and Yang. Yin has a tendency to expand, Yang to contract. We shall see that an individual needs the contrasting effect of both to maintain balance.

Yin and Yang

We have already said that activity is Yang and passivity is Yin. This principle is well illustrated by the sun's heat and activity as opposed to the moon's coldness and passivity. Thus the sun, daytime, heat, and summer are all called "Yang," and the moon, nighttime, cold, and winter are called "Yin." The activity of Yin and Yang can be demonstrated in thousands of ways. For example, there is more "visible" activity taking place in summer than in winter. This is not to say that in winter there is no activity at all. There is activity, but it is more subtle than the visible kind taking place during the hot days. On a hot day the air is electrified, the fruits are blossoming, people fill the streets and beaches. When the cold days arrive, people enter the home and the country is silent.

Energy is Yang. Let us take the example of boiling water. Heat (Yang) creates a dynamic movement, a complete change in the structure of the molecules and elements found in water. Inertia, on the other hand, is Yin. There is no visible activity taking place.

Most of the fruits that grow in a warm climate are more or less Yin, whereas plants, especially roots which grow in a cold climate, are Yang. This reciprocal relationship between Yin and Yang can be illustrated by the following. A cactus tree thrives in a hot climate. It grows on dry land, yet has a great amount of liquid in it. One can see from this why a hot climate (Yang) produces juicy fruits (Yin) such as oranges, papayas, avocados, etc. On the contrary, a colder climate produces smaller fruits or no fruit at all. That is why most plants die in the winter. Activity is seen again with the approach of warmer days; nature begins to murmur the coming of new plants and fruits.

The activity of both Yin and Yang affects man in his innermost being. When it is cold, man builds a fire to warm himself. When it grows warm, he searches for water to refresh himself. This change from Yin to Yang can affect man adversely if he does not acclimatize himself to the ever new conditions. That is why man should be careful to change his diet whenever he moves from a cold place to a warm one, and vice versa.

Whatever man eats affects his condition to some degree. Just as the weather from the outside affects him, so food, whether liquid, spicy or acid, is a "weather" inside him which can produce a sensation of cold or warmth.

Some food produces more thirst than other types. Salt, which is Yang, certainly does so. That is why a good cook balances it with other ingredients, such as oil, in her cooking. The reverse is also true; a salad prepared with oil but without salt lacks taste as well as balance.

The good cook knows one simple secret, that Yin cannot be delicious without a bit of help from Yang. Salt, when added in the correct measure, helps create the ideal taste. *A potato without salt does not taste like a potato!* One's opposite is always needed to enhance one's quality.

We have already seen that there is a mutual attraction between Yin and Yang. For example, we tend to drink a great amount of liquid to remedy the simple irritations or painful contractions brought about from the consumption of too much salty food. Conversely, the consumption of excess liquid causes salt to be removed from the body and results in a strong desire for more salt.

This attraction of Yin for Yang and vice versa can be controlled, depending on who is experiencing it. The wise and understanding man, aware of the natural attraction between Yin and Yang, is careful not to let his desires overshadow his wisdom. Only the fool is governed by the sudden attractions he brings upon himself—when he is hungry, he eats until full; when thirsty, he drinks until he aches.

Thus we learn that a free man is one who accepts these two forces as an expression of natural law, yet is neither controlled nor overwhelmed by them.

The reader will frequently encounter the terms "Yin" and "Yang" throughout the text. He should not be alarmed. At first he will find it difficult to comprehend what they are there for. However, with time and experience he will begin to grow used to the way of thinking they demand.

We have tried to use these terms as little as possible, in order to make this book accessible to the Occidental reader. Nevertheless, it is very necessary that they be used to a certain extent, since they are so basic to the concepts and techniques of Oriental medicine.   M.A.

THE THEORY OF THE FIVE ELEMENTS

As Applied in Oriental Medicine

MUCH HAS ALREADY BEEN WRITTEN about the Five Elements Theory. Many books have revealed its applicability in medicine, especially in acupuncture. However, it seems that no book has exposed it in a way that reveals it as more than a theory. It is too significant a concept—at least for the student of medicine—to be presented dry and unrelated to the imperatives of life. For the Five Elements Theory reflects the very rhythms of nature. Its far-reaching implications affect a wide range of fields such as agriculture, nutrition, psychology, astrology (see chart, page 18).

The Theory of the Five Elements is Chinese in origin. It is explained at length in the *Nei Ching,* a compilation of ancient medicine first written down in 400 B.C. but reputed to be over 4,000 years old. Chinese philosophers classified everything in the world according to five primary elements—Wood, Fire, Earth, Metal and Water—which represent five forces. This theory has its roots in the concept of the eternal interplay of Yin and Yang, for in the dual interplay of these two complementary opposites, a new entity is always born. Man contains these five elements, for he is the product of heaven and earth. From this we learn that man—being both a heavenly and an earthly entity—uses these elements in his daily actions.

From one comes two—Yin and Yang, heaven and earth—and from two comes three and four—Wood, Fire, Metal, Water. Earth was added in the center to create an all-encompassing, dynamic system of classification. Eventually (see Fig. 2), it found a place indistinguishable from the others, and the pentagon was complete. Today, the complexities and accomplishments

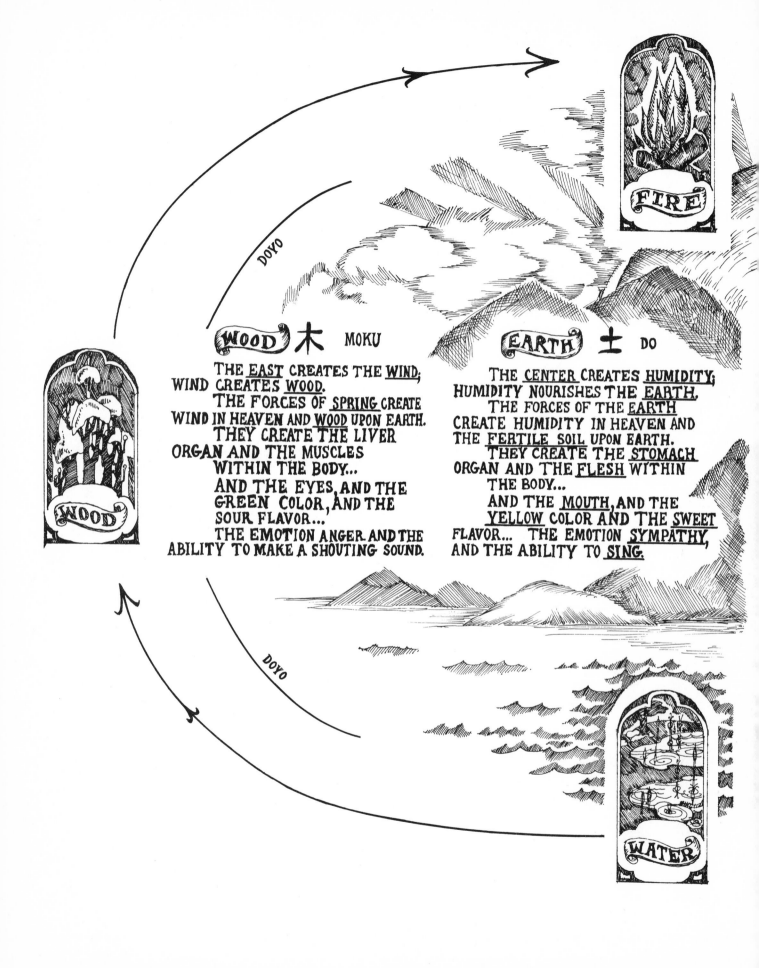

FIRE

WOOD 木 MOKU

THE EAST CREATES THE WIND;
WIND CREATES WOOD.
THE FORCES OF SPRING CREATE
WIND IN HEAVEN AND WOOD UPON EARTH.
THEY CREATE THE LIVER
ORGAN AND THE MUSCLES
WITHIN THE BODY...
AND THE EYES, AND THE
GREEN COLOR, AND THE
SOUR FLAVOR...
THE EMOTION ANGER AND THE
ABILITY TO MAKE A SHOUTING SOUND.

EARTH 土 DO

THE CENTER CREATES HUMIDITY;
HUMIDITY NOURISHES THE EARTH.
THE FORCES OF THE EARTH
CREATE HUMIDITY IN HEAVEN AND
THE FERTILE SOIL UPON EARTH.
THEY CREATE THE STOMACH
ORGAN AND THE FLESH WITHIN
THE BODY...
AND THE MOUTH, AND THE
YELLOW COLOR AND THE SWEET
FLAVOR... THE EMOTION SYMPATHY,
AND THE ABILITY TO SING.

WOOD

DOYO

DOYO

WATER

FIRE 火 KA

FROM THE SOUTH COMES EXTREME HEAT, HEAT PRODUCES FIRE.

THE FORCES OF SUMMER CREATE HEAT IN HEAVEN AND FIRE ON EARTH.

THEY CREATE THE HEART ORGAN AND THE PULSE WITHIN THE BODY...

AND THE TONGUE, THE RED COLOR, AND THE BITTER FLAVOR...

THE EMOTION JOY AND THE ABILITY TO MAKE A LAUGHING SOUND.

DOYO

 METAL 金 GON

THE WEST CREATES SCORCHED DRYNESS; DRYNESS CREATES METAL.

THE FORCES OF AUTUMN CREATE DRYNESS IN HEAVEN AND METAL ON EARTH.

THEY CREATE THE LUNG ORGAN AND THE SKIN UPON THE BODY...

AND THE NOSE, AND THE WHITE COLOR, AND THE PUNGENT FLAVOR...

THE EMOTION GRIEF, AND THE ABILITY TO MAKE A WEEPING SOUND.

METAL

 EARTH

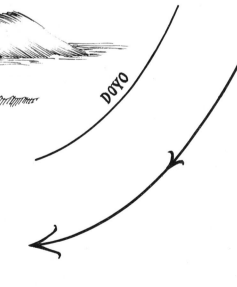

DOYO

WATER 水 SUI

THE NORTH CREATES EXTREME COLD; COLD CREATES WATER.

THE FORCES OF WINTER CREATE COLD IN HEAVEN AND WATER ON EARTH.

THEY CREATE THE KIDNEY ORGAN AND THE BONES WITHIN THE BODY...

AND THE EARS, AND THE BLACK COLOR, AND THE SALTY FLAVOR...

THE EMOTION FEAR, AND THE ABILITY TO MAKE A GROANING SOUND.

of modern science seem to outweigh greatly this simple, ancient theory, and yet even today the Theory of the Five Elements is still proving itself highly effective in medical diagnosis and treatment.

Each element has a corresponding direction and season of the year:

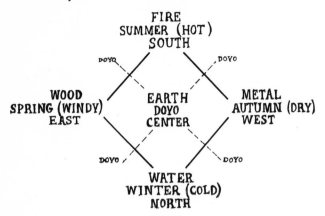

Figure 1. The relationship between elements

This diagram (Fig. 1) is very helpful in showing an important basic relationship between the elements. Spring is the first season of the new year (planting time) and the sun rises in the East every day. Thus, Wood is the premier element, which is indeed appropriate, for Wood represents the force of life—vital, growing life—and its inclusion here as one of the

endar, Doyo would be around the time of the two solstices and the two equinoxes, the points that mark the end of one season and the beginning of the next. The Doyo period lasts about two weeks. It is the period between the seasons as they flow into each other and change. Placed as it is between two seasons, Doyo has in it the active quality of Yin and Yang both, and combines the forces of both seasons. Sometimes the hottest and the coldest days of the year come during Doyo.

The connection between the other elements and their seasons seems obvious (see Fig 1): Fire, summer and the hot South; Metal, dry autumn and the West; Water, winter and the cold North; Wood, spring and the windy East.

The *Nei Ching* explains simply and beautifully the interrelationship between the Five Elements. It says, "Wood gives birth to Fire, Fire gives birth to Earth, Earth gives birth to Metal, Metal gives birth to Water, Water gives birth to Wood." [1]

This is the "Sheng" or "Creation" cycle, producing what is known in Oriental medicine as the "Mother-Son" relationship. It is shown in Fig. 3 by the outer circumference of arrows. Think of how

> WOOD *burns to make*
> FIRE *whose ashes decompose into the*
> EARTH *where are born and mined*
> METALS *which when melted become*
> WATER* (liquid) *which nourishes trees and plants.*

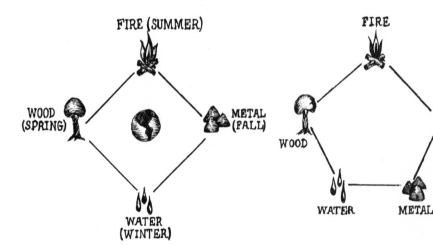

primary elements is what distinguishes the Five Element Theory from any other comparable system, East or West.

Each of the elements is said to come into being through the interplay of Heaven and Earth (Yin and Yang); this is the reason for the central position of the element Earth.

In terms of direction, Wood represents the East, Fire is South, Metal is West, and Water is North. Earth, the ground we live on, is the center connecting them all.

Similarly, Doyo is the season of Earth. In the Oriental calendar, Doyo comes four times a year. In our cal-

The *Nei Ching* also explains the "Ko" cycle, that of "Destruction" or "Control":

> WOOD *is cut down by metal*
> FIRE *is extinguished by water*
> EARTH *is penetrated by wood*
> METAL *is melted by fire*
> WATER *is interrupted and cut off by earth.*[2]

---

[1] *The Yellow Emperor's Classic of Internal Medicine,* trans. Ilza Veith (University of California Press).
[2] Perhaps this last relationship is not clear. A dam, an earthen jug, and mud all dominate water by diverting it, containing it, and absorbing it respectively.

This "Destruction" cycle is depicted in Fig. 3 by the inner arrows. Each of these cycles of interrelationships has great practical applications, as we shall see.

Each of the elements is associated with an organ:

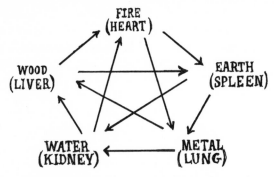

Figure 3. The creation and destruction cycles

The outer arrows, which represent the "Generation" cycle, show how the heart strengthens the spleen, the lungs strengthen the kidneys, the kidneys strengthen the liver, the liver strengthens the heart. It is a circulating process, each organ drawing strength from the one that precedes it and strengthening the one that follows. Improving the state of a weak organ also strengthens the condition of the following organs (its "sons"). Similarly, the weakening of an organ may result in its replenishing its strength by drawing from the organ that precedes it (its "mother").

The inner arrows in Fig. 3 portray the Destruction cycle. This shows how overly strong kidneys make a weak heart, an overly strong spleen makes weak kidneys, overly strong lungs make a weak liver, an overly strong liver makes a weak spleen, and an overly strong heart makes weak lungs.

There is no circulating process in these relationships. For example, if the kidneys are too strong and weaken the heart, the heart alone is weakened. There is no repercussion on any other organ. In other words, this strong-weak "Control" relationship (inner arrows) exists between only two organs. It is complementary-antagonistic but not circulatory as is the "Generation" relationship (outer arrows) where if one organ is strengthened, each consecutive organ will be strengthened accordingly.

In actuality, each element is associated with two organs, since for each organ depicted in Fig. 3, there is another organ which complements it. In addition, there is a sixth pair of organs, the heart governor/triple heater, making twelve organs in all (Fig. 4).

The liver and gall bladder are the organs of the element Wood. Fire has two pairs: the heart/small intestine and the heart governor/triple heater (the two latter organs are described at length in the chapter "The Organs"). Earth has the spleen-pancreas and the stomach (the spleen and pancreas are considered one organ in traditional Oriental medicine). The lungs and the large intestine are under Metal; the kidneys and bladder are associated with Water.

The "Tzang" organs, which we will call Yang,[3] are those whose interrelationship is shown in Fig. 3—the heart, spleen-pancreas, lungs, kidneys, liver and also the heart governor. The "Fu" organs, which we will call Yin, are the small intestine, stomach, large intestine, bladder, gall bladder, and triple heater. Each of these Yin organs is closely related to its complementary Yang organ (this will be discussed in detail in the chapter "The Organs").

The *Nei Ching* describes some more very interesting physiological relationships (notice the application of the "Generation" relationship):

The liver nourishes the muscles and the muscles strengthen the heart; the liver governs the eyes.

The heart nourishes the blood and the blood enlivens the stomach; the heart rules over the tongue.

The stomach strengthens the flesh and the flesh protects the lungs; the stomach rules over the mouth.

The lung strengthens the skin and [body]hair, the skin and the hair protect the kidneys; the lungs govern the nose.

The kidneys strengthen the bones and the marrow, and the bones and the marrow strengthen the liver; the kidneys rule over the ears.

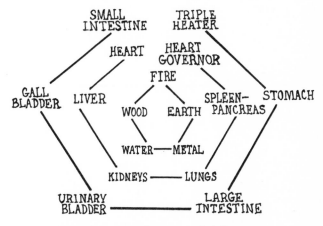

Figure 4. The elements and their organs

[3] Students of the *I Ching* and *Nei Ching* will notice that the Yin-Yang classification scheme used in this text differs from the one with which they are already familiar. We believe that the system used here will prove easier for readers unfamiliar with Eastern thought to grasp and *apply practically.* It was developed recently for modern people who are accustomed to scientific rather than metaphysical thinking. In the *I Ching* and *Nei Ching,* heaven is the source of creative energy which nourishes the earth; therefore, heaven is called "Yang" and earth "Yin." The Fu organs, being closer to the surface of the body, are nearer the sun and thus are called "Yang." However, here, from our physical viewpoint, the solid earth on which we stand is "Yang" and the all-pervasive heavens are "Yin." The Tsang organs, being deeper inside the body as well as being solid, compact, and red or dark in color, are called "Yang" in this system. The Fu, or Yin organs are hollow, soft and pale in color.

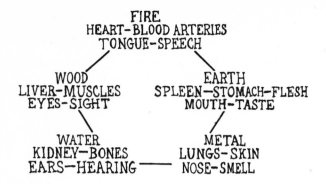

Figure 5. The relationship between the 5 senses and the organs

Figure 5 shows the relationships between organs, tissues and sense organs, and the way in which each of our senses is connected to one of the organs and ruled by it: heart and speech; stomach and taste; lungs and smell; kidneys and hearing; liver and sight.

This diagram also makes clear certain techniques of Oriental diagnosis—for example, it shows why you can learn about the condition of someone's stomach from his lips, and the condition of his heart from his complexion and rate of speech (for others, see Fig. 8 and also the chapter "The Diagnosis").

Each element has an associated emotion in intimate connection with its organ.

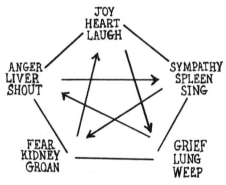

Figure 6. The emotion cycle

The *Nei Ching* says:

> *Anger is injurious to the liver, but grief counteracts anger.*
> *Extravagant joy is injurious to the heart, but fear counteracts joy.*
> *Extreme sympathy [worry] is injurious to the stomach, but anger counteracts sympathy.*
> *Extreme grief is injurious to the lungs, but joy counteracts grief.*
> *Extreme fear is injurious to the kidneys, but sympathy can overcome fear [by diverting one's attention from one's own problems].*

So, an outburst of any one of these emotions not only represents a problem in its associated organ, it also aggravates it. Even more, we see an interrelationship among these organs, which is explained by the "Control" cycle of the Five Elements Theory.

The "Creation" cycle also applies to the emotions. Excessive sympathy or worry will result in grief; excess grief creates fear, etc. Joy, the emotion of Fire (heat, summer), is the most Yang; fear, the emotion of Water (cold, winter) is the most Yin.

Here is a very old story showing the application of the theory of the Five Elements, using these emotional attributes:

> Once, a long time ago, a girl was in love with a boy but her parents would not allow her to marry him. Every day she worried more and more about her problem and refused to eat any food. She became thinner and thinner—a victim of lovesickness. Her parents were very concerned and called in many doctors, but not one of them could cure her lovesickness.
>
> Then one day came a doctor who knew the Five Elements Theory. He determined to make her angry, so he lied to her and tricked her. It worked—she became very angry. That same day she resumed eating regularly; soon she was back to normal. So, the Five Elements Theory can help cure even lovesickness! In this case, Wood (anger) destroyed Earth (worry) (see Fig. 6). Study all these relationships well. Certainly this is a kind of "medicine" that anyone can apply.

Each element has an associated sound. This sound is obviously related to the emotion and organ. The relationships are: Wood—shout; Fire—laugh; Earth—sing; Metal—weep; Water—groan.

These correspondences can help us understand further the way in which each element represents an encounter of Yin and Yang. They can also aid greatly in diagnosis. Excessive laughter is indicative of an overly strong heart. The idea of "too much joy" may seem strange, but in Oriental medicine excess joy is said to be responsible for "slowing the energy." Think of the times when you've laughed so hard you couldn't move. On the other hand, a person with a weak heart may seem dejected and show no joy at all (sadness has a quality distinctly different from that of "grief," which is a very active emotion). It is said that a fine singer with a strong voice probably has a good spleen. Depression and emotional tension are both cause and effect of a bad stomach. Someone who cries easily is almost certain to have lung problems. A person with liver (or gall bladder) trouble may give vent to anger or simply shout.

It is said that each element "creates" a flavor: Wood produces the sour taste, Fire produces the bitter, Earth produces the sweet, Metal produces the hot (pungent), and water produces the salty. Each element's corresponding organ is said to desire the flavor of its element. The different flavors are said to have certain

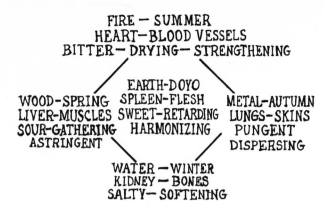

Figure 7. The five flavors

powers. All this becomes clear when considered in light of the respective seasons.

The bitter flavor, which has the power of drying and strengthening, is the taste we desire in summer; the pungent flavor, which is dispersive, is the taste we desire in the season of falling leaves; the salty flavor, which has the power of softening (Water), is the taste we desire in winter; the sour flavor, which has the power of gathering (astringent), is the taste we desire in spring. The sweet taste is desired at all times; accordingly, it is found at the center. It has the power of slowing down, of bringing harmony. Its season is Doyo, the time of change between seasons.

Each flavor is beneficial to its corresponding organ. In excess, however, each will prove harmful. Similarly, the Yin-Yang principle tells us that extreme Yin will quickly become Yang, and vice versa. Thus the *Nei Ching* says, "The sour flavor nourishes the liver," and "the sour flavor is injurious to the liver and muscles." Likewise, bitter food is good for the heart, but too much injures the heart and blood vessels; sweet food is good for the spleen, but too much will injure the spleen (and stomach!—see "The Organs") and flesh; pungent food is good for the lungs, but too much will injure the lungs and skin; salty food is good for the kidneys, but too much will injure the kidneys (see "The Organs") and bones.

The five flavors too are affected by the relationships of the "Creation" and "Destruction" cycles. The powers of each flavor (see Fig. 8) can be beneficial to the organ of the element which follows. For example, sour food, which is astringent ("gathering") can benefit a weak ("tardy") heart.

Too much of one kind of food not only harms its associated organ, but also weakens the organ it controls in the "Destruction" cycle. Thus:

> *Too much salt in food endangers the heart, and "the pulse hardens, tears make their appearance and the complexion changes."*

> *Too much bitter food endangers the lungs, and "the skin becomes withered and the body hair falls out."*

> *Too much pungent flavor in food endangers the liver, and "the muscles become knotty and the finger and toe nails wither and decay."*

> *Too much sour flavor in food endangers the spleen and stomach, and "the flesh hardens and wrinkles and the skin becomes slack."*

> *Too much sweet flavor in food endangers the kidneys, and "the bones ache and the hair on the head falls out" (see "The Diagnosis").*

However, the effects of the excess of one flavor can be remedied by utilizing the flavor which controls it. So, the sour flavor is counteracted by the pungent flavor; the bitter flavor is counteracted by the salty flavor; the sweet flavor is counteracted by the sour flavor; the pungent flavor is counteracted by the bitter flavor; and the salty flavor is counteracted by the sweet flavor.

One must be careful to exercise good judgment when employing the five flavors for treatment. As has been made clear, excess can be dangerous. And it is very easy to make mistakes. In addition to what is mentioned here, there are many possible treatments based on the powers of the flavors and the interrelationships between the flavors and their organs, according to the Five Elements Theory. These methods are too complex to be set forth here, but their implications are all incorporated into the preparation of herb teas.

Each element and organ has a representative color. Fire is red, Earth is yellow, Metal is white, Water is black, and Wood is green or blue (it is said that in ancient times these two colors were not distinguished from one another by name).

A knowledge of these color relationships is very helpful in diagnosis. Always look carefully at the complexion. If a person is too red, heart problems are probable. A yellowish color indicates spleen problems (jaundice—see "The Cure"); a white complexion, although

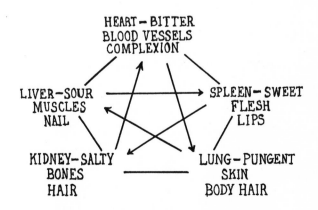

Figure 8. The five flavors and their effects

CLASSIFICATION BY THE FIVE ELEMENTS THEORY

	WOOD	FIRE	EARTH	METAL	WATER
TSANG ORGAN	liver	heart	spleen/pancreas	lung	kidney
FU ORGAN	gall bladder	small intestine	stomach	large intestine	bladder
TISSUE	muscles	blood vessels	flesh	skin	bones
INDICATOR	toe nails	complexion	lips	body hair	hair
SENSE ORGAN	eyes	tongue	mouth	nose	ears
SENSE	sight	speech	taste	smell	hearing
BODY FLUID	tears	sweat	saliva	mucus	urine
DIRECTION	East	South	Center	West	North
ADVERSE CLIMATE	wind	heat	moisture	dryness	cold
SEASON	Spring	Summer	Doyo	Fall	Winter
TIME OF DAY	morning	noon	—	evening	day
PLANET	Jupiter	Mars	Earth	Venus	Mercury
NUMBER	8	7	5	9	6
EMOTION	anger	joy	sympathy/worry	grief	fear
EXPRESSION	shout	laugh	sing	weep	groan
MANNER IN TIME OF EXCITEMENT AND CHANGE	control	sadness/grief	belch (stubborn)	cough	trembling
FACULTY	spiritual	inspirational	intellectual	vital	will
TASTE	sour	bitter	sweet	pungent	salty
GRAIN	wheat	red millet/corn	yellow millet	rice	beans
FRUIT	plum	apricot	dates	peach	chestnuts
VEGETABLE	leeks	scallions	mallows	onions	coarse greens
DOMESTIC ANIMAL	fowl	sheep	ox	horse	pig

very striking, indicates bad lungs; a blackish (dark brown) color indicates kidney problems; a green color indicates a liver disorder.

Each element has a particular climate which, while being appropriate to the season of that element, is said to affect its organ adversely (see Fig. 9).

Thus, heat is bad for the heart, dryness affects the lungs, cold damages the kidneys, wind is harmful to the liver, and moisture is dangerous for the spleen. So we can expect heart trouble to be most prevalent in the summer, lung trouble in the fall, kidney trouble in the winter, and liver trouble in the spring. Spleen and stomach troubles are equally likely at all times.

According to Oriental medicine based on the Five Elements Theory, each of these problems indicates a certain general body condition and has a specific type of cure appropriate to it.

The meaning of Full-Empty in relation to Yin-Yang, and the corresponding treatments, are explained in depth in "The Diagnosis." Here they are given as presented in the *Nei Ching*. These treatments are an important consideration in the preparation of herbal teas.

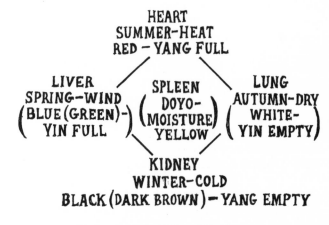

Figure 9. The Full and the Empty

A person with a red complexion has a Yang-Full type of condition and is prone to heart trouble, especially in the hot summer. The appropriate treatment is to induce vomiting and diarrhea (thus reducing excess energy).

A pale, white person has a Yin-Empty type of condition and is prone to lung trouble, especially in the dry

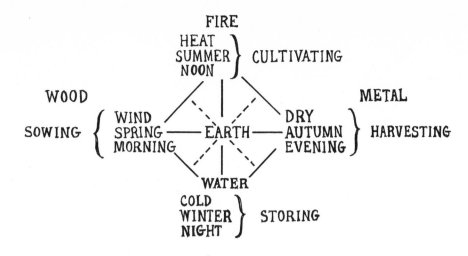

Figure 10. The rhythm of Nature

fall. The appropriate treatment is to induce harmony (harmony is desirable in every case of illness, but especially here where the person is weak).

A person whose complexion has become dark brown has a Yang-Empty type of condition and is prone to kidney trouble, especially in the cold winter. The appropriate treatment is to create warmth.

A person with a greenish complexion or with blue vessels showing in the face (especially between the eye and ear) has a Yin-Full type of condition and is prone to liver trouble, especially in the windy spring. The appropriate treatment is to induce sweating (thus reducing excess heat).

Problems of the spleen and stomach are more general and are not restricted to any particular type of treatment. The condition of the spleen (at the center) can affect all the other organs (see section on the spleen in "The Organs").

The Five Elements Theory also shows how food is an important factor in restoring and maintaining health. In addition to a specific flavor (see Fig. 7), each organ has a grain that is considered especially suitable for nourishing its force: liver/wheat, heart red/ (glutinous) millet, spleen yellow/millet, lungs/rice, kidneys/beans. Glutinous millet is admittedly rare, but here in the Americas we have found corn to be very good for the heart. It is interesting to note that corn is harvested in the summer (heat/heart trouble), rice in the fall (dry/lung trouble), and winter wheat in the spring (wind/liver trouble). Thus, according to the Five Elements Theory, each grain appears in the season when it is most needed.

In ancient China, the small, red "aduki" bean was considered the equivalent of a grain, grains being recognized as the principal food of man.

Each element has its corresponding secondary foods as well—fruits, vegetables, animals. These are listed in the chart on the opposite page.

The elements are related to the times of day as well as to the seasons and the specific agricultural activities appropriate to each. Spring is the season of sowing and sprouting, summer is the season of growing and cultivating, fall is the season of harvesting, and winter is the season of storing.

This is obviously accurate concerning the agricultural cycle; it also provides sound advice for the conducting of individual lives. It applies to the flow of the seasons and to the rhythms of each day. For example, just as crops are planted in the spring, so each person should sow the seeds for his activity early in the morning; and just as it is natural to sleep at night, so in winter one should "rest his Yang"—that is, let one's creative, active force rest and gather strength—just as the deep roots of trees rumble under their blankets of snow until springtime brings new life, activity and change.

The reader may find it helpful to refer back to this chapter to deepen his understanding of the chapters that follow. The chart on page 18 will provide insight into the pattern of the Five Elements Theory. Of course, by itself the chart is insufficient to provide complete understanding; therefore, one should not become too infatuated with it. For the Five Elements Theory is a reflection of changing, flowing life, and cannot be contained in rigid categories.

It is useful to conceive of the Five Elements as forces, and of everything classified under an element as sharing its force. The chart lists but a few of the many categories to which the Five Elements Theory can be applied. The diagram on pages 12 and 13 follows the *Nei Ching*'s poetic expression of the genesis of the Five Elements.

THE DIAGNOSIS

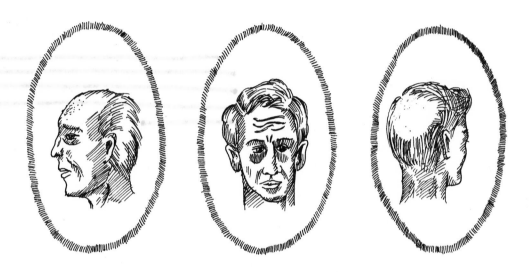

A QUICK GLANCE at a man tells us much about his health. The shape of his face alone reveals his condition. The following simple and practical method of diagnosis can be mastered by anyone in a few months. One can learn it by making a practice of observing other people. It is as accurate as reading from a book. Bad intestines, bad stomach, tired kidneys—each is revealed in the face by a specific sign, a warning to the owner of the troubles ahead.

There are different ways to determine which organ is diseased.[1] Examination of the face is important, but there are several other approaches which are equally important and accurate. These others serve to confirm that which the face might already have shown.

Before committing oneself to a final verdict on the condition of the patient, one must consider the whole person, not just a specific aspect or organ. The environment—city, country, etc.—should be considered. One should even ask questions regarding the patient's family, close relations, and occupation.

These factors are of great significance in determining the treatment to be advised. One should find out whether the patient is highly emotional. Discussing with him subjects of interest will reveal his level of judgment. Once aware of these character traits, you will be in a position to decide whether the patient is likely to follow the diet you would recommend, or whether a different method of treatment will be necessary. It is useless to advise a particular medicine if you sense that, for one reason or another, the patient won't take it. Some people won't give up their eating habits but would be willing to cure themselves with herbs or acupuncture.

In seeking out another person's character, we ourselves grow. Not only do we help other people, but in learning more about human nature we learn other possibilities for cures. In giving simple advice which helps relieve a sickness, we instill confidence in others, inspiring them to seek a more lasting cure.

Healing oneself through the way of eating takes longer, but it is more permanent. Here it is less a ques-

---

[1] A few organs in the Oriental system are slightly different from that which is designated by their English names.

tion of patience than of judgment. Impatient people have decided already that they have no time to deal with the real cause of their sickness. "Good judgment" to them means the ability to take care of the problems of the day—which they may do quite well. However, true judgment involves being in a position to take care of one's life as a whole, for surely a wise man does not let himself be ruled by the urgings of his immediate desires.

Let us not forget that we are *treating a person, not a disease.* If we keep this in mind we will avoid making our diagnosis an abstract oracle neither connected to the immediate needs of the patient nor directed to the capabilities of his temperament.

Diagnosis can reveal information about an individual's basic constitution as well as his present condition. A person's general condition is determined to a great extent by the food he has eaten recently. When diagnosing someone, we usually look first for indications of imbalance in his present condition and recent diet, for these are problems that can be rectified immediately. However, no diagnosis is complete until there is a total picture; the basic constitution must be taken into account. Even before the patient sits down, a quick glance from a distance can determine much about his basic constitution. Later, after the present condition has been ascertained, various diagnostic techniques can be used to obtain more specific information about the basic constitution.

The extent to which your basic constitution leaves you susceptible to disease is the extent to which disease is hereditary. The quality of your basic physical constitution is determined mainly by your mother's constitution and by her diet during pregnancy.

Constitutional problems are fundamental, deep and long-lasting. It is very difficult to alter one's constitution. A baby's constitution can be altered by strong Yin or Yang food; that of an adult, however, takes much longer to change.

The Four Shins

There are four kinds of diagnosis in Oriental medicine. In Japanese they are called Bo-Shin, Bun-Shin, Mon-Shin and Setsu-Shin.

Bo-Shin is diagnosis by observation, which begins with an examination of all the parts of the body, using the eyes and the intuition.

Bun-Shin is diagnosis employing hearing and smelling.

Mon-Shin is diagnosis which involves questioning the patient—regarding job, family situation, case history, etc.

Setsu-Shin is diagnosis using the sense of touch. It involves feeling the pulse, pressure points, etc.

In Oriental medicine the diagnosis is looked upon as a treatment in itself, for symptoms, diagnosis and treatment are directly connected. Diagnosis is always made by considering the patient's entire condition. Every sickness must be diagnosed in view of the general sickness of the whole body.

It is very helpful to use the Yin-Yang principle in diagnosing someone. In doing this we note all the difficulties, assigning each to one of the two possible basic mainstreams of disease, Yin and Yang. This makes treatment much simpler. The treatment given will include more Yin than Yang in the case of Yin symptoms, or vice versa, depending on the existing condition.

The Yin-Yang principle is fundamental in diagnosis, while the Five Elements Theory is helpful in obtaining important supplementary information. The Theory of the Five Elements is very old, but it is still proving itself highly effective in diagnosis and treatment.

The ideal for the Oriental doctor was to diagnose solely by means of Bo-Shin. However, this technique is not easy to master; thus, in most cases all four methods must be employed before a complete diagnosis can be reached.

Bo-Shin relies on observation alone, the eye being man's most highly developed sense organ. Many years of study and experience are required if Bo-Shin is to be mastered thoroughly. This is the most highly regarded method of diagnosis because it is so universal. It can be used even with babies and with extremely ill people too sick to express themselves. The reward for undergoing all the difficulties involved in learning Bo-Shin is the ability to detect at first glance the patient's general condition.

The color and quality of the skin, the subject's weight, his character, his tendency towards activity or inactivity—all are important factors in defining disease. These are the tools necessary for the successful practice of Bo-Shin diagnosis.

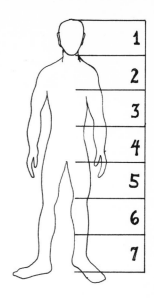

The way the patient walks must be observed. Healthy people walk with their feet parallel. A person who walks with his toes pointing inward ("pigeon-toed") is showing evidence of contraction, of a Yang constitution. If he walks on his heels or with his toes pointing outward (expanding), his constitution is Yin. Bowleggedness is an indication of an overconsumption of meat or, more likely, salt. Walking on the toes and leaning forward is a sign of a Yang constitution. Walking on the heels indicates a Yin constitution. A person who stands erect is Yang; one who slumps is Yin. The head should be one-seventh the size of the body. Someone with a large head is of a Yin constitution, while someone with a small head has a Yang constitution.

Generally speaking, a skinny person is Yin; however, a skinny person who is very muscular and whose skin is dark, is Yang. Older people have the latter type of physiognomy.

Often you will see three horizontal lines on a person's forehead. This indicates a well-developed brain and a great deal of mental activity. If these lines are parallel, they probably indicate an orderly mentality. On the other hand, if these lines go in different directions the mentality is usually chaotic, often schizophrenic.

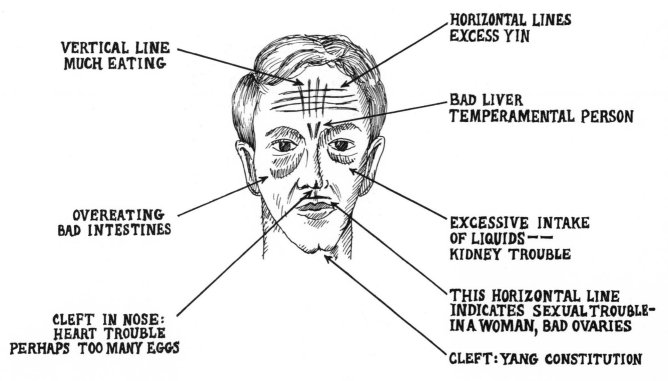

VERTICAL LINE
MUCH EATING

HORIZONTAL LINES
EXCESS YIN

BAD LIVER
TEMPERAMENTAL PERSON

OVEREATING
BAD INTESTINES

EXCESSIVE INTAKE
OF LIQUIDS——
KIDNEY TROUBLE

CLEFT IN NOSE:
HEART TROUBLE
PERHAPS TOO MANY EGGS

THIS HORIZONTAL LINE
INDICATES SEXUAL TROUBLE-
IN A WOMAN, BAD OVARIES

CLEFT: YANG CONSTITUTION

SHELLFISH
MEAT

EGGS, FOWL

RED FISH MEAT

FACE PIMPLES

PIMPLES

According to where they appear, pimples indicate which type of food is being consumed in excess. The presence of pimples is generally termed a "discharge".

Pimples are caused by bad fermentation in the intestines. There is a great amount of waste in the body. Pimples do not come from sugar, but sugary foods initiate the discharge of protein.

Facial Features

THE SHAPE OF THE FACE

Yin-shaped face

The chin is pointed.
The face forms a triangle with base up.
Notice the large forehead.

Yang-shaped face

The chin is somewhat flattened.
The face forms a triangle
with base down.

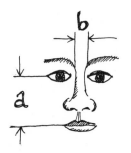

Contraction of facial features (Yang)

The distance between the eyes and mouth (a) is relatively short.
The distance between the inside corners of the eyes (b) is very narrow.
The nose is contracted and almost flat.
The eyes are small.

Expansion of facial features (Yin)

The distance between the eyes and mouth (a) is rather long.
The distance between the outside corners of the eyes (b) is rather wide.
The nose is long and expanded.
The eyes are large.

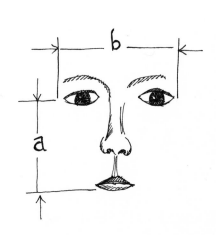

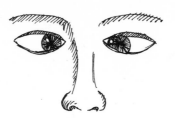

Iris turned toward the nose is a Yang sign. It is in general a sign of blood acidosis and high blood pressure.

THE EYE

Iris turned toward the ears is a Yin sign. Shows a condition of alkalosis in the blood and a proclivity for cancer.

One iris turned toward the nose and one normal sometimes indicates diabetes.
Thin, "folded" eyes are Yang.
Large, round eyes are Yin.
A Japanese proverb states, "Man's eyes should be like a bow, and a woman's eyes like a ring."
Big eyes indicate an intake of Yin food. People with such eyes are delicate and prone to colds and tuberculosis.
Long eyelashes are Yin. The modern woman is using false eyelashes because she has lost her own, due to an exaggerated intake of animal foods which have destroyed her natural Yin quality.
The iris should be at the center of the eye. If the irises are too close to the nose, excess Yang is indicated. If they are at the far side of the nose, the condition is extremely Yin. This symptom often occurs in people with cancer.

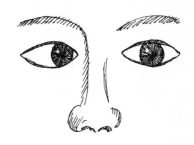

It is normal for the iris of a newborn baby to appear at the bottom, with white showing at the top. A few months later this condition changes and the eye becomes centered. A man whose irises appear at the bottom probably has tendencies toward cruelty. The ideal position is at the center.

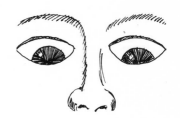

When we grow old, the white at the bottom of our eyes shows. An adult with the white showing is in a very Yin condition. His organs are weakened and, having little reflex ability in case of danger, he is prone to accidents.
Blinking very often signifies the body's attempt to discharge excess Yin in any way that it can. One should not blink one's eyes more than three times per minute.
A prominent red color in the whites of the eyes is a sign of a bad liver. The liver has grown tired due to an over-consumption of food, especially animal food. When the red has spread all over the whites of the eye, the organs are malfunctioning.
If the eyes move constantly or are slow to react (to follow your finger), there is a problem with the heart governor (see "The Organs"). The pace of the heart is not normal. In such cases the pupil of the eye will be too big. A moon on the top part of the iris or a white ring around it indicates a malfunctioning triple heater (see "The Organs").

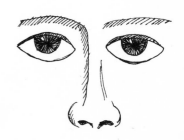

Swelling around the eyes, particularly a swelling of the upper eyelid, indicates gall bladder stones. When the stones pass, the swelling drops immediately.[2]

A dark brown color under the eyes indicates overly Yang kidneys and trouble in the female organs.

Swelling under the eyes indicates kidney stones. A formation of gall stones or blood stagnation may also be indicated.

Dark blue or violet under the eyes reveals blood stagnation, probably caused by an over-consumption of fruit, sugar and meat.

Bulging eyes indicate a Yin condition and thyroid trouble.

Pimples on the interior of the eyelid (sties) signify excess protein. They usually appear and disappear relatively quickly.

An eyelid that is almost white signifies anemia. The inside of the eyelid should be red. To examine, gently pinch the eyelid and pull it away from the eye.

EYEBROWS A broad, thick eyebrow is Yang. A thin eyebrow is Yin. Too much sweet food, especially sugar, makes the eyebrows thinner and eventually causes them to disappear. People with almost no eyebrows are prone to cancer.

**EYEBROWS UP:
LONG TIME MEAT-EATING**

**EYEBROWS DOWN:
VEGETARIAN, FRUITARIAN**

NOSE

An examination of the nose can tell much about the condition of the person being diagnosed. Reduce your intake of food, and you will see your nose grow smaller. A nose can save your life.

A long nose starting high up on the face is Yin. A short nose indicates a strong constitution.

YIN

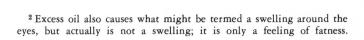

**STRONG
CONSTITUTION
YANG**

A small nose pointing upwards is a sign of strong Yang.

[2] Excess oil also causes what might be termed a swelling around the eyes, but actually is not a swelling; it is only a feeling of fatness.

The center of the nose indicates the condition of the heart. An enlarged nose shows an enlarged heart (excess eating and drinking). The nostrils show the condition of the lungs. The larger the nostrils, the better. Small nostrils indicate weak lungs. Well-developed nostrils are a sign of masculinity.

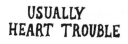

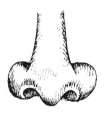

STRONG LUNGS **WEAK LUNGS**

A fat nose which is somewhat oily and sometimes shiny indicates over-consumption of animal protein.
Red vessels on the tip of the nose are an indication of high blood pressure. Heart disease will follow.

THE MOUTH

A small mouth is Yang. A large mouth is Yin. A horizontal line between the mouth and nose shows a malfunctioning of the sexual organs.

LIPS

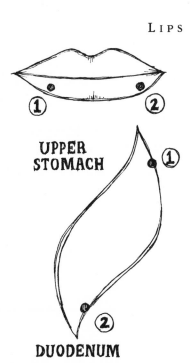

UPPER STOMACH

DUODENUM

The lips should be of equal thickness. In general, thick lips indicate a Yang constitution and thin lips a Yin constitution. The size of the upper lip shows the condition of the liver. If the lip is swollen, the liver is enlarged. The subject eats too much and is prone to mental disorders. The size of the lower lip indicates the condition of the large intestine. When the lower lip is swollen, there is a weakness, a looseness, in the intestines, and thus constipation. Epilepsy is a possibility when both lips are enlarged. This condition indicates that as a child the patient was given too much food.

Lips should usually be pink; however, they grow darker with age. A young person with dark lips has blood stagnation. The blood circulation is bad due to an excessive intake of animal protein and strong Yin foods. People with dark lips tend to develop cancer, pineal troubles, and diseases of the sexual organs.

The texture of the lips reveals the condition of the stomach.

(1) A cyst on the right side of the mouth indicates stomach trouble—acidity or the beginnings of an ulcer on the left side of the stomach.

(2) A cyst on the left side of the mouth indicates a problem in the right side of the stomach.

Chapped lips can indicate stomach problems, but they may simply be a sign that the skin is changing. If the latter is the case, the old skin will peel off easily.

TEETH

Buck teeth are a sign of a Yin constitution. When the teeth angle towards the inside of the mouth, the subject's constitution is Yang.

Pointed teeth reveal a large consumption of meat during childhood.

Weak teeth (tooth decay) are a sign of weak bones.

If a woman's gums and lips are dark in color, irregular menstruation or a tumor in the womb is indicated.

The various teeth have different functions, as shown in the above diagram. When a well-balanced diet is taken, the teeth retain their normal size and shape. When too much Yin food is taken, the teeth decay. Excess animal food makes the canine teeth become larger, more pointed and sharp. Sometimes the incisors and bicuspids right beside the canine teeth also take on the appearance of canine teeth. Vinegar is the worst food as far as the teeth are concerned. It is the food quickest to produce decay.

TONGUE

In general, the tongue shows the condition of the heart and stomach. A white tongue is an early sign of stomach trouble.

When the tongue cannot be stretched out straight, there is trouble in the nervous system or the brain.

When the tongue trembles, there is likewise some nervous or brain trouble indicated.

Ideally, the tongue should be pink. If it is all red, heart trouble is indicated.

A broken tongue also means heart trouble. However, small cracks in the tongue are normal.

If the tongue becomes red, smooth and shiny, there is heart trouble. Usually, a normal tongue is not smooth but has small bumps.

A deep middle crack also means heart trouble.

When one adopts a more balanced diet, i.e. switches from animal products to a more vegetarian diet, white or yellow moles may appear at the root of the tongue and later at the middle, and still later at the tip. We call this condition "tongue mushroom." It is a *discharge*.[3] The internal disease is being healed. If during the period when the tongue is furred one takes strong Yin such as sugar or alcohol, this discharge will disappear. It usually takes one to two months for the mushroom to move from the root of the tongue to the tip. Sometimes it takes much less time.

When the root of the tongue is black, cancer is a probability. If black tongue mushrooms appear accompanied by a violet color in the hands and black nails, one can suspect cancer.

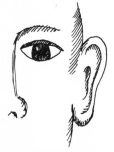

LONG EARLOBES BASICALLY GOOD CONSTITUTION

EARS

A long earlobe shows a good, balanced constitution. The bigger the ear, the better.

Ideally, the top of the ears should be level with the corners of the eyes. A high and pointed ear is Yin, as is an ear that sticks out from the side of the head. A long, low ear with a full lobe is Yang, as is an ear that lies flat against the head.

The ear shows the condition of the kidneys. A red ear indicates a kidney infection and the retention of excess animal protein and salt in the body.

MANY GENERATIONS OF MEAT-EATING

FACE COLOR

In the beginning it will seem hard to distinguish the various degrees of face color. However, a little practice will enable one to differentiate clearly between, for example, a white complexion and a pale one. The meaning of color becomes clear when considered in light of the Five Elements Theory.

Yellow (near orange): Trouble with the spleen-pancreas, liver, stomach and gall bladder. An excess of sweets, such as sugar, harms these particular organs.

White: Indicates a shortage of blood—anemia.

Pale: Pale people with transparent skin become cold easily. The blood collects in certain organs which are probably diseased. The feet are always cold. Pallor is a more Yin condition than whiteness.

Black: Oriental books on medicine use the term "black," but actually dark brown is meant. This color may be indicative of a malfunctioning kidney, unable to filter blood. Overworked by the presence of waste products, the kidney returns the waste to the blood instead of passing it out in the urine. The waste then accumulates throughout the entire body and rises to the surface, giving the skin a dark brown color.

Red: Red always indicates Yang. It signifies an overly Yang condition and probable heart trouble. The color may appear all over the body, or it may be present in certain parts only, as in the case of pimples and rashes.

Red pimples and rashes indicate bad fermentation in the intestines, caused by animal food. Toxins form pimples and rashes.

If the face and nose become red during cold weather, there is blood stagnation, the cold having slowed down the circulation.

If the cheeks and nose become red often, there is an excess of blood, which is an overly Yang condition. The thickness of the blood makes passage through the tiny vessels difficult; this is another type of blood stagnation. When this is the case, it is advisable to avoid animal food.

[3] See also the chapter "Getting Rid of Waste."

When the complexion of an alcohol drinker turns blue or white, the liver has become diseased.

Babies, however, are naturally very Yang (small, compact, and new). With them a red color is a healthy sign. So is a big belly.

* *

When asked if diagnosis by face color could be applied to people of the Negro race also, Sensei Muramoto said, "Perhaps not. In Japan I never had black patients. Now that I am here I must study this. An interesting problem."

* *

Blue: Blue blood capillaries are showing. This is a sign of liver trouble.

Green: Indicates possibility of cancer.

Pink cheeks (called "Yin fire" in Oriental medicine): Appears at two or three o'clock in the afternoon, when the weather warms up. A Yin sign, possibly indicating a tubercular condition.

Blue vessels: Visible in the area of the temples, they show a poor liver condition. They are the mark of an emotional person.

Skin color shows the condition of the lungs in particular, as well as that of the other organs. When there is lung trouble the skin seems beautifully white, but this is not a healthy color. Skin should be light pink or light brown, and brilliant.

We often develop a cold when the skin color is poor.

Hands

Hands, feet and eyes (iridology) can each tell a full story, but these systems must be studied completely before being relied on.

The information a hand can reveal is too extensive to expose in a page or two, even if we were to limit ourselves to the physiological information it contains. A hand is an illustrated book from which every doctor should read. It can confirm for him that which he has already diagnosed elsewhere. Cold hands tell one thing, warm hands another, just as large hands give different information than small ones. He who is experienced in telling what is wrong just by looking at the hand has achieved the excellence of the greatest doctor.

SHAPE OF THE HAND

A thick and full palm is a sign of a strong constitution.

A flexible and thin palm is a sign of delicate health.

Long, thin fingers show delicate health.

Short, thick fingers show strong health.

When the hands are stiff, i.e. when the fingers cannot bend back, the arteries are bad due to cholesterol. This stiffness is normal in people of old age, but not in young people.

TEXTURE AND COLOR OF HAND

Often a person who has changed his diet for the better will notice that his hands, from the wrist down to the fingers, have become red. This means that unclean blood is about to be discharged and filtered by the kidneys. The discharge shows in the hands before leaving the system.

If at this time strong Yin such as vinegar or sugar is consumed, the redness will disappear—the potential discharge having been arrested—but it will return eventually after proper eating is resumed.

When the palms of the hand are yellow, there is probably either gall bladder, pancreas, or spleen trouble. Possibly even liver trouble.

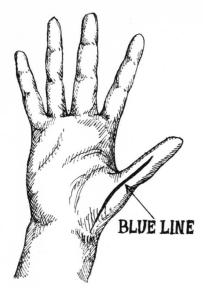

BLUE LINE

STOMACH AND INTESTINAL TROUBLE

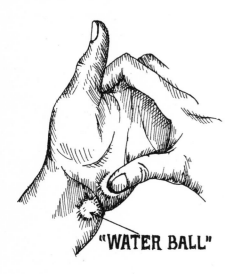

"WATER BALL"

If the heel of the palm is dark red, there may well be problems in the area of the uterus, bladder, or anus. To ensure that one has made the correct diagnosis, one must check to see if the corresponding signs are present. These include:

(a) dark lips

(b) purple gums

(c) violet tongue (present in the worst cases)

A splotchy hand—spotted with different colors—indicates that many different kinds of extreme food have been eaten.

Ideally, the color of the palm should be pink, and the palm itself should be hard. If the palm is purple or blue, excess Yin, such as fruits and sugar, is indicated.

Trembling fingers signify trouble in the heart governor.

The skin of the back of the hand should be very elastic. When pulled away, it must spring back fast. If it is thick and stiff, the individual is not eating a balanced diet—perhaps too much animal food.

Blood vessels should show slightly on the back of the hand, except on a fat person's hand, where there is only a trace of the vessels' color. If you take much liquid, the vessels will bulge; this is a sign that you should drink less.

When the side of the thumb—as far up as the palm—turns blue, there is trouble in the stomach and intestines and probably in all the digestive organs.

Try this: press on the palm towards the wrist. In order to have good results, you must press one-half inch below the wristline, pushing down and in the direction of the line. If a bump appears on the other side of the line, your body is retaining sugar or strong Yin, and you are drinking too much liquid. People who have this *water ball* generally have wet hands.

TEMPERATURE OF THE HAND

The temperature anywhere on the body shows the condition of the person being diagnosed. A high temperature and dryness in the feet and hands is a symptom of Yang. A low temperature is a symptom of Yin, as are warm, wet hands.

The hands should be cool. If they are too warm, the body condition is excessively Yang—probably the liver is overactive.

The hands should also be dry. Wet hands indicate the presence of excess water in the body.

If the hands or fingers tremble, there is probably a heart governor problem.

FINGERS

Each finger is related to a different organ and to the path of energy flow in the body. The relationships are as follows: thumb—lung; 2nd finger—large intestine; 3rd finger—heart governor (nervous system); 4th finger—triple heater; inside of little finger—small intestine; outside of little finger—heart.

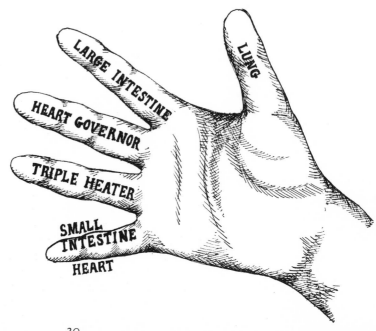

NAILS   Your nails will harden, soften, or become brittle depending on your eating habits. Their quality is affected quickly in a person in delicate health. By simply checking them once in a while, you will learn about your state of health. Sometimes the warning appears suddenly—a bump or a white spot shows up. Such evidence is sufficient to indicate what kind of food, drink or drug is being consumed in excess.

There are various shapes of nails.

YIN   YANG

Long and relatively narrow nails are Yin.
Short, wide nails are Yang.

Flat nails are Yin.   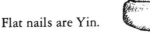   Bulging nails are Yang.

FLAT NAIL
YIN

BULGING NAIL
YANG

CONCAVE NAIL
YIN

When the nail curves away from the finger (concave), parasites are present in the organism. This condition can be double-checked by a look at the whites of the eyes, which would have become blue.

If the nails are hard and crack easily, and if one bites them frequently, there is likewise a probability of parasites in the body. This indication is reinforced if the white of the eye is blue and if the anus itches.

CONVEX NAIL
YANG

When the root of the nail (cuticle) is thick, there is an excess of protein; excess animal protein is indicated especially when this area is red and peeling.

BULGING NAIL
BECOMING FLAT

A significant change in diet is reflected in the nail when the latter becomes either flat or bulging, depending on the person and on the food being consumed. For a while, part of the nail may be flat and the rest bulging.

SIGN OF
EXCESS PROTEIN

White spots in the nail reveal that strong Yin (sugar, chemicals, etc.) was taken in the past. To determine the time of this intake of Yin, observe the distance from the base of the nail to the white spot. However, it is necessary to know the nail's speed of growth, which varies with the individual. Children's nails grow more quickly than those of adults. It might take eight to nine months for an adult's nail to attain full growth, while a child's nail will take only three or four months to grow completely.

WHITE SPOTS
STRONG INTAKE
OF SUGAR OR
CHEMICALS

The moon at the base of each nail should take up no more than one quarter of the nail, especially on the thumb, where it shows most. The small finger should have the smallest moon. The moons should decrease in size when a balanced diet is taken and when food consumption is reduced. It is best to have no moons. The moon on the thumb is the last to go. Older people eat less, so their moons grow more slowly. A moon that is visible on more than one third of the nail indicates too much protein. A pink nail with a white moon signifies good health.

DIAGNOSIS OF ANEMIA

There is a simple way to discover if you are anemic. Stretch your hand, making it slightly tense. Your nails should become white; this is normal. However, if your nails remain white after you relax your hand, you are anemic. Some people do not even have to stretch their hands to show this sign of anemia. Their nails are always white. Such a condition indicates severe anemia. You can double-check this symptom by pulling down the lower eyelid to see if it is pale underneath. It should be red.

Babies that clench their fists tightly have a Yang condition. If they cannot grip tightly, they have a Yin condition.

When the tips of the fingers are enlarged, it is an indication of trouble in the endocardium—a heart murmur or some other problem.

Feet

Most people believe that pain in the feet comes from walking with bad shoes. The answer, they conclude, is to go to a specialist who will correct their feet surgically and recommend suitable shoes to prevent the problem from developing again. It may be necessary for some people to have their feet adjusted because of great pain. The podiatrist's job should not be minimized in these cases. What is being criticized here is the attitude that all foot pain derives from improper shoes.

The feet contain major acupuncture points which, when painful, indicate that the corresponding organ is not in good condition. Everyone can check the condition of his kidneys and digestive organs by walking barefoot on stones. (By the way, it's a good self-massage, especially if you have no calluses on your soles.) If this hurts, you have a sure indication that your digestive organs are in poor shape.

If your feet hurt after you've been standing a long time, you've been taking too much liquid. There is bladder or kidney trouble. The condition that leads to athlete's foot is caused by bad kidneys and is brought about by an excess consumption of animal protein.

The toes should be flexible. One should be able to move each toe and to spread out all of them at will.

Each toe represents an organ. The big toe represents the liver, the second toe the stomach, the third toe the bladder, the fourth toe the gall bladder, and the small toe the kidneys. Pain or discharge in a certain toe always indicates trouble in the corresponding organ. If the second toe is longer than the big toe, the stomach is most likely weak.

A shrunken small toe with a very small nail is a sign of Yang kidney trouble. Cracked nails are a sign that drugs were taken.

Callused skin indicates an over-consumption of protein, especially animal protein. Cracked feet are often caused by some trouble in the spleen-pancreas.

LIVER
STOMACH
GALL BLADDER
KIDNEY

Hair

COLOR

White hair is a sign that one is too Yang. Red hair is more Yang than black hair, though not as Yang as white.

QUANTITY

An abundance of hair is Yin.

TEXTURE

Wavy or curly hair is Yang, while straight hair is Yin. Split ends are a sure sign of serious trouble in the ovaries. Dandruff indicates that the body is trying to get rid of waste, especially animal protein. There is very probably liver trouble.

**TOO MUCH FRUIT
AND LIQUID**

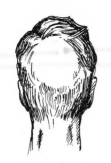

**EXCESS ANIMAL
PROTEIN**

LOSS OF HAIR

Hair falls out because the internal organs are in poor condition. Hair is a living organism. Its life is sustained by the food we eat.

* *

*I have white hair
three thousand feet long.
By too much worry
I got this.*
—Chinese Poem

* *

One can tell what a person eats by the area from which he loses hair. If his hair falls from the front, he is probably consuming too much liquid and fruit. Hair loss from the top of the head indicates excess animal protein. Loss of hair from the back of the head signifies an excessive intake of strong chemicals in the form of drugs or medicine. An extreme intake of sugar and drugs is revealed in the loss of hair from the temples.

The reason hair falls is that the skin has become loose and can no longer hold it. Instead the skin should be firm.

Hair in general is Yin. Long eyelashes are a sign of a Yin constitution, while underarm hair indicates a Yang constitution.

Urination and Feces

THE DAILY CHECK-UP

The morning can be the time of self-evaluation, for your daily urine says more about you than you can guess. This daily check-up is used instinctively by the self-service doctor; it tells him on the spot how much he should permit himself to drink that day, to adjust his body to the liquid intake of the previous day.

URINE

You can tell whether you have been eating or drinking too much just by counting the number of times you urinate in a day. A male should not urinate more than three to four times a day; a female, whose bladder holds more than a man's, not more than two to three times. More frequent urination is a Yin symptom. It is a warning that too much liquid is being consumed.

The color of the urine should be neither too dark nor too light; ideally, it should be the color of beer. It is a bad proportion of food and drink which changes the color of the urine so drastically. If the urine is darker, like dark beer, Yang food (too much meat, fish or salt, or grain exclusively) was taken on the previous day. If it is clearer than beer, like sake, too much liquid was taken. If it is almost like water, you are being warned to stop eating sugar.

* *

Salt, Urine and the Kidneys

The urine of a healthy person is golden in color, like beer. Someone whose condition is too Yang, or who has taken too much salt, urinates less because his kidneys are contracted and release less liquid. His urine is usually brown, like dark beer. On the other hand, if excess Yin food is consumed, the kidneys become too relaxed and filter too much water. This causes frequent urination of a liquid that is pale or colorless, like water.

* *

In general, frequent urination produces urine that is light in color. But it happens sometimes that frequent urination produces dark urine. In this case, the bladder is unable to retain water long enough; it is too contracted.

The condition of the kidneys is indicated by the color of the urine. Dark brown urine is the result of Yang (contracted) kidneys. Urine that is thin and light in color is a sign of Yin (expanded) kidneys.

In general, people whose urine is like water and who always have cold feet have certain kidney trouble.

A child's urine should be thinner than an adult's. Children normally urinate more frequently.

FECES   It is normal to evacuate once a day. The need to evacuate more often is a sign of intestinal trouble.

The feces should be firm, large, and shaped like a banana. They should have no bad odor. Bad odor is a sign of trouble in either the stomach or the intestines.

If fecal matter is light in color, one has been eating more Yin than Yang—more vegetables and fruits than grains and animal food, for example.

The normal color of the feces is brown. If they are very dark, nearly black, there has been a heavy consumption of animal food. If they are greenish, excess Yin (fruits, sweets, etc.) has been eaten.

If the feces are actually black, there may be internal bleeding. Blood from the abdomen or stomach mixes with the feces and produces this dark color. The more severe the bleeding, the darker the color.

The emergence of old feces that are black like coal and contain stones is a discharge which is the prelude to better health (see "Getting Rid of Waste," page 56).

A baby's feces should be yellow and somewhat soft. If they are brown like an adult's, the mother's food is of an overly Yang quality.

When a newborn baby's feces are green, the child is not being given the proper food. Either the mother's milk is of poor quality or the quality of the food being given him is too Yin.

The feces should not sink. When they do, we have been taking the wrong type of food and eating hurriedly. When the food is of good quality and is properly chewed and well digested, it produces brown, firm feces which remain on the surface.

A healthy person needs very few pieces of toilet paper. This is not the case with modern man, who uses rolls of it.

* *

Salt, Feces, and the Intestines

If too much salt is consumed, the large intestine absorbs extra water and one's feces become shrunken and dry. On the other hand, if one's diet consists mostly of milk, fruits and sugar or if insufficient salt is consumed, there is more liquid than is needed by the intestines. In this case the feces have no shape.

* *

In general, constipation is the result of a Yang condition. Sometimes, however, there is Yin constipation. If the stool is small and in balls, like those of a rabbit, and has a good glossiness, there is Yang constipation. If there is no glossiness, there is Yin constipation. With Yang constipation, the intestines are constricted; with Yin constipation they are expanded.

While urination reveals a more recent condition, the stool reveals the condition of the past few days. For example, sugar, fruit and beer will produce a thin urine a few hours after they are taken.

Body Heat

The degree of heat our body generates is an indication of our present condition. By "body heat" we do not mean fever, but simply the heat that everyone generates.

A healthy person is sensitive to this heat and can detect it by running his hand over his body, keeping the hand relaxed and flat, one-half inch or so from the body.

Some parts of the body generate more heat than others. A heated area is an indication that an organ is overactive because it is trying to get rid of waste.

Warm hands and feet may indicate good circulation, but they may at the same time suggest excessive eating and drinking. The feet are the most Yang part of the body and, accordingly, it is proper for them to be warm. The hands, however, should be neither cold nor warm. People with warm hands and feet have a Yang constitution, which means that there is strong bodily activity which quickly distributes the nourishment to produce heat.

Cold hands and feet are a sign of bad circulation due to blood stagnation.

When the top and bottom parts of the body have significantly different temperatures, it is a certain indication of trouble in the triple heater (see "The Organs").

Pressure Points

Manipulation of the pressure points is a method used widely for its accuracy by the Oriental doctor, especially the acupuncturist. Anyone can use it. It is already on its way to becoming very popular in the U.S., for it is easy to practice.

A sharp or dull pain at certain points on the body tells the condition of the organ that one wishes to diagnose. Here is a general pressure point diagnosis which, if followed as shown here, can give valuable information regarding a person's condition.

HANDS

The most common point is the point of the large intestine. Press with thumb and index finger. If pain is felt, the large intestine is not healthy.

If you press the heart governor point and feel pain, there is most likely trouble in the autonomic nervous system. Insomnia, rapid heartbeat, shortness of breath, and irregularity of bowel movements result from the malfunctioning of the meridian on which this point is situated. This point is almost half-way from the line of the arm joint to the wrist.

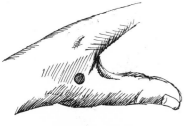

THE POINT OF THE LARGE INTESTINES

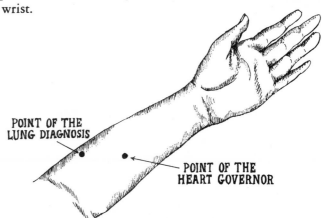

POINT OF THE LUNG DIAGNOSIS

POINT OF THE HEART GOVERNOR

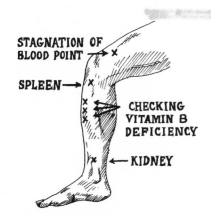

STAGNATION OF BLOOD POINT

SPLEEN

CHECKING VITAMIN B DEFICIENCY

KIDNEY

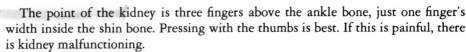

The point of the kidney is three fingers above the ankle bone, just one finger's width inside the shin bone. Pressing with the thumbs is best. If this is painful, there is kidney malfunctioning.

The point of the spleen is situated on the curved point of the leg bone. Pain there shows a disorder of the spleen or pancreas.

The next point to be checked is an important one. It tells accurately whether there is stagnation of the blood (poor circulation). Most people feel pain here. If the pain is sharp, hemorrhoids or pyorrhea is indicated. Women who feel pain at this point may have trouble with their female organs.

Here is a simple way to check whether you have a vitamin B deficiency. Press the flat part of the shinbone. If the flesh does not bounce back, if you press with your fingers and the imprint remains for a while, there is a strong possibility of a vitamin B deficiency.

The abdomen of a healthy person has a bouncy texture. It is neither too soft nor too hard. The muscles are relaxed. There is no pain under finger pressure. The skin should be easy to pinch.

Smell

Sick people have a special smell. When you enter their room or house you can detect a fetid odor. That kind of offensive smell is a discharge of toxins. You will learn later on in this book that odor is the first discharge the body makes before ridding itself of coarser material through either vomiting or anal excretion.

Different races even have different smells. Everyone agrees that Koreans smell like garlic (they eat a lot of it). Oriental people say that white people have a meat smell.

In general, a smell is a discharge of some sort of waste, be it fat or some other kind of food. Some people smell only when they fast. This is because fasting gives the body the opportunity to get rid of its waste. On the other hand, some people emit a bad odor all the time. In this case there is no more room for the waste to accumulate; the organs are trying desperately to clean themselves of the toxins and there is not much they can do.

To the question "Why do people have bad smells in different parts of the body?" Mr. Muramoto gave the following answer: "There is a probable correlation between the smell and the part of the body. I think that people eating much animal food, especially meat, have a bad odor in their feet, whereas people eating dairy food, such as cheese, have the smell in a higher position, perhaps in the sex organs or the armpits."

In general, an exaggerated consumption of animal food produces a bad smell. To cure this, it suffices to eat plenty of green vegetables (chlorophyll)—and to lower the meat consumption, of course.

Voice

Everyone has noticed the not-so-pleasant sound of certain people who normally speak in a high-pitched or loud voice.

A voice suggests the condition of its owner. A very loud voice is the sign of a person who thinks in a disorderly manner. He is screaming to give weight to his concepts.

A high-pitched voice may signify internal disease. Many people have a high-pitched voice sporadically, depending on what they eat.

A normal and pleasant voice is not too high and not too faint. It is vibrating, almost singing.

Fast speech reveals an overactive heart.

Some people express themselves with long sentences and strange noises. This is because they have not found that inner balance which, when expressed in words, has a pleasing effect on the listener. A man in good health speaks very little and makes himself understood with only a few words. Too much food produces too much talk.

* *

What Is Your Sleeping Position?

Most Americans sleep on their stomachs, face down. Western medicine sees nothing wrong with this, even believing it to be beneficial. In Oriental medicine, however, this is looked upon as a sign of swollen digestive organs. From the point of view of a healthy man, this is obviously the position of a sleeping animal.

When man sleeps on his back, he can breathe more easily. In America nowadays, babies are placed on their stomachs. This is not conducive to breathing. Babies naturally breathe through the abdomen, so it is most advisable to lay them on their backs.

American babies feel better lying on their stomachs because of the diet being given them. Improve their diet and they will prefer to sleep in a different position. A new method is often invented to suit a deficiency!

* *

The Yin-Yang principle is quite simple; nevertheless it is usually sufficient for purposes of diagnosis and cure. In some instances, however—with acupuncture and herbal teas, for example—more precision is necessary. Thus Yin and Yang can be subdivided into Greater Yang and Lesser Yang, Greater Yin and Lesser Yin. The distinction is one of degrees of Yin or Yang and is often useful. Of course, there is no thing in existence that is purely Yang or Yin. We call something Yin or Yang because of the dominating force of Yin or Yang present in it. When the dominance is slight, we call it Lesser Yin or Lesser Yang; when the dominance is clear, we say Great Yin or Great Yang, as the case may be.

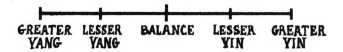

GREATER YANG   LESSER YANG   BALANCE   LESSER YIN   GREATER YIN

An even more useful subdivision of Yin and Yang for purposes of diagnosis is the classification of "Full" (*Titan*) and "Empty" (*Kyo*). This is a measure of energy volume; "Full" people tend to have very much and "Empty" people not enough energy. Accordingly, "Empty" people have a much lower resistance to disease.

By combining Yin and Yang with Full and Empty, we have four basic types of people:

1) Full Yang (*Yang Titan*): He is active, red in color, generally fat, and prone to heart trouble, high blood pressure, cerebral hemorrhage. He is unlikely to develop tuberculosis. *Yang-Full* means the organs are too active.
2) Empty Yang (*Yang Kyo*): He is active, dark brown in color; slim, but still Yang. He is prone to kidney trouble.
3) Full Yin (*Yin Titan*): He is not very active. Blue or yellowish in color and rather fat, he is prone to liver trouble.
4) Empty Yin (*Yin Kyo*): He is inactive, his complexion is pale white. This is the most Yin stage. Such a person is thin and unable to retain energy, prone to lung trouble such as T.B., and anemia.

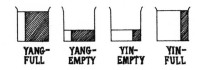

YANG-FULL   YANG-EMPTY   YIN-EMPTY   YIN-FULL

[See also the section on face color in this chapter (page 28) and the section on Empty-Full in "The Theory of the Five Elements."]

The classical treatments for these four basic types are as follows:

Yang-Full: induce vomiting and diarrhea
Yang-Empty: make warm
Yin-Full: make sweat
Yin-Empty: induce harmony

These factors are taken into account in the composing of herb teas. Practically speaking, vomiting, diarrhea and sweating are means of reducing excess energy, therefore these methods are used only with "Full" people. Extremely Yang-Full people may even use all three, while people who are less "Full" should use only one of these. For constipation, either diarrhea or sweating should be induced, but not vomiting. In general, it is better to go slowly; a mild method is more effective in establishing lasting health. For "Empty" people, energy must be given. For people only slightly more "Empty" than "Full," give a little energy. "Empty" and very Yang people should be given Yin-quality food.

THE BLOOD

ACCORDING TO BIOLOGISTS, it takes 120 days for the red blood globules to change completely. This means that there is a 10% difference in the quality of the blood after 10 to 12 days, which is the time it takes for the symptoms of an existing disease to disappear. In other words, although it takes 120 days for the blood to become clean, 12 days of proper eating (no chemicalized, industrial food, no overeating or excess drinking, etc.) are sufficient to remove the symptoms and, in most cases, put us out of danger.

It takes approximately three years to reconstruct the muscle fibers; the same applies to certain organs. But it takes seven years to change the entire bodily constitution. The speed of these changes differs depending on the individual, especially where children, who have a faster metabolism, are concerned. A child's system cleanses itself faster because of its rapid metabolism and superior circulation. Older people, because they usually suffer from blood stagnation, have difficulty in renewing their cells. With the years, their circulation has declined. That is why elderly people always need to cover themselves well. They are sensitive to the cold, while children are able to go out in the cold with fewer clothes.

Every day our blood is renewed while old blood is destroyed. Waste products are expelled by the kidneys and skin. The useful components of the waste products and old blood are retained and used in the bile for the gall bladder.

It is not yet known exactly how blood is made. The small intestine, which is the final organ in the digestive process, starts the manufacture of blood, but the globule is incomplete at this point.[1] The process is too complex for just one organ to complete; there are many further components to be picked up. From the intestines the incomplete blood travels to the liver, heart, lungs, pancreas and finally the spleen. The liver, which makes bile, and the spleen, which is the organ involved in the blood's final stage of development, may be the organs which destroy blood. Thus it is actually possible that the organs which make blood destroy blood.

Is bad blood always discarded? If the treatment is proper, it is definitely eliminated, leaving only new, healthy blood.

---

[1] Many diseases of the blood can arise at this point. See section on leukemia in "The Cure."

Blood attracts the oxygen it needs to renew itself. But how does this process of attraction take place? Red globules contain hemoglobin with iron at the center. Iron and oxygen together (FeO_2) give the blood its red color. Iron (Fe), as everyone knows, is the strongest attractor of oxygen (O_2). Iron left in the open air rusts immediately upon contacting the free oxygen. It is the iron in hemoglobin that enables our blood to attract oxygen. When we eat green leaves, which contain chlorophyll (rich in magnesium), our body extracts the magnesium and, by a process of transmutation, changes it into iron.[2] Chlorophyll and hemoglobin are thus closely related.

Primitive animals have copper in their blood. That is why their blood appears blue or green. When copper (Cu) is left in the open air, it tends to turn green. The blood of octopuses, cuttlefish, insects, etc. is of too weak a quality to attract oxygen. However, highly developed animals have iron in their blood.

Food determines blood quality; good food makes good blood. Good blood, as has already been said, at-tracts oxygen and makes sickness or chronic fatigue less likely.

In order to make good quality blood, one should include green leaves in one's daily diet. These activate the blood and thereby affect the entire body metabolism.

Animals eat plants to form blood and build flesh. By eating flesh we can form blood rapidly, but the quality of this animal blood is poor and short-lived. The process by which a heavy meat eater makes blood is one of decomposition. Plants→blood→flesh is the natural building process. By choosing food from the final stage of this development, we force our organism to make blood by reversing the natural process. This deviation from Natural Law is the cause of many diseases, for no cyclical process takes place. It is most advisable, then, to include greens in our daily meals.

---

[2] See *Good News*, page 54.

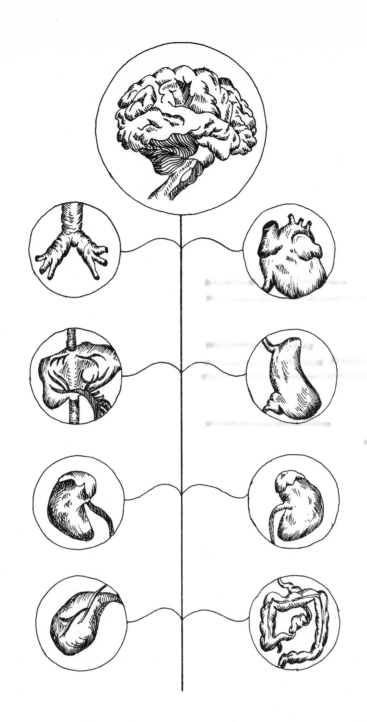

THE ORGANS

IN ORIENTAL MEDICINE, all organs are classified as either Yin or Yang. The Yang* organs (solid and deeper) are the liver, spleen-pancreas, kidneys, heart and lungs. In the *Nei Ching* these five are referred to as the "Tzang" organs (Yin); they are centers for circulation, storage and distribution. The Yin* organs (hollow and closer to the body surface) are the stomach, small intestine, large intestine, urinary bladder, and gall bladder. In the *Nei Ching* these five (plus the triple heater—"three burning spaces"—see below) are referred to as the "Fu" organs (Yang); they are the workshops for nutrition and excretion.

The chapter "The Diagnosis" teaches how to recognize trouble in the organs; the chapter "The Cure" tells how best to heal them. "The Theory of the Five Elements" reveals the significant role of the organs, placing each in a broader perspective.

According to the Five Elements Theory, each Yang organ has a complementary Yin organ. Paired thus, they are: heart/small intestine; liver/gall bladder; kidney/urinary bladder; lung/large intestine; spleen/stomach; and in addition, two organs not recognized by Western medicine: heart governor/triple hearter. In the Theory of the Five Elements this last pair is usually classified under Fire, along with the heart/small intestine.

To explain the heart governor and triple heater in Western medical terms is very complicated; they can best be understood if we say that the heart governor supervises the entire process of circulation, thus connecting together the entire organism. It is approximately equivalent to the autonomic nervous system. The triple heater is traditionally said to control the three systems (respiratory, digestive, excretory) which regulate body temperature. In its function as regulator of body temperature, it is closely related to the skin. These two organs are the most fundamental to life; even the most primitive life forms have an autonomic nervous system and skin.

When there is a formation of many cells grouped around a common entrance for food, there is a stomach/spleen for assimilation and distribution of food.

In more complex life forms, there is a heart/small intestine to regulate circulation of nourishment (liquid) and provide a passageway for waste.

Then come the kidneys/bladder. The sexual organs develop from the kidneys. The kidneys make urine which is passed by the bladder.

The next organs are the liver and gall bladder. The liver filters toxins, stores nourishment, and makes blood and bile; the gall bladder stores and distributes the bile.

The last set of organs, which develops in the most complex organisms, is the lungs/large intestine. Our lungs are the last-developed organ, corresponding to the air bag in a fish (see Fig. 6). In our erect bodies, the lower organs are more fundamental and primitive—more Yang. All the upper organs developed later. In the womb the stomach and small intestine divide, developing a large intestine. From the intestine, the lung develops. Similarly, in the head the brain and eyes are the last to develop (mouth→nose→ears→eyes). There is a close relationship between the brain and the lungs, due to the large amount of oxygen consumed by the brain. Only land creatures have lungs; their brains are more developed than sea creatures' because there is a larger percentage of oxygen in air (20%) than in water (1.8–1.9%).

Heart Governor

Although neither the heart governor nor the triple heater is a concrete and tangible organ, both have basic and important functions and are considered fundamental. The heart governor—which is comparable to the autonomic nervous system—is the body's Yin-Yang coordinator. To give an example: when we take salt we might imagine, as Western medicine asserts, that the initial reaction takes place in the stomach. Actually, as soon as the salt enters the mouth the brain receives the message, and immediately the heart governor begins coordinating the organs to prepare them for this food. The kidneys and large intestine absorb more water, the heart beats more slowly, and the stomach becomes more active.

* See footnote, p. 15.

A malfunctioning of the heart governor affects the pace of the heart. The pulse will be either too quick (Yang) or too slow (Yin). The eyes provide another sign. If they are slow to react or constantly moving, there is a problem with the heart governor. In such cases the pupil will be too large. Often there will be trembling, especially in the fingers and tongue. Repeated constipation and diarrhea, and shallow, dream-filled sleep are also said to indicate a malfunctioning heart governor.

Triple Heater

The triple heater—which controls the respiratory, digestive and excretory systems—regulates our energy. An active person has a strong triple heater.

While the triple heater controls these systems (respiratory, digestive and excretory), the skin connects them. Located at the surface of the body, the skin is thus the antithesis of the heart governor, which is located the deepest inside. The skin and triple heater are therefore closely related.

The organ is called "triple heater" because in the Orient it is held that, for feeling heat, the body is divided into three sections—upper, middle and lower. Sometimes only the trunk feels heat; sometimes the head and feet alone; sometimes only the head or the feet.

Healthy skin has a positive effect on all the organs. Swimming in cold water is good for the skin, as is living in a hot climate. A morning shower using first hot and then cold water is also beneficial; brushing the skin is good too. Best of all is a proper diet.

In its function of controlling body temperature through sweating, the skin is closely related to the lungs. Like the lungs, it takes oxygen directly as a form of nourishment.

The skin not only regulates body temperature through sweating, it also aids the kidneys in releasing wastes from the body. In this function the skin and kidneys are closely connected. Sweat and urine are very similar in composition. If the kidneys deteriorate or become overloaded, and if food heavy in waste products continues to be taken, the waste rises to the skin and gives it a dark hue. If both organs are too overworked to discharge waste, skin ulcers will result as soon as there is contact with bacteria. Although skin conditions can be relieved with "balms" and lotions, these do nothing to help the kidneys, wherein lies the fundamental source of the problem. Skin diseases such as psoriasis, eczema and acne are invariably the result of kidney problems. Treat the kidneys, and the skin will clear up naturally.

When the triple heater is malfunctioning, a white ring often appears around the iris, with a moon above it. The surface of the body may feel cold, or the head may feel hot and the extremities cold.

Stomach

Directly after food is swallowed, the stomach receives it. The stomach is the first organ in the digestive process. It breaks down the food further by mixing it with gastric juices, forming a semifluid mixture called "chyme," and then slowly releases it into the small intestine at a rate suitable for proper digestion by the latter. Fats and proteins remain in the stomach the longest. Carbohydrates have only a mild delaying effect on the emptying process. The stomach secretes different kinds of gastric juices, classifiable as either Yin or Yang, for different kinds of food.

An intake of foods such as sugar and cold drinks which rush directly to the stomach can prevent the stomach from functioning properly. Sugar can inhibit the flow of the gastric juices and produce over-acidity, while cold drinks can actually paralyze the stomach. It is always better to start a meal with relatively hot or solid food to activate the stomach.

Carbohydrates such as grains and bread must be digested very well in the mouth. They must be chewed completely and mixed thoroughly with the digestive juices in the saliva. Gastric ulcers and nearly all other problems of the stomach and duodenum result from poor chewing—and, of course, from excessive amounts of extreme food such as sugar, alcohol, salt and meat (see section on stomach disorders in "The Cure").

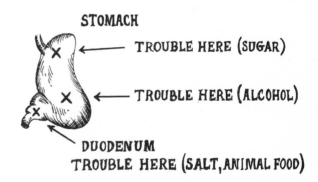

STOMACH
TROUBLE HERE (SUGAR)
TROUBLE HERE (ALCOHOL)
DUODENUM
TROUBLE HERE (SALT, ANIMAL FOOD)

Stomach problems are revealed on the tongue, on the lips and in the feces (see "The Diagnosis"). Excessive or insufficient appetite is also indicative of stomach trouble.

Spleen-Pancreas

Oriental medicine considers the spleen and the pancreas to constitute one organ, the organ complementary to the stomach.

The spleen-pancreas is a digestive organ. Modern physiologists say that the spleen is one of the last organs involved in the formation of red globules. It stores blood and is also an organ where blood is destroyed.

The pancreas secretes hormones; however, the more important functions of the spleen-pancreas are the distribution of nourishment throughout the body and, according to Oriental medicine, the governing of the will and memory. When the spleen-pancreas is malfunctioning, we lose our strength of will and seem foolish. When we become well, our strong will returns.

All diseases which give the skin a yellowish color —diabetes, hyperinsulism, jaundice, etc.—are related to a malfunctioning of the spleen-pancreas. Jaundice, which results from gall bladder trouble, gives the body an almost distinctly yellow color.

For the best method of curing each of these diseases, consult the chapter "The Cure."

Forgetfulness and overworry are both indicative of spleen trouble and can be considered Ki diseases. Jaundice and diabetes-hypoglycemia are blood diseases. While these classifications are not exact, we know that in every disease the Ki is poor.

The spleen is the organ in which Yin and Yang are the most balanced; the empty-full relationship (see "The Theory of the Five Elements") has no specific correspondence with it. In the Five Elements Theory, the spleen is located at the center; when the spleen is sick, the entire body is fundamentally sick. These days it is not rare for the spleen to be diseased. We eat too much sweet food.

Heart

The heart regulates the circulation of blood. It is the body's most Yang organ. There is an obvious connection between the heart and the blood vessels, since the heart is always working very actively to send blood to the whole body through the blood vessels.

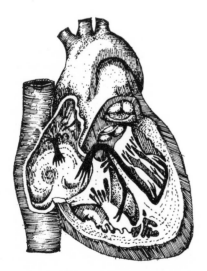

Many cases of heart trouble represent a very Yang condition. People suffering from this condition are extremely active and have a red face color. If the heart is

strong the body is strong; but often the blood vessels become hard—this is sclerosis—causing the blood pressure to rise to an often dangerous level.

A Yin heart condition results when there is some trouble in the heart valve or endocardium, or when a lengthy sickness has made the heart weak. People with this condition are pale and usually have low blood pressure.

High blood pressure is often connected closely to a constriction of the kidneys, which forces the heart to accelerate its function of moving blood (see sections on heart and kidney trouble in "The Cure"). If the heart is weak, the blood fails to reach the extremities and one feels cold. The same feeling may result when salt is eaten. The organs retain blood, and a weak organ does so even more. Salt is a further cause of blood retention in the body centers. Thus, when one takes salt one feels cold initially, but later, when circulation has been established, one feels warm. Sugar has just the opposite effect. Because of its many calories it initially produces warmth, but eventually leaves one feeling cold. Alcohol works in the same way.

Heart problems reveal themselves in the facial and body color and in swelling in various places such as the nose and fingertips (see "The Diagnosis"). Too much or too little laughter is also said to be indicative of heart trouble.

Small Intestine

The small intestine completes the digestion of food and begins the formation of blood, which is completed by the liver (see "The Blood"). The bacterial flora in the small intestine accomplish this work. The small intestine may be compared to the root of a plant. The soil is the home for bacteria which constantly break down what once grew out of the earth, to produce nourishment for what will grow later. In the same way the flora in our intestines break down food and begin the process of making the blood needed to nourish the entire organism. Oriental medicine considers man's body as one with the soil. Just as the earth is barren due to man's shortsighted conquest of the land, so our intestines lie barren, stripped of their beneficial flora by the effects of an artificial diet. When we return to eating natural food, we find that we suffer from the inability to transmute the necessary elements from our food, due to the damage wrought by the modern diet (see section on vitamin B deficiency in "The Cure"). Meat, sugar and chemicals expand and weaken the intestines and destroy the flora. They are not foods for biological transmutation.

When the small intestine does not function properly, there is likely to be blood disease (anemia) and loss of weight. Disorders of the small intestine can be detected in a pale lip color.

Liver

The liver stores and distributes the nourishment for the entire body and is involved in the formation and breakdown of blood. It forms bile from the useful components of the blood and filters toxins from blood which has been newly made in the small intestine. When the liver is overloaded, some of these poisons may remain. Then they cannot be ejected by the kidneys. The liver expands, its functioning deteriorates, and the blood is left uncleaned. The worst "food" for the liver is drugs and chemicals, followed (in this order) by vinegar, alcohol and cold drinks. Poisons from drugs and chemicals linger longest in the liver and are the hardest to discharge. Cold liquid passes quickly through the stomach and intestines, then to the liver and around the body. The effect of alcohol is felt more rapidly in a person with a healthy liver.

An enlarged liver is a very dangerous condition which is caused by overeating. Liver troubles can become acute. Too much of any food is bad for the liver, but especially too much alcohol, vinegar, chemicalized food, drugs, oil and meat. These carry too much nourishment to the liver from the stomach and small intestine, filling and expanding it. While you are in a sitting position, press your liver; if there is pain, you have a liver disorder. Fast or eat little, taking care to avoid the foods just mentioned which are so antagonistic to the liver. Reduced eating is very important for this organ and for the entire body.

Dandruff and hair loss, eye trouble and many other problems are caused by liver trouble (see "The Cure"). Both mental and visual problems are related to a bad liver. A bad liver will reveal itself in many places including the forehead, the eyes, and the facial and body color (see "The Diagnosis").

Gall Bladder

The gall bladder stores bile and regulates its flow into the duodenum (entrance to the small intestine). This process aids the digestion of fat and oil and gives color to the feces.

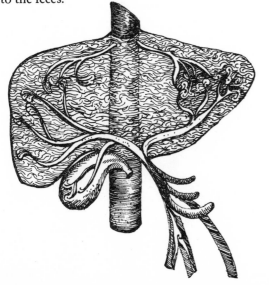

Jaundice is bile poisoning, associated with the gall bladder and spleen. If the passage from the gall bladder to the duodenum is blocked—by a "stone," for example—the bile goes directly into the blood. A greenish-yellow color then appears on the surface of the body, and the feces become white. Usually the feces take the color of the bile, but when the bile is prevented from reaching the duodenum, they become white.

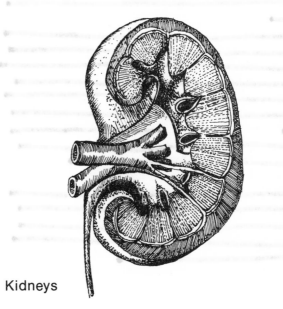

Kidneys

The kidneys are not very large—only about the size of your ears—but their interior is filled with many thousands of tiny porous vessels which serve to filter blood toxins and wastes. Their function consists in filtering the blood and converting waste products into urine. Useful liquids, hormones, etc. are returned to the blood stream. Approximately 100 quarts of liquid pass through the kidneys daily. Of that amount, about 1½ quarts are eliminated; the remainder returns to the blood stream (Diagram 11).

If you take too much of the type of food that produces great quantities of waste products—food such as meat and fowl—then the kidneys cannot effectively filter the large amount of toxins, and a great percentage of the waste is returned to the blood stream. A heavy meat diet induces a contraction of the kidneys, in addition to overloading them with waste. Both conditions force the heart to beat more strongly and the blood pressure to rise in order to aid the kidneys in pushing down the liquid. High blood pressure stems from kidney trouble.

The kidneys are the hosts for the adrenal glands, which Oriental medicine says control the sexual function. The kidneys are considered the governors of the sexual organs, the physical source of all sexual problems. The measure of sexual potency is determined by the kidneys' state of health. Perhaps for this reason the kidneys are known as the "seat of life."

The kidneys affect the condition of the bones. When the kidneys function well, the bones are white inside and strong. Poor kidney functioning resulting from a diet heavy in meat makes the interior of the bones dark.

The kidneys and the skin are closely related. The kidneys eject waste through urination, and the skin ejects waste through perspiration. Sweat and urine are very similar in composition. A skin disease is always the result of the kidneys' inability to filter all the waste effectively; the waste goes to the skin in an attempt to escape.

The kidneys are among the most afflicted organs in modern man. This is due to his heavy consumption of meat. Most Americans, as well as all heavy meat eaters, have overly Yang, constricted kidneys which contribute to arterial and heart disease, high blood pressure and cholesterol, skin problems, swollen thighs, and other illnesses (see "The Cure"). Symptoms of kidney trouble appear in the feet, under the eyes, in the skin, in the urine, and in the overall face and body color (see "The Diagnosis").

Eating and drinking sparingly or not at all is a good method for healing diseased kidneys along with leg and general body swelling, which is a related condition. It is especially important to consume less salt, for salt creates a need in the body for more water. The urine becomes dark brown from excess salt, for one effect of excess salt is liquid retention.

Bladder

The urinary bladder is the liquid-container for the body. It collects and stores liquid from the kidneys prior to urination. Only excessively Yang people suffer from bladder problems. In such cases there is often tenderness along the line that runs down the middle of the back of the leg.

TO FIND OUT IF THERE IS BLADDER TROUBLE PRESS THESE POINTS WITH THUMB.

CHECKING THE BLADDER CONDITION

Large intestine

The function of the large intestine is to complete the absorption of nutrients from food matter, to destroy the texture of food matter by bacterial action, to absorb water, to form the feces, and to store the feces until elimination.

The average adult passes about 1.5 quarts of fluid a day. However, this quantity is much smaller—about one quart or less—for people who eat no meat and who eat mostly grains and vegetables. With such a diet, extra liquid is not needed to counteract the effect of meat on the system. Furthermore, one does not become as thirsty; thus, much less liquid is taken.

When the large intestine fails to absorb enough water, diarrhea ensues. If it absorbs too much water, the result is constipation. Food that has been digested in the small intestine is about 90% water; the large intestine reduces this amount to 80%.

The large intestine secretes a fluid which contains virtually no enzymes for digestion but is strongly alkaline and aids the living bacteria in fermenting and decomposing food. This fluid stimulates bowel movement and also produces gas. Nearly all feces and gas are located in the large intestine.

In addition to diarrhea and constipation, a malfunctioning large intestine may produce convulsions (see "The Cure"). Problems in the large intestine are revealed in the lower lip and in the hand (see "The Diagnosis").

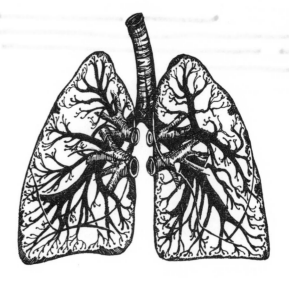

Lungs

By our lungs we are connected directly with our environment. Our lungs take oxygen from the air and feed it to our blood. Just think: millions of green plants are alive for our benefit, providing us with oxygen. The leaves of a tree are very wide; they touch the air and change CO_2 into O_2. Our lungs do the opposite: they take in O_2 and release CO_2. Within the lungs are tiny balls of tissue around which air and blood circulate. If we were to open one of these miraculous balls of tissue, we would find it to be as wide as a tree leaf. Red blood cells travel around these balls, release their CO_2, and pick up O_2.

The lung is the organ that distinguishes the most highly-developed forms of life. It is the last organ to develop in the womb. The more fundamental organs are lower in body position and more Yang. The lung is the most Yin organ. It is special in that its activity can be controlled by our will. All the other organs are moved only by our autonomic nervous system.

Our lungs connect us directly to our environment by breathing, just as our stomach connects us to our environment by receiving food. Without a constant supply of oxygen for his cells, man could not live. Our capacity as thinking beings is dependent on the relationship between the lungs and the brain, for the brain demands much oxygen. If you weigh 150 pounds, your brain probably weighs about 3 pounds, or 2% of your total body weight. Yet the brain requires 25% of all the oxygen used by the body. Compare this to the 12% used by the kidneys, the 7% used by the heart, and the varying smaller percentages used by the other organs. We may prefer mental work to physical work, thinking it easier, but actually physical work is much less fatiguing.

All fatigue is caused by an oxygen deficiency in the cells. Vigorous physical work is always accompanied by an increase in breathing and heartbeat, as well as in the flexing of muscles and the movement of various parts of the body. These factors cause a rapid exchange of O_2 for CO_2 on a cellular level. Though the brain requires much blood for its work, mental work is rarely accompanied by deeper breathing and better blood circulation; in fact, the opposite is usually the case.

The mental effort involved in reading, writing, thinking and worrying is very taxing to our bodies. Thus, good breathing is extremely important for mental and physical health. Meditation or exercises involving proper breathing from the abdomen can be most beneficial. These are much better than massage, acupuncture or herbs, because you do them yourself. You don't have to rely on anyone else. If our breathing is sufficient, we can sustain activity over a long period of time without fatigue. Sensei Sakurazawa said that fatigue is the first sign of disease, and that good food is the best cure for any illness. But clean air is more important than food. We are breathing all the time, while we eat only two or three times a day. Proper food must be complemented with deep breathing and good air; neither is sufficient by itself.

Lung problems can be detected in the cheeks, nostrils, skin color, and other places (see "The Diagnosis"). Respiratory ailments such as asthma and tuberculosis are related to the lungs (see "The Cure"). They are caused by an excessive intake of meat, sugar and chemicals. The act of smoking disturbs the natural respiratory cycle by overstimulating inhalation. The tar and nicotine may adhere to the uric acid deposits in the lungs, thus making lung cancer a possibility. Uric acid deposits, however, are a result of excessive consumption of animal protein. Thus, while it is clear that smoking is not a good habit, smoking alone cannot be blamed for the lung cancer that is so prevalent today. The true cause, which makes this and all other diseases possible, is faulty diet.

ON UNDERSTANDING DISEASE

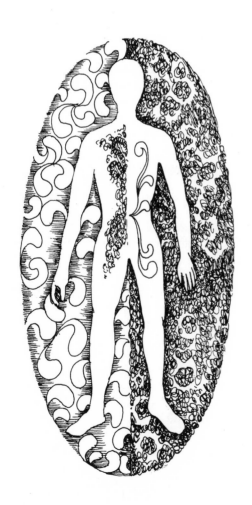

SINCE ANCIENT TIMES, Oriental peoples have recognized that our bodies are merely a part of nature and that man is always living under nature's influence. Each human body is a miniature cosmos, a replica of the great cosmos that is Nature. There is an order, a principle of constant flux in nature, and it is in accord with this fundamental principle that our world is always changing. In Oriental philosophy, this principle is known as the "Yin-Yang theory." Our bodies are one with the universe; body and soil are not two. All phenomena are born from the Ki (or "Chi") of Yin and Yang.

"Ki" is the energy of the universe. It is more fundamental than the energy of "light," "electricity," "gravity," "magnetism," etc. The Ki of Yin and Yang is continually emerging from and returning to the infinite source itself.

Sun, planets, air, water, plants, animals and man all have Ki in differing degrees and combinations of Yin and Yang. The movement of the sun, moon and planets, the cycle of the seasons, the changing of day into night, and even our thoughts are products of the Ki of Yin and Yang.[1]

---

[1] As was already mentioned in the chapter "Yin and Yang," the most fundamental aspect of Yin is centrifugal (expanding) force, while Yang is basically centripetal (contracting) force. From the simultaneous antagonism and attraction between these two opposing forces, energy and change are born, and from energy all physical-material phenomena are produced. Yet Yin and Yang are but relative forces. Neither expansion nor contraction can be maintained forever; all matter and all created phenomena are always in flux. Nothing can be constant or permanent except the infinite source of Yin-Yang itself.

Our bodies are a combination of Yin and Yang, and our minds work by means of Yin-Yang Ki energy. If our bodies maintain a harmonious balance of Yin and Yang, we will be healthy; if we lose that harmony, we become sick.

We are constantly receiving energy from magnetic forces, cosmic rays, etc.; however, the strongest energy we receive is the energy from the sun.

In daytime we wake up and move into activity; at night we rest and sleep. In the spring, plants awake from their winter sleep and blossom into flowers and leaves. Summer is the height of visible activity, when everything grows and ripens. In autumn, grains and seeds are harvested. At last comes winter, when plants and animals take their rest. On the earth the tropical zone is hot (Yang), the polar regions are cold (Yin). Everything in the world is under the influence of the sun.

The Cause of Disease

Today we tend to think that disease is caused externally—by bacteria, viruses, chemicals, etc. In truth, this is only a partial answer. While certain bacteria may make some people sick, the same bacteria will have no apparent effect on other people.

It is important to realize that the source of disease is twofold; the cause of disease lies both outside the body and within. In actuality, the inner cause is the more significant, for it is one's own physical condition which is the major factor in determining one's health. The inner causes of disease include physical strain from excess eating and drinking, too much sex, overwork, and emotional strain from excess or overly intense anger, worry, fear, and even laughter.

Despite these many factors, Oriental medicine often states that there is only one cause of disease—improper eating. It is food which makes up our body; our basic physical constitution and present physical condition are determined mainly by the food we eat. On the simplest level, those who are sick because their condition is too Yang should eat Yin-quality food, while those who are too Yin should take food that is more Yang. The best way to prevent disease is to eat a balanced diet of good food in moderation.

Classification of Disease

In Oriental medicine we have a different way of understanding disease. An ancient Chinese classic *Lu Chih Ch'un Ch'iu* (The Annals of Spring and Autumn) by Lii Pu Wei, who died around 230 B.C., says that we are constantly receiving the Ki of the universe either directly or through the sun, the earth, our food, etc.; that we are born by the Ki of the combining of Yin and Yang and that we die when Yin and Yang separate. All disease comes from a stagnation of Ki or a disharmony between Yin and Yang.

Even today the Japanese word for disease is "byoki," which means literally "all Ki" or "the evil of Ki." Stagnation or imbalance in the flow of Ki within the body leads to imbalance and abnormalities in body fluids and blood. Thus, in the later development of Oriental medical theory, disease is broken down into the general categories of Ki disease, water disease and blood disease. Diseases within each of these classifications can be either Yin or Yang.

Ki Disease

"Ki" (Japanese—"Chi" in Chinese) may be described as the force of the universe. It circulates in the body and animates it. When this force is prevented from circulating properly, disease immediately arises. The Ki of the body functions as the motor of the nervous system, relating all bodily functions to each other. It also connects the body to the outside world.

The proper circulation of Ki creates harmonious movement throughout the body. A poor Ki circulation brings impaired actions and disease.

Every disease, no matter how classified, indicates a Ki stagnation. When the flow of Ki is impeded, sickness may manifest itself as a result of an excess of Ki in one area (meridian) or from a subsequent deficiency of Ki somewhere else.

Ki disease is present, for example, when the stomach feels cold. A hospital examination will reveal no problem, but still the stomach is cold.

People suffering from Ki disease may feel constant discomfort in the throat when there is no visible problem.

Sleeplessness, mental disturbance, unexpected pain in any part of the body, and diseases of the nervous system are all manifestations of Ki disease. Ki disease affects the nervous system and brain and is the direct cause of mental problems such as melancholy, hysteria, and neurosis.

Oriental medicine considers someone to be sick *when that person considers himself sick, even if no symptoms are present*—at the very least there is a mental problem (Ki disease). And when someone says he is healthy when he is obviously suffering, he is also considered unhealthy. Yet while an individual may know himself to be temporarily sick, if he still has a relatively good Ki circulation he knows he can cure himself quickly without too much difficulty.

Ki disease can often be healed with strong-smelling foods such as onions, garlic, hot peppers, scallions, ginger, and chiso leaves. Sometimes it is only necessary to smell these foods to effect a cure. A proper circulation of Ki is restored thanks to the property these foods have of stimulating the organism.

The Anniversary of Your Conception:
A Day of Celebration!

The period of time from conception to birth determines an individual's endurance throughout life. Oriental medicine considers this period to be a very important factor in diagnosis. For a traditional Oriental doctor, the most significant period in the life cycle is the first three months in the womb. During this time the foetus is molded to produce a certain kind of person; personality traits as well as the most important physiological characteristics are determined.

Here is an interesting fact: at the time of the conception anniversary we are the strongest and are unlikely to become sick. On the other hand, at the regular birthday we are more prone to sickness.

All this brings us to one point: if at the conception anniversary, when we are strong and unlikely to fall ill, we do contract a disease, we will be more likely to develop a sickness that will be very difficult to uproot—having been weakened at the very moment when we should have been at our best. However, a disease contracted at the time of our actual birthday is easily cured, for we are not expected to be strong at this point in our life cycle. We still have the opportunity to strengthen ourselves.

Modern medicine has not yet conducted adequate research into the beneficial effect strong-smelling food has on the Ki. In Japan and China such food has traditionally proved to be a radical method for curing certain ailments. (The West also has this tradition: cayenne pepper is used extensively in American folk medicine remedies—Ed.)

Many Ki diseases are considered Yin diseases. Ki disease leads to water disease. The fundamental tea remedies for Ki disease are Hangekobokuto and Sashikokito. Sometimes these troubles can be cured simply and quickly. Other times Ki disease proves to be the most difficult to cure, as in cases of mental disorder.

Water Disease

The liquid inside the body is called, simply, water. Water disease relates to the amount of water present in the body. Too much or too little water in the body or in any part of the body is the cause of many troubles.

Excess water causes swelling. Water is Yin. Swelling (expansion) is also Yin, but one should not hasten to assume that all water diseases can be classified as Yin diseases. A Yang body retains water. The controlling center for our body liquid is the kidney. Thus, water disease is always connected to the kidneys. For example, taking too much meat or salt brings about a Yang condition of the body and particularly the kidneys. When the kidneys are too contracted (Yang), they do not pass water freely and the body becomes bloated.

Too much mucus, tears, sweat or urine are all easy-to-detect signs of water disease. Coughing, accelerated heartbeat, noise in the stomach or intestines, and a bloated appearance are other sure signs of water disease.

Aduki beans (small, red beans) are an old and excellent remedy for kidney problems.

Water disease leads to blood disease. The fundamental tea remedy for water disease is Goreisan.

Blood Disease

Almost all blood diseases are considered Yang diseases, although a few, such as leukemia and hemophilia, are Yin.

When the blood quality and circulation become poor, various troubles arise throughout the entire body. This is blood disease. As soon as the blood has been cleared of pollution and the circulation restored, there is an immediate restoration of health.

Yang people and Yang-type diseases are the easiest to cure, for Yang changes very quickly. It is not as deep-rooted. Remember, however, that at every stage of disease the proportions of Yin and Yang vary, depending on one's constitution, condition,[2] diet and type of activity.

The most efficient and lasting way to cure blood disease is by means of good quality food, for food becomes blood at the end of the digestive process (in the intestines). New blood is constantly being created; therefore, a significant improvement in blood quality can take place rapidly. To bring this about, one must use good judgment in choosing a proper diet.

If we take animal food, the body can make blood easily, but the quality of the blood will not be good—it will be too thick (Yang). As a result, we instinctively tend to take a lot of sugared food and fruit; then the blood becomes too thin (Yin).

Blood disease affects the bladder, anus, uterus, ovaries, and certain other sexual organs. Blood stagnation is Yang and affects primarily the organs of the lower abdomen. It also causes ulcers of the skin and ulcers and tumors in general. Leukemia and anemia are Yin blood diseases. Alkalosis is also a Yin type of blood disease, while acidosis is a widespread Yang disease which can lead to more serious ailments. (See also section *Blood Disease* in chapter "The Cure.") The fundamental tea remedy for blood disease is Tokaku Jokito.

The simplest way to classify diseases is according to Yin and Yang. Every case of disease is connected with a particular condition of the body. Yang people get Yang diseases, Yin people get Yin diseases.

---

[2] For the distinction between "constitution" and "condition," see "The Diagnosis," page 22.

Yang diseases have pronounced symptoms. This type of disease is active and quick to change. High fever, strong pulse, body pain, dry throat, heavy coughing, etc., are all symptoms of Yang disease.

Yin diseases usually do not manifest such strong symptoms. A person with a Yin disease always wants to lie down, lacks energy, and appears pale. Although a Yin disease often may not seem serious, the condition is slow to change and thus Yin diseases are actually more difficult to conquer than Yang diseases.

A typical Yang disease is high blood pressure and cerebral hemorrhage; a typical Yin disease is tuberculosis. In fact, these two diseases are opposites in Yin-Yang quality; it is extremely rare for someone to get both of these diseases.

A similar example: tooth decay is Yin and pyorrhea is Yang. People who have many decayed teeth very rarely have pyorrhea as well.

The Different Stages of Disease

Everything in nature is constantly changing, disease included. Usually an acute disease changes very quickly. Almost all disease starts as acute and after a long period of time changes to chronic. Therefore, the changes that take place in the early stages of disease are very important.

About 1800 years ago, Chang Chung-Ching, the author of *Shang Han Lun,* wrote that disease advances through six basic stages. This method of classification proves most useful, for it simplifies and defines clearly the progression of disease.

The three stages of disease above the horizontal line are dominated by Yang. Below the line are the three stages of disease dominated by Yin. At the beginning of disease, signs of vigor are still present, but if the disease persists, the patient becomes weaker and weaker. This decline may occur over a period of days or years, depending on the nature of the disease.

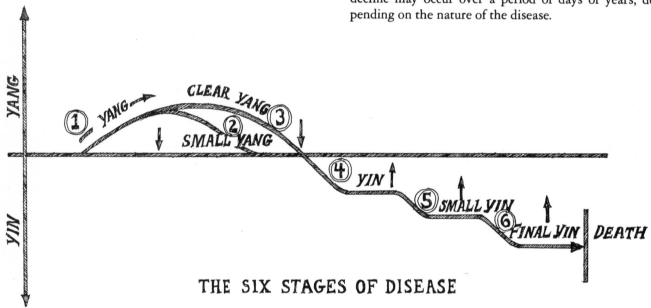

THE SIX STAGES OF DISEASE

STAGE 1

THE BEGINNING OF A YANG DISEASE

Here, Yang is felt on the surface of the body. The superficial pulse is strong; there is pain in some parts of the body, accompanied by chills, high fever, and often headache, forehead pressure, coughing, stiff shoulders and painful joints.

The cause of this illness is Yang. This means that it was contracted after great activity. Such symptoms are an indication that the patient has enough strength within himself to repel waste. Persons with weak constitutions cannot even produce fever; they lack sufficient internal energy. When these symptoms occur, we are at the first stage of disease; therefore, we can effect a rapid cure—without the use of medicine—simply by wrapping ourselves in blankets to induce sweating.

STAGE 2

THE SMALL YANG STAGE OF DISEASE

The disease is still somewhat apparent on the surface; it has also gone into the stomach. There is headache, strong superficial pulse, a heavy feeling in the stomach, and a hard and swollen abdomen. In many cases, tongue mushrooms appear—the tongue looks white or yellow. There is usually constipation.

STAGE 3

THE CLEAR YANG STAGE OF DISEASE

Here the Yang is no longer on the surface; it has moved into the stomach and intestines. The stomach is heavy, sometimes aching. There is constipation, the deep pulse is strong, the higher abdomen is hard. Other symptoms include: bitter taste in the mouth, thirst, dizziness, fast heartbeat, loss of appetite, nausea, and sometimes vomiting.

A Yang disease can change quickly. If the treatment is good, the disease will disappear soon. If the treatment is not suitable, however, the disease changes to Yin disease.

STAGE 4
THE BEGINNING OF
YIN DISEASE

The initial stage of Yin disease takes place in the stomach and intestines as does Clear Yang, but at this point Yang has changed to Yin. The abdomen is soft, there is no appetite, the stomach aches, constipation often changes to diarrhea and sometimes vomiting, the deep pulse becomes weak and the feet are usually cold.

STAGE 5
THE SMALL YIN STAGE
OF DISEASE

Now the heart too becomes weak. At this point the patient will not sit up. The pulse is weak, the appetite has disappeared, and there is diarrhea, vomiting, and a noticeable loss of weight. This is a critical stage; at this time the disease may become fatal. Yang-type people can die in a matter of days, for they change very quickly; for them, the disease affects the heart and liver. Yin-type, weaker people, however, can last for years in this stage. Unlike their strong, Yang-type counterparts, they are accustomed to fighting illness and disease.

STAGE 6
THE FINAL YIN STAGE
OF DISEASE

This stage is the most serious. All the organs become weak. There is a desire to eat, but if food is taken vomiting results. There is severe diarrhea or sometimes constipation, depending on what the patient is given to eat. The upper body, especially the head, is hot; the lower body, including the hands and feet, is cold. There is no high fever, although the temperature may approach 100 degrees, for a Yin type of disease cannot cause high fever; the body hasn't enough energy for that. The patient may also sweat and urinate excessively—a dangerous condition at this point, because all the liquid may leave the body.

It is obvious that these six stages of disease must be treated differently, and that each stage is progressively more serious. There are particular treatments for each stage, specifying what kind of food or herb tea must be taken. The reader can see that it is easier to heal oneself at the first stage of disease than at the last, for at the end the patient has no strength of his own by which to recover. However, the first stage can also be very dangerous, for it is the most Yang and the condition can change very quickly for the worse. The chapter on teas contains the various kinds of herbs used for each stage of disease (page 97).

****

Good News

M.D.'s, nutritionists, and agronomists are now being offered the opportunity to study their own field in depth, thanks to a new trend of thinking in science. It has been proved that elements do change their structure at low temperatures. This discovery—made by Professor Louis Kervran —confirms that there is no need to take a specific element and lock it in the organism.

Today thousands upon thousands of people are practicing this new science—M.D.'s, nutritionists, agronomists, biologists and laymen included. This science is called biological transmutation, *and it is here to clarify for us that which a few hundred years of progress in science has been unable to discern—that, for example, manganese changes into iron, and vice versa; that sodium changes into potassium; that magnesium changes into calcium, etc. In his book* Biological Transmutations,* *Louis Kervran provides insights into many different fields of science. To nutritionists he advises against the giving of calcium directly, especially if the calcium is in mineral form. To persons suffering from arthritis or bone fractures, he recommends horsetail, a plant rich in* silica. *He warns doctors against prescribing medicines which may do more harm than good. A full explanation is provided regarding this point, especially concerning delicate illnesses such as heart disease, Cushing's disease, etc. Mr. Kervran proves that the injecting of one particular element into a patient can prove fatal, since that element, upon entering the blood stream, can change into its opposite by way of transmutation.*

One who reads this book will undergo a complete change in outlook regarding most fields of science, especially nutrition, medicine and agriculture.

Louis Kervran has worked with thousands of colleagues throughout France during the past 25 years. He began proclaiming the news only 12 years ago, when it became clear to him beyond the shadow of a doubt that there is transmutation of the elements.

Certainly this is good news for all of us.

* *Available from Swan House Publishing Co., P.O. Box 170, Brooklyn, N.Y. 11223.   Hardcover $5.75, softcover $2.75 plus 35¢ for postage and handling.*

****

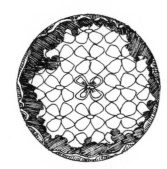

GETTING RID OF WASTE

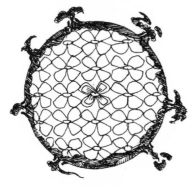

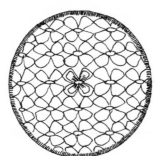

A PASSAGE from an ancient "Sho Sutra" states, "If tea or medicine does not *meigen,* disease cannot be cured." *Meigen* refers to what happens during the last stage of a disease, before the disease releases its hold. Because of the curative process taking place, one actually feels worse. This condition is a sign that health is being restored. At this time one should not try to stop the pain by artificial means, even though one will feel still worse before recovering. It is important to let the curative process take place naturally, with no interference.

Grave problems may accompany this sudden eruption of pain. During this period the patient becomes worried and may, in a state of panic, act out of poor judgment. Not realizing that health is close at hand, he may resort to the pain killers usually prescribed at this stage by modern medicine. To suppress the pain is to retard the cure, since the pain signifies imminent release.

When people change from one diet to another, especially from a diet of dairy food and meat to one of grains and vegetables, they eventually experience what is called a "discharge." This is always a positive sign indicating that toxins are leaving the body and that health is about to be restored.

Discharge generally begins with pain. Pain progresses through the body in ordered stages during the elimination of toxins.

The pain begins in the neck area and travels both downward and upward.

It moves from the neck to the lower abdomen and down the arms and legs.

The last stage in the downward progression occurs in the tips of the fingers and toes.

The pain also travels upward from the neck to the head, the last stage occurring at the top of the head.

At this stage, mucus may be released abundantly through the nose. There is generally pain in any part of the body that is already weak or malfunctioning.

In the most severe cases, vomiting occurs. Some people are quick to discharge, some are slow;

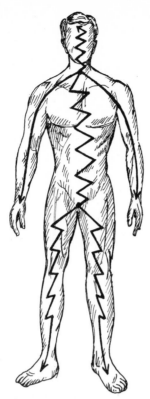

PROGRESSION OF PAIN

it depends on the individual constitution. Some people even react after eating one simple meal. So accustomed are they to meals consisting of dairy food, meat, sweets, soft drinks, etc., that something as foreign to them as a simple, healthy meal can produce a very rapid reaction.

In the first stage of discharge, the body may exude a bad odor. This symptom is often followed by vomiting —the food is being sent back to the mouth. When no food is left in the stomach, liquid bile (green in color) may emerge. Suffering may be acute at this point, but one should not panic. During the next stage a sticky and colorless substance, similar in consistency to a spider's web, may come out. At this time the suffering may be at its peak. However, when this sticky substance— which comes from the intestines—has been expelled, the suffering is over. This last stage is usually accompanied by a headache.

When vomiting occurs at the first stage, suffering and loss of appetite can be relieved by the plum-soy-ginger-bancha drink. During the second stage, simply take bancha, habu seed, or hato (wild barley) tea. At this point a salt plum would probably taste too salty. If the patient feels hot at this time, green leaves or a chlorophyll plaster (see "External Treatments") may be applied over the whole body.

The reason such vomiting occurs is that excess matter inside the body has started breaking down and is trying to get out in any way that it can. The odor is the first stirring of this, followed by the heat. During these

various reactions people usually dislike eating simple food such as grains and vegetables, and often groan at the sight of it. They may even dislike the same salt plum-bancha tea drink that they had gladly taken before.

During discharge, old feces, black in color and usually containing tiny stones, are expelled. In some cases the skin peels off the entire body, leaving beautiful new skin. At this time the thinking is clear and the body clean. Hato tea or tea made from roasted barley can aid in the elimination of old feces.

A long history of bad food intake causes old feces to collect. This accumulation is the cause of most diseases. People who fast extensively may break up this blockage, but not always, for a severely weakened patient has insufficient energy left to discharge waste. One should be very cautious in such cases, for weak people cannot stand the strain of a rapid elimination.

An enema may be tried by Yang people, but enemas are rarely effective when the blockage is in the upper intestinal tract, as is the case with old feces. A better and more natural treatment is to softly massage the abdomen with your hand in the area around the navel. The bowels will soon move.

A diet consisting of a large proportion of brown rice (or other whole grains) and white noodles is another natural means of accelerating the discharge of old feces. This diet should be complemented by steady exercise, such as a five or ten mile walk daily.

Different symptoms appear in the body at each stage of discharge. During the first stage, the root of the tongue may be covered with white or yellow moles. This yellowish color moves to the middle of the tongue in the second stage, and to the tip of the tongue in the third stage. Finally it disappears, at which point health is restored. If the color of the moles is black—a condition which is usually accompanied by a violet color in the hands and nails—we can suspect cancer.

During the first stage of discharge, the hands and feet become red. In the second stage the red color travels downward, and in the third stage the redness remains only in the fingers and toes. This means that bad blood is being released into the blood stream and is about to be eliminated.

At the time headache occurs, one must be wary of a possible disorientation. Individuals have been known to experience prophetic visions, seeing distant places and predicting the future. In some cases, ghosts, from ancient times right up to the recent past, have appeared and vanished in succession. At the next stage of discharge, health is restored and these special powers disappear altogether. Only an ill person will see these apparitions. It is interesting to note that people who wish to retain these visionary powers tend to eat a great deal of fruit.

When head pain occurs, it is inadvisable to take any drug to alleviate the discomfort. Rather, one should

56

allow the pain to run its course, letting the body discharge whatever is causing the suffering. If and when this pain occurs, one should be careful to resist any strong cravings for bad food.

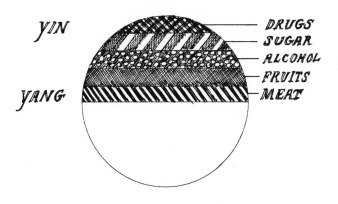

ORDER OF ELIMINATION

Toxins reside in different levels of the body and are released accordingly in their own time. When these toxins begin to be released, there will be a craving for a specific type of food—meat one day, fruit another day, alcohol the next, etc. Animal food, vinegar, alcohol, sugar, drugs, is the usual order of elimination. Usually, the craving is for that which is being discharged.

An alcohol drinker usually retains alcohol in his body for twenty-four hours. Precisely when the alcohol leaves his body, he will crave another drink. A regular drinker who gives up the habit suddenly, often has a sensation of madness when he craves another drink. Sugar works in the same way, producing a very strong craving in one who has to free himself from it. Satisfying these urges will most likely bring temporary relief, for the discharge will be halted for the moment. However, the toxins are still in the organism and the process will have to be completed eventually so that the organism may be rid of this potential threat to health.

There must be a good understanding of what these cravings signify. Otherwise, the pressing desire will be followed and the person will once more lose himself in harmful eating habits—soft drinks, alcohol, candy bars, whatever. Eventually the quality of the cravings will change as the condition of the body improves. Meanwhile, however, this stage is the most critical, for now when the floodgates are open, one brief indulgence can cancel out weeks or even years of steady progress.

A proper diet is the most highly recommended treatment for establishing health. For this, the Yin-Yang principle can be of great help when applied in the choice of food for a particular cure. If a patient is strong enough to walk and chew, a rigorous method may be employed. First he can try a diet of brown rice (whole grain) alone for 3 days. If this does not work

—if the discharge of waste fails to occur—he can alternate a one-week diet of Yin food with a one-week diet of Yang. For example, he can try one week of cereals with both cooked and raw vegetables in equal amounts, followed by a week of cereals combined with cooked vegetables exclusively and accompanied by sesame salt, pickles, and more salty food in general.

For those too weak to chew thoroughly or walk (people of the Yin type), rice milk, rice cream, buckwheat cream or vegetable soup is advised.

A person with a strong constitution (a Yang-type person) should abstain from animal food; instead, he should take raw vegetables. If upon eating raw vegetables he feels weak, the Yang has changed to Yin. In such a case it is then advisable that he switch to cooked vegetables and saltier food so as to establish balance.

When using the radical method (rice only, and some tea), you may become constipated. If this happens, take buckwheat or aduki beans.

Whenever a diet of mostly Yang or mostly Yin food is ineffective, try the opposite. If neither is effective, alternate one week of Yang food with one week of Yin. With the latter method the body "swings" from Yin to Yang and from Yang to Yin, alternately drawing out either Yin or Yang toxins. Weak people, however, cannot stand the strain of a sudden elimination of old feces. For them, this method may be dangerous.

The amount of salt and water is very important, for too much or too little of either will interfere with the positive effects of a good diet. Salt should enhance the flavor of the food, not dominate it. If salt is the main ingredient tasted, rather than the food itself, too much salt is being used. The correct measure of salt always brings out the ideal taste.

To hasten the discharge, it is best to drink less than usual. For example, try abstaining from all liquids for two days, drinking only a few sips of tea. While you refrain from drinking, you will have little desire to eat; this lack of appetite is beneficial, for an empty stomach accelerates the discharge process. When you resume eating, it is advisable to take vegetables in order to establish a good, balanced blood condition.

In general—both for losing weight and for other purposes such as cleansing ourselves from a disease—we should avoid any sudden restriction of liquid intake. In almost any American, a drastic restriction will cause a heavy discharge of toxic matter. In most of the States the air is dry, as compared with Japan; the climate is relatively warm, and meat is consumed abundantly. These are Yang conditions which must be taken into consideration. Therefore, Americans in general have a tendency to take more moist foods (Yin).

If a meat eater should restrict his drinking, he would feel hot by way of reaction. This condition should not be interpreted as fever; it is merely a sensation of warmth. Sometimes a headache will follow. When we advise someone to restrict his liquid intake, we must at the same time tell him how to handle the possible reactions. What happens most of the time is classic—most people fail to recognize their resultant cravings as a positive sign of discharge, and start drinking strong liquids such as whiskey. A more violent reaction will most likely happen in a person with a strong constitution who eats too much salty food. Such a reaction is always the result of a quick discharge of toxins.

A discharge can last one week, sometimes two, and in some cases even longer. The strength and duration of the discharge depends generally on past eating habits and the method of cure being employed. For example, the use of compresses or herbs will hasten the discharge.

In some cases the discharge occurs through the normal excretory channels with no violent reactions. This is good. But in other cases, when, for example, one has followed a strict diet for a certain period of time and is still unsuccessful in getting rid of latent disease, it may be that he is chewing poorly or is eating in an unbalanced way (taking a disproportionate quantity of liquid, salt, or oil). In this case, limiting food intake will prove helpful. Such a person will know that he is not doing well because he will be in constant pain, a sign that toxins are still present in the organism.

Sometimes an herbal tea will cause a discharge. This reaction is called "meigen" and is distinctly different from a side-effect. Soon after this unexpected discharge, the patient becomes well.

There is an important point to note regarding newborn babies. It concerns the release of old feces which collect in the baby while it is in the mother's womb. It is essential that the baby get the mother's first milk as his first food. This milk causes diarrhea and releases the old feces. It is the common practice of many hospitals to teach mothers to throw away that first milk since it causes diarrhea. This is foolish advice, for there is nothing more natural than for the baby to have that milk. To follow such advice is to prevent the old feces from being released, thus running the risk of serious complications.

CASE HISTORY

A Tale of Weight Loss,
Black Blood,
Orange Ghosts and Ice Cream!

I once met a fat woman (5'5" tall, 160 pounds) who complained of not having conceived a child after three years of marriage, even though she had switched to a good diet of grains and vegetables. Her feet were very cold and her female organs were in poor condition. I advised her to lose thirty pounds; she answered that she had dieted strictly for several years, but without much success.

Usually in such cases, the problem stems from the reten-tion of much excess protein. However, according to my observations, this woman had lost most of her excess protein by following a grain and vegetable diet for two years. Nevertheless, she remained fat. I could see that her trouble was due to retention of excess water, sugar and drugs taken in the past. Thus, I advised her to come with her husband and stay for a few days at the camp where I was lecturing on Oriental medicine. I advised her to eat anything she pleased from what we were serving, except, of course, that which she was having difficulty discharging; namely, liquids (we never serve sugar in any form!). I told her that she could increase her salt intake without danger, for I could see that she was not storing much animal protein.

When she arrived at the camp two days later, she told me that she had succeeded in drinking no liquids but that she had seen a ghost and had been unable to sleep. When I learned that her husband had been with her during that time, I knew that the ghost could not have been the product of any great fear. Rather, it was a by-product of the discharge. So I answered, "Your ghost vision is an illusion. Sleeping less is better for you anyway, for it will help you lose weight by being more active. Please continue the same diet, no liquid or sugar."

It was safe for her to continue abstaining from liquid, for I could see that the discharge was almost finished. How did I know? Because, upon being questioned she had told me that the ghost was orange! Discharge occurs in a Yin-to-Yang order, and the color orange is located at the Yang end of the spectrum.

She said that she had no appetite, to which I replied that she did not need to eat anyway and should instead have a mixture of salt plum, soya sauce, ginger, and bancha tea. This drink is beneficial for people with no appetite; it also strengthens the heart, an important factor for people who are losing weight suddenly.

When I asked her what she craved most, she immediately replied, "Ice cream!" It is always very important to know what people crave most, for this is an indication of what advice to give them.

The craving is always for that which is being discharged. This woman's response to my question showed that she was eliminating sugar as a result of having eaten large amounts of ice cream in the past. It was not the needs of her body expressing themselves, but the memories of her brain—"sugar-poisoning."

After a short while she regained some appetite, but still she could not eat rice.

I gave her some vegetable soup. At first she was very thirsty—after two days of drinking nothing—but that feeling passed quickly. The next morning she was able to eat fresh cream of rice cereal. In six days she lost sixteen pounds. She returned home, and soon afterwards she eliminated a large clot of black blood through her vagina. This was a uterine tumor. The black color indicated that the blood was very old. The woman lost fifteen pounds more, and I predicted to her that she would conceive within a year. Sure enough, in March she called long-distance to say that she was pregnant. However, in April she miscarried. How unfortunate! Her uterus was still weak from the effects of the tumor. This is not unusual. First babies are often difficult in such cases. But at least now she can conceive. The next time she will probably do well.

KEEPING OURSELVES
HEALTHY WITH FOOD

IT IS NO SECRET that food is fundamental to health. In the act of choosing food, we are already committing ourselves to health or disease. By eating the proper food we can make ourselves strong and healthy enough to resist disease in all its forms. In this way we can avoid the hardship of mental and physical pain and the difficulty of trying to cure ourselves with various external remedies. By giving our body and mind to a stranger who knows nothing of us but the symptoms of our disease, we jeopardize the precious human faculties which help us function on our own. By choosing a quick needle injection in order to avoid the seeming hardship of a simple privation of food, we lose sight of the true nature of man and disease and sink into an animal-like world of aimless desires.

Due to the increasing awareness of the importance of food, America is now experiencing a phenomenon unique in history. Diets of all types are flooding the market. There is the raw food diet, the grapefruit diet, the Weight Watcher's diet, the honey diet, the water diet, the steak and salad diet, . . . *ad infinitum.* Every individual tries to find a method of eating compatible with his makeup, and everyone who succeeds is happy. There remain those who stand in between, who hesitate between this or that diet, perhaps even trying all the methods—getting sick or healthy depending on how long they follow each particular method. It is to them that this chapter is addressed primarily. However, even those who are already set on following a specific diet should look with an open mind at what is written here; there is always more to learn. In reading this chapter devoted to food, they will be brought to a crossroad in the field of diet. This perspective may prove very helpful in case of future trouble. Both the person who is still searching and the one who has already found what he was looking for will enrich their understanding of nutrition in general by learning a simple principle—the Yin-Yang principle—which helps us judge what food we should eat. This means that instead of ran-domly trying each of the diets in turn, we choose food by taking into account factors such as the climate, our individual condition, our immediate environment, our needs and our goals.

* *

Where Has Man Gone?

Nyoiti Sakurazawa once said, half jokingly and half seriously, "Healthy and happy people are becoming so rare, one ought to keep a good specimen of man in a museum so that it will be remembered what he looked like." Man is becoming markedly abnormal with all the chemicals and hormones he is subjected to, and with the prevalence of sexual and mental problems, yet such aberrations do not seem to seriously disturb the general public. Although these distortions may be recognized in some degree by individuals, the governments do not seem greatly concerned about the situation. The decline in the quality of our food is just one example. Using hormones and antibiotics on livestock is now common practice. New chemicals are produced every day for no other reason than to make money. Cattle breeders are always ready to use any method that will fatten their animals, without concern for the terrible consequences for human health. What will happen to man if he continues polluting his food?

* *

If our desire is to become healthy, we will select the appropriate food accordingly. If we are already healthy, our choice is easy to make; thoughts of Yin and Yang will intervene only when it is imperative for us to draw upon them. A person with a Yin constitution and condition (for example, a person with pale skin, low blood pressure and cold feet) should avoid eating Yin foods, while a person of the opposite constitution and condition will have to include some fruit and salad in his meal, or he will soon experience trouble of some sort. Your own condition is a most important factor. A particular diet that you have heard or read about may seem perfect theoretically, but that does not guarantee that it is suitable for you, or even viable! All people are physically and psychologically different from each other. Therefore, each person requires a diet different in both quantity and quality, depending on his individual constitution and type of activity. In short, Yin and Yang are included in this chapter to enable those who are lost in indecision to see their situation more clearly and decide with better understanding what they should eat.

This is not necessarily to say that health can be achieved solely through the study of Yin and Yang, though this approach is an excellent one for the person who is learning to cure himself. There comes a time when true health involves forgetting about Yin and Yang when choosing food, and instead choosing food intuitively, with respect to one's condition, environment and needs.

In general, we can classify food from Yin to Yang. In doing so we must consider the climate, the method of cultivation, the length of the ripening period, and the food's shape, size, color and taste. A Yang vegetable is most likely a plant that grows in a cool place and in the ground—a carrot, for example. All root vegetables that grow above the ground are also more or less Yang, depending again on their shape, ripening period, color, etc.

A vegetable that takes time to ripen is more Yang than one that grows in a few days. It takes 8 to 10 weeks for a carrot to grow, and only a few days for mushrooms and asparagus to reach full size.

There is an important factor which we ourselves can employ to affect greatly the quality of a plant; and that is fire. In general, people who are sick or in delicate health should eat cooked rather than raw vegetables. In cooking a vegetable we cause it to lose many of its unstable, undesirable elements. In other words, any vegetable, no matter how acidic and full of liquid, can be changed with fire—and salt, time and pressure—into its opposite.

The reverse effect is achieved by adding liquid or spices, or by refrigerating after cooking.

The part of the plant that has been chosen is also significant. Leaves, stems, and roots (from Yin to Yang) are each different in composition. Cereals, seeds, and nuts are usually eaten whole—without the shell, of course. This is the preferable way to eat any food, for in so doing we gain a greater share of the food's nutritional value, and in a naturally balanced form as well. People are accustomed to peeling carrots, whereas they should simply brush them under running water.

Each part of a plant has its own particular value. When composing a meal, one should be careful to keep in mind the quality and quantity of the various elements, for by doing so one learns how to achieve balance. For example, some people always prefer to eat only part of a vegetable and leave the rest, not realizing that the second part complements the first, that both parts are needed to achieve balance and complete nutrition. Some people even prefer to eat only one or two kinds of vegetables the year round, forgetting about the added nutritional value they could derive from other plants.

It is important to understand that all sicknesses arise from excess. In every case of sickness the quantity of eating should be reduced. In the case of excess Yang, it is advisable to adjust one's diet to be proportionally less Yang, while for excess Yin, proportionally less Yin food should be eaten. Too much of both Yin and Yang is a sure sign of overeating. It is worthwhile to note that fasting never causes death unless carried to the point of starvation, while many people literally overeat themselves to death (heart attacks, cancer, etc.—see "The Cure").

People who switch from a diet composed mainly of animal food to a grain and vegetable diet generally lose some weight very quickly. This is because the body has been allowed to release its stored excesses. When we eat less or fast, our body makes blood from stored nourishment. The supply is first taken from the liver; then fat is lost, followed by protein. The body building process follows this order: blood→muscles→fat. When we fast, this process is reversed. If the liver becomes enlarged from overeating, it will contract when we eat less. We can go for several days with no food at all—ten days, sometimes fifty days. The liver will release its stored nourishment and its functioning will be improved as it becomes more active. Overeating is the worst thing for the liver, for it causes the liver to be unable to provide nourishment for the body, by hampering its ability to filter toxins from food (see section on the liver in "The Organs").

Abstention from eating is not such a strain on the body. It is by not drinking that we can endanger ourselves. However, this is a problem that should never arise. When we fast, we should continue to drink; otherwise our organs and cells contract too quickly, and all sorts of problems can result.

Fasting is a good curative method, but it is not necessary to prolong it needlessly. Nor is it advisable to make a regular practice of fasting. People fast to balance the effects of an extreme kind of diet. They feel the urge to fast in order to eliminate the excess. However, a balanced diet is necessary if health is to be maintained without undue strain.

People who wish to fast because of a weight problem should not do so completely. They are better off continuing to eat food that contains no calories, in order to strengthen the heart. Kanten, a gelatin-like sea vegetable, is excellent for that purpose for it contains no fat or protein but does have a large mineral content.

Eating must be orderly. Some people proceed to eat whatever presents itself first. It is inadvisable to do this; instead we should discipline ourselves to adhere to an order. It is preferable for people in delicate health—with a weak stomach or generally weak digestive system—to begin with hot soup, followed by grain or animal food, vegetables, and finally fruit, pastry, or a cold drink. Any kind of sweet food inhibits the digestive system; cold drinks do the same (see section on the stomach in "The Organs"). Therefore it is wisest to take them at the end of the meal. Eating something solid or hot first and chewing well activates the secretion of digestive juices. The food is assimilated well, causing no indigestion or heartburn.

It is important to chew all food thoroughly. Chewing is a sacred act by which we can prevent most diseases. When we chew well, we are more careful and thoughtful with the food we are eating. Giving thoughtful consideration to each spoonful or dish is a worthwhile habit to develop. In the act of chewing we show our care and gratitude for both the food and our body.

Healthy people can take extreme foods of all kinds at the same time and still make balance, but weak people must avoid such indulgences. In attempting to establish health, we should limit our food primarily to those foods most balanced in themselves. This is why grains and vegetables should be the principal food in your diet. You remain free to eat whatever pleases you, as long as you become aware of the balance of food.

The Nature of Food

More scientific research must be carried out concerning the composition of food. It will be interesting for doctors and nutritionists to know each element—not only in terms of the quantity contained in various foods, but also the element's relation to the other elements. This might be the key to their discovery of balance. About 80 years ago a Japanese researcher found that the K/Na (potassium/sodium) ratio in the human body is between 5:1 and 7:1. This discovery has proved useful in defining the proper balance in food; however, it is still incomplete, for there are other elements which could also be taken into account (see box).

Here is a succinct presentation of foods, to serve as an aid in understanding their nutritive value and their place in a balanced, healthful diet. From it an individual can decide what foods are best suited for him, at the same time learning more about their relationship to his particular condition and state of health. Let us start with the grains, which hopefully will comprise a regular part of the daily meal.

The Grains

Cereals (or grains) are the most suitable food for man. We are referring here to the whole grain cereals, as these afford complete nourishment. Grains that have been separated or refined, such as white rice and white flour, lose precious nutritive components and thus are reduced considerably in food value. Whole grains are very high in vitamin B and have six of the major amino acids. The other two or three can be supplied by beans, vegetables, seeds, nuts, etc., as long as they are eaten simultaneously with the grains. It is said that grain is acid-forming, but this statement can be misleading; if grains are chewed a long time, they will be alkaline in the body.

* *

The Acid and the Alkaline

The classification "acid-forming" embraces a wide spectrum of foods. Meat, grains, and sugar are all considered acid-forming. The acid or alkaline quality of a food is determined by the inorganic mineral residue which remains after oxidation. Changes in the biochemical nature of the food as a result of the cooking and digestive processes (see Good News, *page 54) are not taken into account.*

acid-forming elements	alkaline-forming elements
sulphur	*sodium*
phosphorus	*potassium*
chlorine	*calcium*
	magnesium
	iron

Meat and grains are both high in sodium, yet are still acid-forming. Meat proteins are nearly all high in sulphur, which is very difficult for the kidneys to eliminate. Grains are high in phosphorus, an important element for the brain. Sugar and processed, chemicalized food are also high in phosphorus, but they contain little or no sodium. Salt is high in sodium and is definitely alkaline-forming since it has very little phosphorus and sulphur. Fruits and vegetables, which contain potassium, calcium and iron and are low in phosphorus and sulphur, are also alkaline-forming.

The addition of a little salt when cooking grains will have an alkalizing effect.

* *

There are seven cereals: millet, rice, wheat, barley, rye, oats and corn. Millet can be classified as the most Yang cereal; corn is the most Yin.

Corn is harvested in August. Rice, millet, and rye are harvested in the fall. Wheat and barley are harvested in both May and October.

BUCKWHEAT

Buckwheat can be eaten with noodles as a cereal, or as a stuffing for cabbage, green pepper, etc., in place of meat. It is excellent for cold and humid weather since it produces heat quickly. If eaten in warm weather, it should be taken in the evening. Buckwheat is high in vitamin E and is a good blood-building food which is beneficial for the kidneys.

RYE

Rye is excellent as an ingredient in breads and morning cereals. It is similar to wheat but lower in gluten. Both rye and wheat are good for providing muscle power; they give energy and endurance.

MILLET

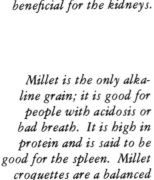

Millet is the only alkaline grain; it is good for people with acidosis or bad breath. It is high in protein and is said to be good for the spleen. Millet croquettes are a balanced and delicious food.

Oatmeal is best when made from fresh steel-cut oats or whole oats cooked overnight. Oat flakes or rolled oats are excellent in soups and cookies. Oats are high in fat and are good for people with a slow thyroid gland. Those people who have much stored protein tolerate oatmeal much better than rice or buckwheat cream.

OATS

RICE

Whole grain brown rice is the best food for daily consumption. It is the grain highest in B complex vitamins and the easiest to digest. Rice is beneficial for the nervous system and the brain and good for people with allergies. The germ of brown rice contains phytin acid which helps expel poisons from the body.

Barley is excellent in soups or cooked and served with vegetables. Barley flour can be made into an excellent morning cereal. Next to rice, barley is the grain easiest to digest. It is the secondary grain of many cultures. It can also be used in making tea or miso.

BARLEY

WHEAT

Whole wheat flour is the basic ingredient in home-baked bread. Wheat can be made into morning cereals and pancakes, and other products such as noodles, bulghur and couscous. Wheat is the grain highest in protein and gluten. It is beneficial for the liver, and from ancient times has been acknowledged to be food for thinking.

Dried-corn meal and flour are excellent used in bread or made into polenta. Fresh corn-on-the-cob is a delightful summer vegetable. Corn is a good cooling grain for hot weather. It is also excellent for blood building and gives high energy. Corn is the sweetest grain and easily changes into sugar in the body. It is good for the heart.

CORN

Autumn is Yang; a crop that bears grain and ripens in autumn will be Yang, whereas a crop that bears grain during the spring will be Yin. Therefore, the wheat and barley that ripen in May are more Yin than the wheat and barley that ripen in October.

Barley, wheat and oats are called *mugi* in the Orient. A Chinese saying expresses the effect of each of these grains in a few words; it says: "Mugi makes cool." These grains are considered more Yin than rice and millet and are used as summer food. Rice and millet give more warmth than mugi. If one takes wheat and feels warm, this is an indication of a very strong condition. Corn can be eaten beneficially every day during the summer. It is an excellent replacement for the winter cereals.

Buckwheat is not one of the cereals, although it is often grouped with them. It is a seed grass and is more Yang than any of the grains. Cereals are eaten throughout the world, but buckwheat is found only in colder climates. It grows very quickly, maturing in only two months, and can be harvested in spring, summer and autumn. The essential attribute of buckwheat is that of quickly supplying calories. A regular intake of buckwheat tends to give one's character a volatile quality. Buckwheat is quite different from wheat, which tends to make one's character more durable and consistent. Perhaps this is because wheat has such a long growing season, even longer than that of rice.

It is said that brown rice has more condensed electromagnetic energy (Ki) than any other grain. Perhaps this is because rice grows in paddies and thus gains energy and nourishment directly from water as well as from the sun, air and earth. Brown rice is a very desirable food which should be a staple for everybody.

Brown rice, buckwheat and millet are the only soft-shelled grains and are the best cereals to be eaten whole. The outer shell of hard-shelled grains is indigestible unless cooked for a long time. When hard-shelled grains are used as flour, the dough must be well-kneaded and leavened (sourdough is best—see section on whole wheat bread in "Food Is Best Medicine"), and allowed to rise.

Pressure cooked rice is good for people with weak constitutions and people unused to eating whole grains. It is soft, sticky and delicious. However, people with strong constitutions are better off eating rice cooked without pressure. It may also be advisable for many Americans to cook their rice without salt.

Bread

When whole grains are cracked or ground into flour, they begin to lose much of their nutritive value upon contacting the oxygen in the air. This is why it is so important to use fresh flour. Eighteen hours after it is ground, flour is virtually a dead food. People could cure themselves three times as quickly if they would eat no flour products except bread, and no nut butters. Bread, however, is a very important food (see "The Daily Bread").

Noodles

Although made from flour, noodles have the virtue of being a very light food that is easy to chew and digest. This makes them a good food to eat occasionally in the summer. Noodles may be prepared as a main dish with a broth or sauce poured over them, or used as an ingredient in soups and casseroles. It is not complicated to make noodles from fresh flour. Try it sometime.

Greens

Most people think it is too much trouble to buy fresh vegetables; frozen ones take up less space in the refrigerator. Most people prefer food that is convenient to prepare. Vegetables must be washed and cooked, whereas canned food simply has to be heated. People are always willing to "kill" time rather than give it full meaning. By preparing vegetables in a human way, one performs a sacred act. Indeed, it takes time to prepare vegetables, but what a reward! Eating them is always a pleasure, not only for their nutritive value. Their taste brings us down to earth and leads us to enjoy being part of this natural world.

Green vegetables—all leafy plants—are an indispensable source of chlorophyll, which is instrumental in creating healthy red globules, the carriers of oxygen in the body.

If we eat green vegetables our brain functions better, the thinking is clearer. The brain needs a fairly large supply of oxygen to function at its best. It is of the utmost importance that our body receive enough oxygen, especially while curing any disease. Not only must the air we breathe be clean, but the blood cells must be healthy in order to attract and accept the oxygen and carry it throughout the body.

* *

Vegetables should preferably be cooked, especially in this part of the country (New York). It is best that each person discover for himself which cooking method is most suitable. The various methods to choose from include sautéing, baking, steaming, boiling. In sautéing, one must take care not to overcook the vegetables. In baking, one must make sure that they are not undercooked. A well-cooked vegetable retains its color and yet is soft.

* *

64

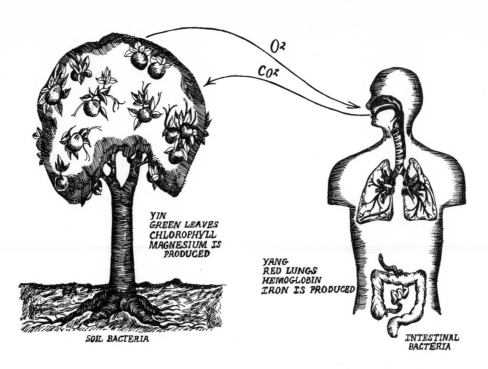

YIN
GREEN LEAVES
CHLOROPHYLL
MAGNESIUM IS
PRODUCED

YANG
RED LUNGS
HEMOGLOBIN
IRON IS PRODUCED

SOIL BACTERIA

INTESTINAL
BACTERIA

Green leafy vegetables are very good for the gall bladder as well as for the brain, while root vegetables are good for the small intestine. The skin and bark of plants are good for the skin, and naturally sweet vegetables such as squash, pumpkin, carrots, onions, etc. are good for the spleen. In cases of body tightness and contracted organs, the kidneys, bladder, liver and large intestine will benefit from both raw and cooked vegetables in large quantities (a little fruit is fine too).

Wild green vegetables such as dandelion and mugwort are very good for the heart and blood.

It seems that many people who have chosen a diet of mostly grains and vegetables have an anemic condition. If they would eat more vegetables—especially green ones—they would be cured quickly. Greens are abundant in the earth. They are freely offered—for what reason then should one deprive oneself of them?

Green leaves receive sun and air and, with their chlorophyll, carry on the process of photosynthesis.

They take in CO_2 and release O_2, while our lungs do the opposite, taking in O_2 and releasing CO_2 (see section on the lungs in "The Organs").

In green plants chlorophyll is responsible for bonding carbon dioxide with nourishment (sap). In human beings hemoglobin is responsible for bonding oxygen with nourishment (blood). Chlorophyll contains magnesium. Hemoglobin contains iron. Otherwise the two are quite similar. When we eat green vegetables we consume chlorophyll. In the blood stream the magnesium is replaced by iron from our bodies and hemoglobin is produced. Thus chlorophyll and hemoglobin are related (see also "The Blood").

From this we see the importance of eating green leaves. They are like a miniature garden which we introduce into our system, thereby providing ourselves with a source of oxygen while at the same time giving the intestines ideal nourishment for the production of bacteria.

* *

You may eat everything that is listed on the following page. Know, however, that good health is the prize of an orderly manner in choosing one's food. Upon turning this page you will find a chart which will guide you in your selection. May what you select help you acquire the best possible health.

* *

He who needs to have this every day should see a psychoanalyst. He who needs it once a week should read elevating books to forget about it. He who needs it once a month should ask himself, "Why in the world should I really have it?" And he who wants it at least once a year, because it is reminiscent of his childhood, should ask himself whether he has yet grown up.

* *

This is good in its own time. The trouble is, people usually take it because they have a problem. Worse, they take it to forget. When there is a gathering to celebrate some great event, one drinks to remember that event . . . having a small glass or even two. A happy occasion nullifies the bad effects of alcohol. Ask yourself how many occasions are like that.

* *

List of Foods *

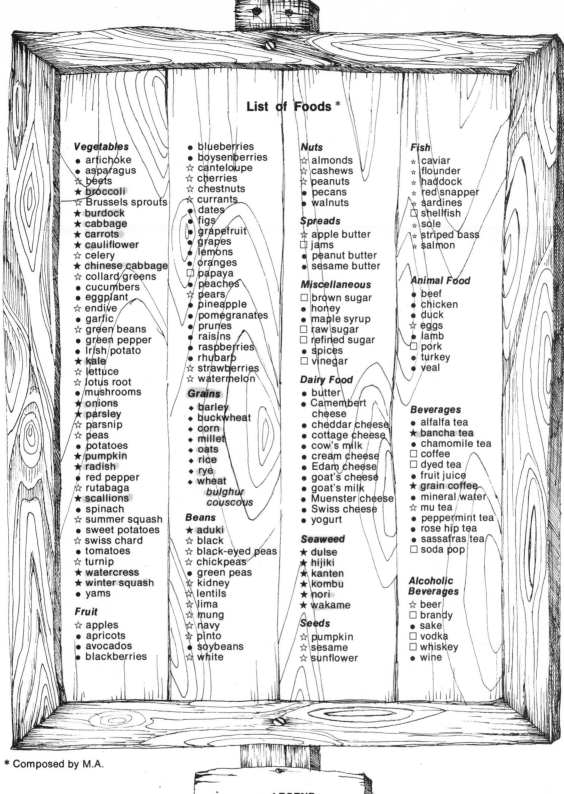

Vegetables
- artichoke
- asparagus
- ☆ beets
- ★ broccoli
- ☆ Brussels sprouts
- ★ burdock
- ★ cabbage
- ★ carrots
- ★ cauliflower
- celery
- ★ chinese cabbage
- ☆ collard greens
- cucumbers
- eggplant
- endive
- garlic
- ☆ green beans
- green pepper
- Irish potato
- ★ kale
- ☆ lettuce
- ☆ lotus root
- mushrooms
- ★ onions
- ★ parsley
- ☆ parsnip
- peas
- potatoes
- ★ pumpkin
- ★ radish
- red pepper
- ☆ rutabaga
- ★ scallions
- spinach
- ☆ summer squash
- sweet potatoes
- ☆ swiss chard
- tomatoes
- ☆ turnip
- ★ watercress
- ★ winter squash
- yams

Fruit
- ☆ apples
- apricots
- avocados
- blackberries

- blueberries
- boysenberries
- ☆ canteloupe
- ☆ cherries
- ☆ chestnuts
- ☆ currants
- dates
- figs
- grapefruit
- grapes
- lemons
- oranges
- ☐ papaya
- peaches
- pears
- pineapple
- pomegranates
- prunes
- raisins
- raspberries
- rhubarb
- ☆ strawberries
- ☆ watermelon

Grains
- ◆ barley
- ◆ buckwheat
- ◆ corn
- ◆ millet
- ◆ oats
- ◆ rice
- ◆ rye
- ◆ wheat
  - *bulghur*
  - *couscous*

Beans
- ★ aduki
- ☆ black
- ☆ black-eyed peas
- ☆ chickpeas
- green peas
- ☆ kidney
- ☆ lentils
- lima
- ☆ mung
- ☆ navy
- ☆ pinto
- soybeans
- ☆ white

Nuts
- ☆ almonds
- cashews
- ☆ peanuts
- pecans
- walnuts

Spreads
- ☆ apple butter
- ☐ jams
- peanut butter
- sesame butter

Miscellaneous
- ☐ brown sugar
- honey
- maple syrup
- ☐ raw sugar
- ☐ refined sugar
- spices
- ☐ vinegar

Dairy Food
- butter
- Camembert cheese
- cheddar cheese
- cottage cheese
- cow's milk
- cream cheese
- Edam cheese
- goat's cheese
- goat's milk
- Muenster cheese
- Swiss cheese
- yogurt

Seaweed
- ★ dulse
- ★ hijiki
- ★ kanten
- ★ kombu
- ★ nori
- ★ wakame

Seeds
- ☆ pumpkin
- ☆ sesame
- ☆ sunflower

Fish
- ☆ caviar
- ☆ flounder
- ☆ haddock
- ☆ red snapper
- ☆ sardines
- ☐ shellfish
- ☆ sole
- ☆ striped bass
- ☆ salmon

Animal Food
- beef
- chicken
- duck
- ☆ eggs
- lamb
- ☐ pork
- turkey
- veal

Beverages
- alfalfa tea
- ★ bancha tea
- chamomile tea
- ☐ coffee
- ☐ dyed tea
- fruit juice
- ★ grain coffee
- mineral water
- ☆ mu tea
- peppermint tea
- rose hip tea
- sassafras tea
- ☐ soda pop

Alcoholic Beverages
- beer
- ☐ brandy
- sake
- ☐ vodka
- ☐ whiskey
- wine

* Composed by M.A.

LEGEND
- ◆ staple food
- ★ side dish
- ☆ once in a while
- • on special occasions
- ☐ try to avoid

Salt

Western medicine believes that salt is a major contributing factor in the development of heart failure. This is true to a certain extent—if, for example, salt is not accompanied by oil or physical exercise; in other words, if it is not balanced.

In the Sahara Desert of Morocco, the standard monetary unit is the salt bar. Yet heart trouble is not a major problem there. It takes a weak heart and unbalanced food to produce heart failure; that is why we cannot directly impute the trouble to salt (see also the section on heart trouble in "The Cure").

Western medicine also holds that salt is first released in the stomach, beginning to work only when it reaches that organ. Actually, however, as soon as salt is consumed it begins working in the mouth. The brain receives the message that salt has been put into the mouth; immediately it sends a message to all the organs, warning them to prepare themselves for the salt that is coming. The kidneys take more water, the large intestines take more water, the heart and lungs decrease their pace, and the stomach becomes active.

Salt provides power and energy. At least one dish at every meal should include salt. A lack of salt can lead to lack of strength and sexual appetite. (Those who thrive on a salt-free diet always prove to have much salt stored in their bodies—usually they have a long history of heavy meat eating.)

Excess sugar or drugs will remove salt from the body and thus give rise to a craving for salt. Excess salt produces excess saliva; water is drawn from the entire body. The more salt we take, the more water we need; however, salt is a highly astringent food, and an excess of salt can actually lead to excess water retention in the body. It can also lead to constipation, high blood pressure, heart and kidney troubles, and duodenum ulcers. Fatigue and insomnia often result, and sometimes violence and insanity.

Symptoms of excess salt are: dark skin; hard muscles; red blood vessels visible in the whites of the eyes; tightly clenched teeth; protruding lower teeth. The most reliable sign is in the urine: if the urine is brown, too much salt is being consumed.

Is overconsumption of salt responsible for Western medicine's theory that we should take great quantities of water for kidney disorders? This practice may work in the beginning, but eventually it will prove to be a dangerous method that tires the kidneys by overloading them with water. It is much more practical to simply eat less salt.

When we take too much salt, the large intestine absorbs much water, causing a loss of water in the feces, which will subsequently become dry and hard. The feces will then usually be round and dark brown and look like rabbit stools. Yang constipation often results from this excessive intake of salt; the feces become shiny and bright.

It is recommended that those people whose bodies are storing too much salt—especially animal salts—and those who eat meat, include raw vegetables and fruit in their diet. A little beer or wine may even be advisable—liquid washes out salt. Hot baths and showers are especially effective. These are all safe ways to eliminate stored salt from the body. If bathing causes rather than eliminates fatigue, the individual needs more salt.

It is harmful to maintain the habit of taking much salt along with meat while including no vegetables in the meal. If salt is being taken without animal food, there is less likely to be trouble. However, if one has a long history of meat eating, it is advisable not to take much salt. Only when the animal food has been eliminated from the body can we afford to take more salt.

* *

The words "salt" and "solar" have the same root. There is a connection between salt and the sun; both are basic to our lives. Since the beginning of sea life, body cells have contained salt (sodium chloride). All body liquid contains salt. Our bodies can manufacture salt from sodium, but grains and vegetables haven't enough of this element. Meat is very high in sodium—and salts—but its salt is not the best quality for us. Sea salt is better.

Salt can be very shocking to our system. In the Orient the following foods are used to aid in the assimilation of salt:

tamari—18% salt
miso—13% salt (U.S.A.: 10-13%)
miso soup—10% miso→0.9% salt
old pickles (1-2 years)—20% salt
fresh pickles (3 days)—3% salt
umeboshi salt plums—20% salt

* *

It is impossible to say how much salt should be consumed; the amount varies for each individual. In fact, for one individual it differs from day to day, depending on the weather, the type of activity in question, and other factors. Perhaps the best guideline is to use as much salt as makes the food most delicious to you.

Orientals prefer to use salt in different forms (see box above). Soya sauce (*tamari*) and soya paste (*miso*) are often used in place of salt—in soups, main dishes, in condiments and as medicine. Soya sauce contains 18% salt (compared to sea water, which contains 2.8% NaCl) and is a very practical and safe means of salting food. One must, of course, be careful not to overindulge even in this case. These seasonings are very tasty, so it is easy to use too much of them.

Salt does not enter the cells alone, but oil and salt are held in the cell when they are combined. That is why soya sauce is good; the fat from the soybeans combines with the salt.

Another example: a combination of soya sauce, ginger, salt plum and bancha tea is a good mixture for strengthening the heart. Ginger has a good quality of Yin which, when combined with soya sauce and hot bancha tea, helps promote good circulation (see also "Food Is Best Medicine").

To summarize, it is better to develop a method whereby we can learn to balance salt taken in moderation than to eliminate salt altogether from our diet.

Meat

Meat provides an abundant amount of calories which stimulate the body by providing quick energy. This kind of energy does not last long, however; to maintain the energy given by meat, one must eat meat constantly. On the other hand, cereals and vegetables provide energy that is much less explosive. When we eat them, our body is allowed to assimilate the nutrients into the blood at a slower and more even pace. This in turn gives us energy that is less violent and of a much more enduring nature. The energy supplied by grains and vegetables is less dramatic than that of meat. It allows one to go on doing one's work. There is no feeling of heaviness, no need for rest and recuperation.

Building our body with cereals and vegetables is more natural than building it with animal food. In the former process plants become blood and then flesh. When we eat meat, the process is reversed, the flesh becomes blood. Because this process is quick, we receive great energy. However, this energy represents a process of decomposition rather than a building process. Those who eat meat heavily are often subject to sudden attacks of fever. The meat, once it is broken down to be assimilated and rejected, gives energy but doesn't build good quality blood or tissue. The process is too fast, the need to eliminate too strong. Thus, what does not follow the natural building process is continually rejected. This is the body's attempt to burn away "dead" matter. Fever results when toxins are not eliminated fast enough.

Fever generally comes from excess animal protein. In this sense, fever can be considered a kind of discharge. If you try eating large quantities of Yin food—fruits, for example—you will see that no fever results. This is very interesting. But take a large amount of meat, fish, etc., and you will see that fever quickly arises.

A fever indicates that the animal protein has become a poison to the system. At first the protein is not poisonous, but whatever is not quickly burned to become energy, is stored in the body and ultimately becomes toxic. At this stage, bacteria and viruses may be present. This storage of protein can eventually lead to diseases such as uremia and produces numerous ill effects in body organs and blood.

* *

On Ecology and Overpopulation

Historians inform us that the world population was about 250 million by the first century. In the year 1650 it was only 500 million, which is very small considering the rate of increase in modern times. Within about 200 years, the population increased drastically. By 1850 there were 1,250,000,000 people on earth. That number literally doubled by 1950, just a hundred years later. And from 1950 to 1970, in only 20 years, it is estimated that the earth's population grew to 3,630,000,000. This means that at the present rate of growth we will total 7 billion by the year 2000.

This situation, in which acute overpopulation combines with the desperate need of man to take care of his health, is seemingly being handled by the food industry. The reasoning is thus: "The world needs food, and the only way to provide enough of it is to manufacture it industrially. It may not be very natural but it serves the immediate purpose. People at least do not die from hunger." It may be said without exaggerating that the majority of our population is consuming strange foods which are effective only in temporarily prolonging life. It seems that there is just enough "life" in modern food for man to survive.

The U.S. population is now 250 million. The country is 2.3 billion acres large (including Alaska and Hawaii), 20% of it being used as inhabitable land. Every acre of land supports one person. If the land were used as pasture, 460,000,000 would then be the maximum the U.S. could support. Scientists tell us that our population will exceed 500 million by the year 2000. If this calculation is correct, 40 million people will starve at that time.

In light of this possibility it is most urgent to point out that a cultivation of grains and vegetables and fruits can support a population 8 times greater than that provided for by the present diet, which includes too much animal food. Cattle need large areas of land which, if used properly, could give forth the best of food. Our problem is not only to try and nourish people, but to save the land from exhaustion. The earth is burning with chemicals. It is time for everyone to demand that peace be given to the fields. We should, in our efforts to save man from malnutrition, consider a diet for the earth itself. Large industries are behaving like disabled ship captains who do not foresee that the journey will be long and that food should be given out sparingly. We have to think of the generations to come.

* *

A calf, which has a strong body, eats only grass. A cow, which has a huge skeleton, eats only grass and builds that skeleton from grass alone. One thousand pounds of grass eaten by a calf might produce, say, one pound of meat. But if that calf were to eat only one hundred pounds of grain, he would produce the same amount of flesh—one pound—for grain is a more concentrated form of energy than grass. In other words, this is the process: grass or grain→meat, Yin→Yang. Meat, then, is an extremely concentrated form of energy, for huge amounts of either grass or grains are necessary to produce a small amount of it.

Americans usually eat a great deal of meat (concentrated, heavy) and as a result eat huge amounts of sugar (dispersive, light). Each American eats, on the average, 340 pounds of meat per year as compared to the Oriental, who eats 70 pounds. Each American eats an average of 110 pounds of sugar per year; the Oriental, 50 pounds. The American eats two to three times more fruit than the Oriental. While the American suffers from meat and sugar consumption simultaneously, the modern Oriental suffers mainly from excess sugar. The Japanese eat white rice as their main food, plus many sweet condiments and other kinds of poor quality food. The result is blood stagnation. Many Orientals have dark lips because of this condition. Americans also suffer from blood stagnation as a result of their excessive consumption of both meat and sugar.

There is a practical and safe way to expel animal food toxins. It is not enough simply to stop eating so much meat; many toxins will remain stored in the body. One can take radish to expel fish toxins; mushrooms for egg and fowl toxins; lettuce with cheese, and onions and scallions (raw and cooked) for beef and lamb toxins. For the latter, potatoes (prepared properly—see "Food Is Best Medicine") are also often effective.

PROTEIN DEFICIENCY

People with a past history of relying on meat as the mainstay of their diet may undergo a difficult period when they first begin eating grains and vegetables as their main food. Their organism cannot manufacture blood easily because their digestive system is no longer able to perform the work it was designed to do, i.e. to transmute plant nourishment into flesh. In other words, after years of reliance on animal protein, the body becomes accustomed to doing without plant food, thereby losing its innate ability to effect the complete process of transmutation. Therefore it takes the body some time to reestablish its natural ability, and in the meantime the individual is going to lose some weight. After a while —how long depends on the individual—the ability to transmute is reestablished and there is a weight gain. If, however, one continues to lose weight, and if this tendency persists over a long period of time, there may be serious trouble. At this point he should include some cheese or carp soup in his diet, for he has become seriously weakened and needs a longer transition period to reestablish his bodily functions.

On Eating Chicken

The way things are going it would be wise for man to return to a simpler and healthier way of eating. Animal food has in some degree been part of the traditional diet of many countries; however, the meat that is currently available is a great threat to mankind. A simple story can illustrate this fact:

An American boy came to see me about a problem he had. He could not understand why he had girl's breasts. When I inquired whether he had taken hormones in any form, he answered in the negative. I wondered what could have caused the breast growth until I asked him if he had eaten much chicken in the past few years. This time he did not hesitate to confirm my suspicions as to how this growth could have come about. He even informed me that girl's breasts in men are not uncommon in America. Before we parted he asked me whether he could have any children. He had been married for quite a few years and had no children. A doctor whom he had consulted told him that there was no hope of his ever fathering a child. I expressed hope that his sexual condition would return to normal if he could abstain from animal food and adopt a grain and vegetable diet. After all, in this world nothing is constant.

One year passed. Last summer I heard that his wife had become pregnant.

Beans

Beans are a good quality food which supplies the organism with a fairly large quantity of protein and energy. This does not mean that one should consume huge amounts; usually a tablespoon or two per meal is quite sufficient. It is an unhealthy habit to worry about protein and eat more than is necessary. Also, it is better to get protein from many different sources rather than to center one's attention on one particular source. Such an attitude causes our body to lose its ability to assimilate and transmute other kinds of food.

Beans are sometimes used as medicine, internally as well as externally. Aduki beans are excellent for kidney disorders. Black beans are good for the sexual organs —for example, in cases of irregular menstruation, barrenness, lack of sexual appetite (see recipes in "Food Is Best Medicine"). White beans (navy, lima, etc.) contain less oil than other beans and thus are good for people with liver problems. Green peas are good for the stomach.

Soybeans are not recommended as a bean dish, despite their high protein content. They contain a certain harmful acid which can be eliminated only by elaborate cooking methods. This is why Orientals usually eat soybeans in the form of tofu, a sort of "soybean cheese."

However, tofu is not desirable either. Protruding eyes are often a sign of a large consumption of soybeans. It is better to eat soybeans in the form of miso and tamari, unless they are being used medicinally (see page 130).

Seeds and Nuts

Nuts are closely related to seeds. Both contain oil. Seeds and nuts have a high protein content. They contain vitamin E, an important vitamin for the sexual organs and the heart as well as for pregnant women and newborn babies.

Sesame seeds are known for their high protein and calcium content. Buckwheat, which is considered a seed rather than a cereal, is very rich in vitamin E.

The seed of any fruit contains life-giving force in concentrated form. The flesh of a fruit is soft, but the seed is very hard. Ninety percent of the flesh composing the fruit is water and therefore decays quickly. The other ten percent, which constitutes the seed, can live through the winter. If the plant did not have this concentrated, hard component, it would die and decay, for from this concentrated, hearty seed springs forth new growth.

Seeds and nuts are excellent for maintaining health. It is advisable to include them in one's regular diet. They are good body builders but, like everything else, should be taken in measure and chewed thoroughly, especially walnuts and almonds, since their skin creates acidity. It is recommended that all seeds and nuts be toasted lightly before being eaten.

* *

Tomatoes

Tomatoes are not recommended for regular consumption, for they contain too much potassium and oxalic acid. It is oxalic acid which is responsible for melting down the calcium in our bones and bringing about gall and kidney stones. Taken occasionally by people with much stored animal protein, it will help to eliminate the undesirable excess.

* *

Sugar and Honey

When sugar is used in moderation, it can prove to be a good medicine. It is unfortunate that modern man overuses it for purposes other than medicine or even simple satisfaction. These days sugar is a drug taken to lift up a worn-out body in need of the instant energy that sugar can supply. Unfortunately, sugar is addictive. It creates an infernal circle in which sugar comes to be depended upon more than any other food. Meat gives quick energy also, but not as fast as sugar. Sugar is the sweet friend which has taken the place of a nonexistent will; eating it is what enables one to go on working. Modern man depends on sugar to give him the push he needs to accomplish his immediate actions, be they sports or a day's work.

* *

Your Meal

If you wish to avoid trouble, we suggest that you include grains and vegetables in your daily meals. They are the staff of life of the ancients. Both provide excellent nourishment. You may eat other things on the side—vegetable pies, desserts, fish, occasional animal food; only keep in mind that the simpler the meal, the better your health will be. Here are some suggestions which may help you choose your meals. Of course, do not make your eating habits a rigid system. Some days you may need more vegetables, soup or liquid than others. In summer you would not eat the same things as in winter. When it is cold, eat good hot soups with lots of grain to keep the body warm. When it is hot, eat some raw food—if your body can digest it, of course.

an ordinary meal may be composed of:

> 50% grains
> 15% vegetables
> 10% beans
> 25% soup & salad

A fancy meal may be composed of:

25% fish or animal food	15% soup
25% grains	10% dessert
25% vegetables & salad	

─────── *Suggested Menus* ───────

barley soup	miso soup	oat soup
fried sole	vegetable pie	bulghur
rice	string beans	buckwheat croquettes
carrots	zucchini	carrots
watercress		broccoli

─────── *Some Soups* ───────

barley—carrot, onion,	barley—lentils—celery
mushroom	pumpkin—onion
oat—onion—carrot	carrot—potato—onion
barley—beans	celery

Eat in good health!

* *

The sweetest of all simple sugars is *fructose.* When *glucose* and *fructose* combine, they form what is commonly called a *double sugar, sucrose,* which is a less sweet sugar extracted from beets and cane. Another form of sugar, called lactose, is found in milk. It is barely sweet.

Honey is also a combination of fructose and glucose. It is quite different from sugar, for it contains numerous enzymes and minerals.

In the Orient, honey, when it is used as medicine, is diluted in hot water and used in small amounts to reduce its strong effect. This is a good cure which can be used safely in case of difficulties with menstruation. It is particularly excellent for people with strong constitutions.

For many centuries honey has been used as medicine the world over. It used to be very expensive. Now it is so cheap that people consume it in great amounts, straight and undiluted. This is not a very wise thing to do, for in this case the honey's effect is too strong.

The ideal way to take sugar is in its natural form —in food. The sugars found in rice and in most grains, vegetables and fruits are called polysaccharides —complex sugars. When we take sugar in this form, our body is forced to break down the polysaccharides into monosaccharides—simple sugars. This is the natural process of assimilation. Refined sugar, which passes directly into the blood stream without needing to be digested, gives too much of a shock to the stomach, pancreas, and other organs. It is much better to take sugar in its complex forms as it is found naturally in most foods. The energy obtained from breaking down and assimilating complex sugars is of a better quality, for it is energy of a constant and enduring nature which the whole digestive system has worked collectively to provide.

Sugar in its refined form causes an acid condition, for there is no chance for it to be broken down slowly and alkalized. An acid condition uses up the body's minerals very quickly, and this inevitably causes a severe loss of calcium which in turn causes tooth decay.

Refined sugar, when taken more than occasionally, weakens the intestines, which are not used to this excessive consumption. When sugar destroys the intestines' ability to digest food, disease follows—physiological and psychological diseases, acidity, headache, nervousness and even violence.

Heavy meat eaters usually consume large amounts of sugar regularly. They would be better off eating plenty of salad which, although not as light as sugar, is without the same dangerous side effects.

Oil

I was once asked at a lecture whether oil remains as such in the body or transmutes into a different substance. Answer: everything changes; oil turns into carbohydrates, which change into protein, which in turn can change into oil again.

If we take an excessive amount of carbohydrates, our body will store the surplus. The unneeded portion of the carbohydrates is transformed into fat and stored under the skin. Whenever there is a lack of carbohydrates, the body gets what it needs from an indirect source: protein changes into oil which changes into carbohydrates.

Nuts and seeds are a good natural source of oil. It is best to toast them briefly in a pan before eating; this will reduce their oil content.

Vegetable oil is usually used for sautéing vegetables. It is a good quality fat which does not form cholesterol as animal fat does. The sautéing serves to seal in the flavor of the vegetables and preserve it during further cooking. Sesame and corn oil are excellent for sautéing vegetables. Sunflower seed oil is just as good, although less tasty. Olive oil and other oils should be used in small quantities, especially peanut and soybean oil, which are hard to digest.

Actually, in America we do not need to sauté our vegetables all the time, although sautéed vegetables are very delicious. Most of us consume too much oil and fat to begin with. This provokes liver trouble. Too much oil makes the skin rough, especially the skin on the hands. The desire for oil is carried over from a time when large quantities of fat were eaten along with meat.

Seaweed

The time is perhaps not too distant when a large majority of people will turn to the sea for their nourishment. This is happening already on a small scale. Natural food stores throughout the world are offering various kinds of seaweed, all of which are selling fast.

Seaweed as food might not appeal to everyone. The first time you eat it, it definitely tastes like seaweed! However, if and when you develop a taste for it, you will not be able to sit at your table without it. After eating it one feels that one has eaten something truly nourishing. It is a kind of food on which one can depend.

Seaweed is an important source of many minerals which are not found so abundantly in vegetables from the earth. It is a natural food for man, which should be included in everyone's diet.

According to Oriental medicine, an intake of fish should be balanced with seaweed, for there is a harmonious relationship between sea animals and sea vegetables—just as land animals and vegetables depend on each other for nourishment.

Except for certain kinds of fish, seaweed is our only natural source of iodine, an important trace element. Seaweed is also high in vitamin E. Vitamin A is contained in nearly all types of seaweed; B_1 and B_{12} are also universally present. Nori is the highest in protein and in vitamins B and C. Kombu, wakame and other types of kelp are the highest in calcium, while dulse is the highest in iron.

The minerals and enzymes contained in seaweeds aid the body in eliminating the effects of animal food and help it adapt to vegetal-quality foods. In addition, seaweed helps the body discharge radioactive wastes imbibed from the atmosphere! It has been proved experimentally that alginic acid, an important element in brown algae such as wakame, kombu, other types of kelp, and hijiki, acts on metallic elements in the intestines, turning them into insoluble salts which are then discharged from the body.

WAKAME

Seaweed: Food Content and Minerals (per 1000 grams) *

	PROTEIN	FAT	CARBOHYDRATES	Ca	K	Na	Mg	P	Fe	I
Kombu	7.3	1.1	51.9	800	—	2500	—	150	—	—
Wakame	12.7	1.5	47.8	1300	—	11	—	260	13	—
Kelp (powder)	—	—	—	1100	5300	300	760	240	100	150
Nori	34.2	0.7	40.5	470	—	—	—	580	23	—
Hijiki	5.6	0.8	29.8	1400	—	—	—	56	30	—
Dulse	—	—	—	300	8100	2100	220	270	150	8
Kanten	—	—	—	450	—	—	—	—	—	0.2
Irish Moss	—	—	—	880	2850	2900	—	160	9	—

— indicates insufficient information available   * Reprinted from *East-West Journal*

* *

The Liquid Story

Liquid is the number one panacea of the person who eats a lot of meat. The modern theory which prescribes the drinking of much liquid was born out of necessity. It is important indeed for the meat eater to drink great quantities of liquid, in order to wash down that which can pollute his sytem. Otherwise, he may develop kidney trouble.

Eventually, however, the person who eats a great deal of meat, being obliged to take more liquid than anyone else, tires his kidneys with excess work. The theory of flushing out the body with water is very widely observed, but it leaves man everything but free. His pathological desires run his life and he is forced to submit to their consequences.

Small amounts of liquid should be sufficient for those who do not make meat their main food. Liquids should preferably be taken after or between meals. Liquid drunk during meals blocks the digestive process, and that, as most people know, leads to all kinds of disorders.

Some foods are digested in the mouth. The chewing process combined with the saliva breaks down the food into a liquid form which can be assimilated easily by the digestive organs. Grains (including bread, cookies, etc.), generally called "carbohydrates," must be chewed thoroughly. Failure to chew causes minor to major stomach problems—acidity, ulcers, etc.

It is always better to drink liquid that is neither too cold nor too hot. For example, a very cold drink inhibits digestion, freezing the intestines, and that alone is a great source of troubles such as diarrhea, rheumatism, sore throat.

Coffee and tea are good day-starters, and modern, will-less man needs them badly. He needs their stimulation, since he does not possess any true strength with which to finish the day's work. It is advisable to drink these only occasionally. There are excellent herbs and teas on the market which taste as good as coffee and tea and are moreover quite harmless. Bancha twig tea (*kukicha*), which is used by hundreds of thousands of Americans, is a very satisfying tea, undyed, perfumed and non-stimulating. You can drink it before going to bed and still have a good night's sleep.

To summarize, drinking should not be a perfunctory action involving no decision of mind or body. Excess drinking harms the digestive process, prevents one from chewing properly and dulls the thinking. It is advisable to sip liquids rather than gulp them down. That improvement alone will prevent much trouble.

About Milk

Contrary to popular belief, milk is not "a perfect food for man," "supplying all or most of his daily needs." In fact, there is much evidence that a heavy consumption of milk and other dairy products can be quite dangerous. The specific details have been reported in popular magazines such as TIME and LIFE as well as in nutrition periodicals and even Department of Agriculture publications.

It is true that people have been drinking milk for thousands of years, but what is called milk today has very little in common with the fresh raw milk drunk by our ancestors. Such milk is unavailable to most of us today. Oxidation, pasteurization (a process intended by Pasteur for wine) and the addition of chemical preservatives all serve to destroy the lactobacilli and vitamins present in milk, and most of the other nutrients as well. This is as it should be. Milk is designed to be taken directly from the breast. It is nature's perfect food for babies, to be supplied by a loving mother. For human babies, as well as with other species, there is no more need for milk once the child is weaned and has teeth. Adults simply don't need it.

This is not to say that there is anything wrong with indulging occasionally in a little milk, yogurt, cheese or other dairy products. After all, these foods are delicious and can be very soothing as well. There is one exception: HUMAN BABIES SHOULD NEVER BE FED COW'S MILK. Indeed, they never used to be. The first recorded incidence is in 1793! Body size has increased dramatically in the last century; the main reason is the large consumption of meat and milk products.

As Dr. Morishita points out:

A baby calf weighs about 130 pounds when born. He will weigh about 240 pounds one month later. By that time he is already walking around. This rapid growth rate requires quick development and . . . bone growth in order to meet the needs required by activity and weight. This is the reason why cow's milk contains so much more calcium than mother's milk.

On the other hand, human's milk contains phosphorus. This element is very important for brain growth and development. The human baby develops his brain first, while the animal develops his bone structure first. Therefore, milk for a human and that of an animal naturally should be different. Giving cow's milk to the human infant, without thinking about such an order of nature, is too simpleminded.

Cow's milk contains more protein than human milk, but this protein is *caseinogen*, which is insoluble and very difficult for babies to digest. Probably 50% is wasted. The protein in human milk is mainly *lactal bumin*, which is soluble and easily digested. The protein in mother's milk is utilized by the baby with virtually 100% efficiency.

The amount of fat in cow's milk and human's milk is equal, but in cow's milk it is mostly saturated fat and fatty acids, while the fat in human's milk is of a more finely emulsified type. A baby raised on mother's milk will have more body flexibility and adaptability.

Human's milk has more lactose than cow's milk, which is easier for an infant to digest than other sugars and aids the utilization of proteins and the absorption of calcium. The sugars in cow's milk are mostly galactose, glucose and other compounds.

Each form of milk has a different pH reaction which in turn affects digestibility and blood quality in the body. Cow's milk is acid while human milk is alkaline.

Mother's milk transfers immunization to many diseases to the baby, and implants enough intestinal bacterial flora (lactobacilli) to be the basis for a lifetime supply, needed for resistance to infectious disease. (*For mothers who have difficulty producing milk, see page 130.*)

Today in the U.S.A., 28% of the food consumed is dairy. Isn't this—along with refined sugar—perhaps one of the causes of the continual emergence of new diseases and allergies?

Wild Plants

Many people like to hunt for wild plants which can be used as vegetables and herbs.

There are four steps in the investigation of wild plants. The first three are looking, smelling, and tasting. The fourth and final step is to eat a reasonable quantity of the plant and see how the body reacts. (This is what the ancient herbalists did. Some would even fast for three days to become extra sensitive, then eat nothing but the plant and wait to see what would happen.) With mushrooms, it is often necessary to wait several days to observe the reaction.

It should be remembered that most wild plants have both strong Yin and strong Yang qualities in combination and should be prepared by a strong cooking method. The methods of food preparation, from Yin to Yang, are: salad, parboiling (no salt, no extra water), steaming, boiling, sautéing, pressure cooking, baking and roasting, deep frying.

"If you know how to create balance, there is no such thing as poison—only extreme degrees of Yin and Yang."

THE PREPARATION
OF MEDICINE

THERE IS NO "perfect" medicine known to man. There is, however, the most appropriate time for curing every disease, and the most suitable method to apply in each individual case. The ideal, then, is to find the right medicine for that moment. So that this may be possible, it is the duty of each person to cultivate confidence in himself. For that, he must learn to recognize his basic constitution and his condition at a given stage of disease. Every disease should be treated with particular care, even if it is a recurrence of a previous disease. For example, if we once cured a certain disease with a specific type of medicine, it does not necessarily follow that we will always treat that disease with the same medicine. For in the meantime we may have changed our condition and would, therefore, be dealing with a different situation. Or, we might contract the same disease in a different environment.

For example, let us say that you spent the winter in Vermont and while there developed a particular sickness which you treated successfully. Then you decided to spend the summer in Arizona, and there had a recurrence of the same illness. You would have to be careful in dealing with this new situation, especially in terms of food. What you would eat in the South would have to be quite different from what you were eating in the

North. In a hot climate, one is inclined to drink more liquid. That alone—in addition to hundreds of other factors—necessitates a change in eating habits.

We should not depend on any specific technique as the only cure, even if that technique has proved beneficial to thousands. Some people, for example, believe exclusively in the pills and injections of modern medicine, rejecting the possibility that there are other cures, that there may be other civilizations with a highly evolved culture and a deep understanding of man and his world, which could have developed a sound and human medicine. Some people rely only on herbs, others on food, and still others rely exclusively on exotic spiritual exercises. Such people, blind to all the possibilities, make of medicine a rigid system.

Here, presented in three chapters, are three different methods for curing disease. All of them leave room for you to develop the ideal way to cure each specific disease. "Food Is Best Medicine" explains how food can help. By eating properly we strengthen ourselves, body and mind, so that in the event of disease we do not have to panic and put ourselves at the mercy of the first curative technique that is presented to us.

"Using Herbs and Teas" explains the proper use of herbal remedies, precious companions which can be used in their proper time. For example, a case may arise in which food cannot cure the disease quickly enough. In such a case one would utilize the proper herbs, thereby speeding up the curing process (simultaneously maintaining a fairly good balance in eating, of course). Herbs teach us one thing, that we can always rely on their help as long as we observe decent eating habits. Not even the best herbs will have as rapid an effect if we keep making the same mistakes in our way of eating. An improper diet, if it continues to be followed, will only cause the same sickness again. Even worse, it may cause another sickness, indicating that the disease has taken on greater proportions.

The chapter "External Treatments" presents an ancient healing method which is always efficient in speeding up the cure. Here again it is advisable to continue eating well, "well" meaning the avoidance of overeating and excess of any sort. By remaining sober in our way of eating, we arrive at an understanding of the full meaning of the disease and its cure. By showing how modern diseases can be handled with very simple means, this last chapter provides one with the means of gaining self-confidence.

Good work, then!

FOOD IS BEST MEDICINE

The Five Tastes

Usually our tongue distinguishes five basic tastes. From Yin to Yang they are: hot, sour, sweet, salty and bitter.

According to Oriental medicine, the hot taste is good for the lungs, the sour taste for the liver, the sweet taste for the spleen/pancreas, the salty taste for the kidneys, and the bitter taste for the heart (see "The Theory of the Five Elements"). While a small amount of one particular taste is beneficial, an exaggerated quantity is always harmful to the very organ it is supposed to aid. Quantity destroys quality.

Spices have a hot taste. Raw vegetables and certain fruits are naturally sour. Carrots, onions, scallions and squash have a sweet taste. Seaweed usually tastes salty, although it is a little sweet and sometimes even slightly bitter. Many herbs and certain vegetables have a bitter taste; burdock root and dandelion, for example, are bitter.

The tongue is constructed in such a way that each part of it is receptive to a particular taste. The front of the tongue is for tasting sweet food, the sides are for sour food, and the back for bitter food. The entire tongue, however, can taste salty food. The hot taste is rather complicated. Generally it is felt on the tip of the tongue, but other places can taste it as well. Ginger, pepper and mustard, for example, are each tasted at different points on the tongue.

Shibui and Egui

In addition to these five tastes, there are two other important tastes, known in Oriental medicine as *egui* and *shibui*. In the classification from Yin to Yang, egui comes before the five tastes and shibui comes after. The order is thus: egui, hot, sour, sweet, salty, bitter, shibui. While the Yin tastes arise and subside quickly, the Yang tastes are slower to be sensed and remain longer.

Potatoes, especially Irish potatoes, have the egui taste. Bamboo shoots and asparagus have this taste also to some extent. However, sweet potatoes and yams have almost no egui taste. Jinenjo, which is considered to have very strong Yang qualities (since it is a root vegetable that grows deep in the ground), strangely enough has some egui taste. This egui taste is related to the plant's potassium content.

Shibui is found generally in teas. Green persimmons and the outer skin of nuts also have this noticeably bitter taste. Too much shibui food constricts the anus and produces constipation. The Japanese take *sake* (rice wine) to remedy this condition, but any similar alcoholic beverage will do. Conversely, persimmons are an effective remedy for a hangover.

People all over the world are trying to find the best way to remove the shibui taste from green persimmons, for then they would be very sweet. In Paris this has been done by soaking the persimmons in alcohol; in Texas, refrigeration has been used with the same result.

Choosing Food

Classification by taste can be useful in selecting food to help cure disease. For example, one should not make the mistake of giving a person with blood stagnation food which is on the bitter side. Blood stagnation is the result of constriction, so the patient should have hot food to disperse the stagnation and allow the blood to circulate actively. Similarly, if the liver is congested, it is wise to give more sour food.

People who switch from a primarily meat-dairy-sugar diet to a healthier way of eating often undergo certain changes accompanied by pain in various parts of the body. This phenomenon is explained in the chapter "Getting Rid of Waste" and comes about because waste products, including various toxins, are leaving the body. The organs ache from their effort to expel these wastes.

The first winter following such a change in diet is usually a "cold" winter. The individual feels chilly due to a sudden loss of fat and waste and the abandoning of the usual quick-calorie food. The second winter should be much smoother. No coldness should be experienced, for by then the circulation should be good. If one still feels cold at this time, and if he is still pale, proper circulation has not yet been established. Such a person should eat more buckwheat and millet and more Yang quality food in general, at the same time increasing his physical activity. This brings about good circulation in the lungs and makes the blood flow throughout the body.

The Recipes

Here are some basic recipes needed for the particular remedies mentioned in this book. Hundreds of thousands of people are using them as part of their daily diet. These recipes have existed for hundreds of years, some for thousands of years, and have proved both practical and effective. You will find them very handy whatever the sickness, from minor to major disease. Some are suitable for regular consumption, others are simple medicines in the form of drinks or thick mixtures (which generally do not taste bad at all!) to be taken when necessary. They are listed alphabetically rather than according to function. In other words, we have grouped together all the highly curative recipes which more or less resemble food, liquid or solid.

Many of the ingredients listed here can be found in a supermarket. However, all of them can be purchased in a natural food store.

ADUKI BEANS

Aduki beans are small, red beans used commonly in Japan, known for their rich quality as both food and medicine.

Beans can be cooked best in a pressure cooker or heavy clay pot.

Rinse the beans in a strainer. Combine 1 cup of beans and 2½ cups of cold water in a pot. If you are using a pressure cooker, bring up the pressure, lower the flame, and allow the beans to cook for one hour. Remove pressure cooker from the stove and hold under running water to bring down the pressure. Then open and add a small amount of water and the necessary salt (for 2½ cups of water, ½ teaspoon of salt is quite sufficient). Cook uncovered for ten minutes or so. The beans are then ready to eat.

If you wish to cook the beans in a heavy pot you may do so, but in this case you must add more water —½ cup, perhaps. You can start cooking the beans over the stove. When they begin to boil, put them in a hot oven for two hours or so.

Aduki Beans As Medicine

Use 5 cups of water rather than 2½ cups. Boil the beans for one hour; then remove the juice (you may continue cooking the beans, of course). A half-cup of aduki juice taken at least half an hour before meals for two days is excellent for most kidney complaints. If it is kept in the refrigerator to prevent spoiling, the juice should be heated before being taken.

Aduki beans themselves may be used as medicine. For kidney trouble and symptoms related to kidney trouble (swelling, etc.), eat only aduki beans, nothing else, for two or three days. This is often quite effective.

For prolonged menstruation, try eating five raw aduki beans, being careful to chew them well. This is often effective in terminating the bleeding.

Black Beans As Medicine

Black bean juice, prepared in the same way as aduki bean juice, is also used as medicine. It is particularly effective for treating hoarseness and laryngitis. Black bean juice taken over a long period of time (two or three months) helps regulate inconsistent menstruation. Take ½ cup three times a day.

For insensitivity during sexual intercourse, use the following recipe: steam one cup of black beans until soft, then dry them (taking whatever time is necessary). Add ½ cup of black sesame seeds and grind the mixture into a powder. Take one teaspoon mixed with hot water three times a day before meals.

BREAD ("The Daily Bread" page 139)

BUCKWHEAT CREAM

There are two ways to make buckwheat cream: with buckwheat flour or with toasted buckwheat groats ground in an electric blender or hand flour mill.

1) Use 1 cup of flour and 1 teaspoon of corn oil. Heat the oil, taking care not to burn it. Keeping the flame low, add the flour and stir constantly and rapidly with a wooden spoon so that the flour won't burn. After five minutes, the color of the flour will be light brown and even. Set aside to cool. Then put the flour in a pan with 4 cups of water. Place over a high flame, continuing to stir until mixture reaches boiling point. Lower the flame considerably and simmer 15–20 minutes, stirring and checking occasionally. Keep covered while cooking.

2) Grind groats in a blender and use the same procedure as above. Use 1 cup of buckwheat groats and 4 cups of water. Salt to taste.

Excellent for obtaining energy and warmth.

CARP SOUP

    4 lbs. carp
    1 dozen burdock roots
    3 heaping tablespoons miso
    2 tablespoons sesame oil
    1–2 cups used bancha tea leaves

Fresh carp is best. Ask fisherman to remove only the gall bladder. Cut the fish into half-inch slices, using everything—head, fins, scales. Shred the burdock roots into shavings. Sauté these shavings in sesame oil for 20 minutes over a low flame. Place the slices of fish over the burdock, adding enough water to cover. It's best to cook carp soup in a heavy pot.

Now tie the tea leaves in cheesecloth, placing the bag over the fish. Cover, bring to a boil, and simmer until the bones become soft enough to eat (6–8 hours). Then add miso paste previously diluted in a small amount of warm water, and let the soup simmer another hour.

You can eat everything in the soup—bones, scales, fins, head—everything should melt in your mouth. The soup has a strong but excellent taste.

Very beneficial for people in delicate health. Especially recommended for tuberculosis, anemia, arthritis and rheumatism.

Carp can be made into a plaster that is a good treatment for pneumonia (see "External Treatments").

CHISO

In this country, chiso leaves are known as "beefteak leaves." There are two kinds of chiso. One has purple leaves and stems. The other is green. The green variety is more delicious as food, while the purple is more often used as medicine.

Chiso is one of the foods richest in calcium and is thus highly effective for bone, tooth and joint troubles. Chiso leaves can be used to stop coughing. They induce sweating and urination and are good for cases of food poisoning, especially fish poisoning. They can also relieve mental disturbances. Chiso leaves are effective against fever and coughing, stomach trouble and neurosis.

CORN SILK TEA

Dry some corn silks. Take 20 grams (about one handful) and boil in 3 cups of water until the liquid has been reduced by half. Take three times a day, ½ hour before meals. An excellent remedy for kidney troubles.

EGG OIL

An excellent treatment for a weak heart. Take at least 5 eggs; roast the yolks in a frying pan until black. At this stage, oil will emerge. One-half teaspoon twice a day may be taken for a long period of time.

EGGPLANT

Eggplant can be made into miso pickles, which are effective against gout. When included occasionally in one's diet, eggplant can prove very beneficial for certain Yang conditions, especially for a Yang kidney condition. A recommended method of preparation is to fry it in oil and then continue cooking in a small amount of water. Before frying it, slice thinly and sprinkle with salt. Then let it sit a while.

Eggplant has the advantage of satisfying a craving for Yin food. After eating it, one feels satisfied and thus escapes the nagging desire for lots of different kinds of food.

GRATING GINGER

GINGER JUICE

The juice of the ginger root is an ingredient in many recipes—drinks, food, and external treatments. To make ginger juice, simply grate ginger with a Japanese grater or regular grater, using the side that produces the finest consistency. Press the shavings through a cheesecloth or simply squeeze by hand, and you will obtain juice.

KANTEN

    1 stick white kanten
    3 cups of water (approximately)
      vanilla extract, lemon rind,
        or mint for flavoring
      a small amount of currants, raisins,
        or apple concentrate for sweetening

Soak kanten in water for about 30 minutes. Then boil until kanten melts. Add flavoring and sweetening. Remove from stove. Pour into a pan, preferably a flat one. Allow to cool in refrigerator. Cut into cubes and serve.

Good for people who are trying to lose weight. Contains no calories except what is in the apple concentrate.

Kuzu Root

Kuzu could have been listed with herbs and teas as well. It is a very deep root (perhaps 3 or 4 feet long) which grows in Japan. It is used for curing colds, healing weak intestines, neutralizing acidity, alleviating body pain, relaxing tight muscles, etc. Most health food stores now carry it.

Here is the recipe:

1 level teaspoon kuzu
3/4 cup water
1 teaspoon soya sauce

In a saucepan dilute kuzu in cold water. Place over flame, stirring constantly. The mixture will change from opaque to clear. Keeping the flame very low, add soya sauce and continue stirring for a minute or so. It should be thick but in liquid form.

Kuzu should be taken one hour before meals, preferably in the morning when the stomach is empty. Try for two or three mornings; if extended treatment is necessary, see Kuzu Root Herb Tea in "Using Herbs and Teas."

Kuzu-Soy-Plum-Ginger Drink

Kuzu mixed with the following ingredients has proved very effective against colds, diarrhea and stomach cramps.

1 salt plum
10 drops juice from grated ginger (approx.)
1 tablespoon soya sauce
1 rounded tablespoon kuzu
1 cup bancha tea

Dilute kuzu in a little of the bancha tea. Heat the remaining tea and add the diluted kuzu. Leave preparation on low flame until it starts boiling and becomes clear; this should take only a few seconds. Add salt plum, soya sauce and ginger juice. Stir over fire 2–3 minutes. Drink it hot. Do not eat for an hour or so before and after taking it. (See also Kuzu Root Herb Tea in "Using Herbs and Teas.")

Miso

There are three kinds of miso: Hacho, Mugi and Kome. Hacho miso is made with soybeans, Mugi with barley and soybeans, and Kome with soybeans and rice. Hacho is aged 3 years in wooden barrels, Mugi 18 months and Kome 6 months. In Japan, Kome is the most popular type of miso. Hacho is too strong for everyday use, especially in the summer; it is advisable for Americans to use the other kinds.

Miso looks like a dark paste. It is very salty. Its spicy flavor enhances soups and various other dishes. A good medicine for anemic and arthritic people, it is valued for its beneficial effect on intestinal bacteria.

Miso Soup

Austin Carroll and Embrée de Persis Vome recommend miso in their article which appeared in the July 1972 issue of *Women's Day*. Hundreds of thousands of Americans are now using it either for health reasons or simply for its good taste.

Miso soup is a precious part of the Japanese food tradition. It is an excellent alkalizer and helps promote proper metabolism. Its other properties include providing or improving resistance to sickness and aiding in the digestion and assimilation of food. For this reason it may be taken once daily by those who feel they need it.

Recipe

Several combinations of vegetables may be used. The most popular are:

daikon (Japanese radish) — wakame (seaweed)
daikon greens — wakame
turnip — turnip greens — wakame
cauliflower — cauliflower greens
onions — wakame
onions — cabbage
onions — dulse (seaweed)
onions — swiss chard

Proportions (using the onion — cabbage combination):

2 onions, minced
½ cabbage, shredded
1 tablespoon oil (corn, sunflower or sesame)
4 cups water
6 rounded teaspoons miso paste

Sauté the vegetables in oil. Simmer 10–15 minutes. Boil water and pour into the deep pot in which the vegetables have just been sautéed. Cover, bring to a boil, and simmer 30 minutes. Dilute miso in 1 cup of the simmering broth and add to mixture 5 minutes before the end of cooking. Do not boil soup after adding miso, for that will make it bitter. Stir well. You may serve miso soup with finely chopped scallions sprinkled on top.

MOCHI

Mochi is very popular in Japan. It is a miracle worker. Japanese people recommend it for a variety of sicknesses. Excellent for convalescents and breastfeeding mothers, it provides strength for the weak, and abundant milk of high quality for the newborn baby. Children like it in all forms. Especially recommended for anemia, it is a good body builder and easy to digest.

Mochi is made from a special kind of rice called "sweet" or "glutinous" rice, which is indeed sweeter than common rice. Since the rice is pounded in a bowl, it is necessary to use a strong bowl that won't break or chip. To pound the rice you will need a large wooden pestle (called *kine* in Japanese). You will also need a steamer.

POUNDING RICE

Recipe

Rinse sweet rice until water is no longer cloudy. Soak for 24 hours. Then steam rice until soft (approximately 2 or 3 hours for brown sweet rice). Next, pound until all grains are broken. Finally, shape into balls, patties, squares, etc.

Mochi may be eaten just after it has been pounded. After about 12 hours it becomes hard. Then it should be baked, toasted, deep fried, pan fried, boiled or added to soup before eating. These methods improve its flavor. After several days mochi dried in the shade becomes hard as a rock. If it is then baked or fried, the result is rice cakes.

MUGWORT

Mugwort is an organic source of iron. Beneficial for people whose blood lacks iron, it can be taken as tea or incorporated into food recipes. Mugwort tea is recom-

mended mainly for expelling worms or stopping bleeding, but it is not as effective for anemia. Mugwort should be eaten (in mochi, etc.) to cure anemia. The American mugwort is of good quality but is very bitter compared to the Japanese version, which tastes better.

To prepare mugwort tea, boil one handful of mugwort in 3 cups of water for 30 minutes. One-half cup may be taken 3 times a day.

MUGWORT MOCHI

A combination of mochi and mugwort is good for leukemia and anemia patients. Effective against internal bleeding, it builds blood and is excellent nourishment for pregnant women.

Use mugwort picked in the spring. The top of the plant picked in summer or autumn is fine too, since it is very soft.

Boil the soft part of the mugwort leaves in salted water. Dry the leaves by laying them out flat. Allow to dry completely. They will keep for one or two years.

To make mugwort mochi, follow the instructions for mochi. The only difference is that before pounding the rice you will add mugwort to it. Whether the mugwort used is fresh or dried, it should be cooked lightly before being added.

Pieces of mugwort can also be added to miso soup. They should, of course, become soft enough to be eaten. Mugwort leaves prepared in this manner are good for anemia and weakness.

For leukemia, it is recommended that mugwort, brown rice, buckwheat and a few cooked vegetables be included in the diet.

Mugwort is also good for cancer patients. It is helpful for heart, stomach and intestinal troubles. Generally speaking, it benefits people whose condition is weak.

PICKLES

Just as the roots of trees take nourishment from the soil, so man's intestines draw nourishment from his food. And just as countless bacteria in the soil help provide proper nourishment for the tree, so man requires bacteria to provide him with proper nourishment. These bacteria are called *intestinal flora*. If you have an unbalanced culture of bacteria, B vitamins will not be assimilated from the grains you eat and you will develop an acute vitamin deficiency accompanied by symptoms such as fatigue, body pain (especially in the legs), mental dullness, rapid heartbeat and difficulty in breathing.

The cure for this condition is rice bran pickles, which stimulate the intestinal flora. Vegetables pickled in bran contain lactic acid bacteria, upon which intestinal flora thrive. When the intestinal flora are healthy, they will digest food properly and provide the body with sufficient vitamin B.

WOODEN KEG
THE ANCIENT METHOD

Pickles have a strong and delicious taste and are an excellent condiment. They should be taken in small quantities, one or two pieces at every meal. Here are a few recipes. Choose whichever method is most practical for you. Rice bran pickles are the most highly recommended. Vinegar should not be used; it is unnecessary and has a disastrous effect on the kidneys.

Bran Pickles

This is Rebecca Wood's recipe. It has been modified slightly for our purposes.

    10 pounds rice bran or wheat bran
     2 pounds salt (preferably gray)
    20 cups water
     1 ounce kombu seaweed

Heat a dry skillet and lightly toast as much of the bran as the skillet will hold comfortably. When the bran releases a light aroma and begins to darken, it is done. Repeat this process until half the bran is toasted. Place the toasted bran, the untoasted bran, and the salt in a 3–4 gallon container. A crock is ideal, but a wooden barrel or enamel bucket will also work.

Place the kombu in the water, bring to a boil and simmer twenty minutes. Remove the kombu (which may then be used in a vegetable dish). Add the cooled stock to the bran mixture and stir well. This is now the basis of your pickle barrel. Into the barrel put vegetables which have been scrubbed thoroughly to discourage undesirable bacterial growth. Firm vegetables such as radishes, carrots, cauliflower and turnips work best. The smaller the pieces, the sooner the vegetables will pickle. A small slice of radish will be ready to eat in two or three days, while a larger piece may take a week to pickle. Be careful not to add too many vegetables; their surfaces should not touch each other.

Cover the container with something light to keep it clean, and store in a cool place. Daily you can retrieve pickled vegetables and add fresh ones. When you add new ingredients, be sure to give the contents a thorough stirring to maintain an even distribution.

Soft vegetables such as cucumbers may take as little as 12 hours to pickle if cut into slices; the blossom should be cut off to prevent softening. If they are put in whole, however, they take longer to pickle.

Apples pickled in rice bran are an excellent treatment for children's colds and fevers. The entire apple should be used.

If possible, pickle barrels should be started during the cold season. The best time is during a cold spell, after the temperature has dropped below freezing.

There are other methods for making bran pickles. We have chosen this one because it seems the easiest. A method very popular in Japan involves using stone weights on the lid to create pressure.

Other vegetables can be put in the bucket besides those recommended in the above recipe. Daikon (Japanese white radish), daikon leaves, celery and cabbage are excellent. You may leave the vegetables whole if they are small.

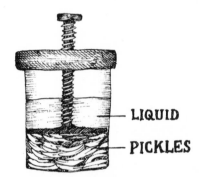

— LIQUID

— PICKLES

SALAD PRESS:
A FAST METHOD FOR
MAKING PICKLES

Making Pickles With a Salad Press

This is a very simple method for making pickles. It is fast and practical. However, you will have to purchase a salad press at a Japanese store. This press will prove very useful, especially in summer. You can pickle practically any vegetable in this press; you can even mix together three or four kinds. Cucumbers can be pickled in two or three hours. Other vegetables take much longer, anywhere from several hours to days.

Chinese Cabbage Pickles

Wash a Chinese cabbage and cut into one-inch slices. In a bowl mix the cabbage with approximately 1 tablespoon of salt, using your hands. Put in the press and apply as much pressure as you can. Increase pressure twice a day for the first two days. Pour off any liquid that rises to the surface. These pickles should be ready to eat in three to five days.

Variations

Onion pickles — Make rings. Takes a few hours.
Radish — A few hours.
Daikon — A few hours.
Broccoli — Cut into small pieces. Takes two days.
Cauliflower — Same as broccoli.
Carrot — Cut into thin slices. Pickles in a day or two.
Cucumber — Pickles in a few hours.
Lettuce — Takes a day. Prepare in morning for same night.

You may use combinations of vegetables, such as carrot-onion, cauliflower-onion, etc. Powdered mustard or bay leaves may be added for flavor.

POTATO

Good for stomach ulcer, duodenum ulcer and stomach acidity.

People with strong constitutions can eat potatoes. Be sure to remove the sprouts, for these sometimes contain poisons. People with weak constitutions who wish to eat potatoes should use this special preparation, which lessens the potentially harmful effects of the potato:

Peel potatoes, sprinkle with salt, and let soak for a while. Wash and put in a pot in water already salted. Cook for several hours. To make the potatoes even more Yang, slice and sprinkle with salt to draw out the liquid. Then fry in oil previously salted.

The following preparation can be used as medicine for gastric, stomach or duodenum ulcers:

1) Wash and grate raw potatoes. Squeeze with cheesecloth to remove juice. Take ½ cup of this juice three times a day before meals. Red potato is best for this; next best is blue-skinned potato. White and yellow are a little less effective.

2) Grate fresh potatoes, squeeze, and place juice in earthenware or porcelain pan. Simmer uncovered until water evaporates. This will take a long time. When it is finished, only black carbon from the potatoes will remain. This is almost complete protein. Take 1 teaspoon with water once a day. This can be used to stop pain and cure gastric ulcers; it is also good for a person prone to allergies.

PUMPKIN

For trouble with the spleen or pancreas, cook pumpkin (or squash) with aduki beans. Take 1 cup every day.

For throat trouble, pain, or excess mucus, baked pumpkin is good. The same results can be obtained with a tea made by boiling pumpkin seeds in water (20 seeds to 2 cups water).

Both cooked pumpkin and roasted pumpkin seeds are effective in expelling worms and parasites. Pumpkin leaves may be used as well.

RADISH DRINK

Recipe I

3 tablespoons grated radish [1]
½ teaspoon grated ginger (approx.)
1 teaspoon soya sauce
1 pint boiling water or bancha tea

Boil water/bancha tea and add ingredients. Let simmer a few minutes.

Do not squeeze the grated radish. It is better to use the entire radish, not just the juice, so that the mixture will remain longer in the stomach. If only the liquid is used, the drink will pass through the body too quickly. This drink is good for causing sweating and thus breaking a fever. Although the body may at certain times require more heat, an extended high temperature is dangerous. In such cases, the drink should be taken once a day.

Do not take this drink when your temperature is rising. It is better to wait until the fever reaches its peak.

Radish Drink I is also beneficial for liver trouble, since one of the functions of the liver is to adjust body temperature.

When the weather turns hot, liver trouble is most prevalent. At this time, radish drink is excellent for causing perspiration and thus lowering body temperature. Traditionally, Oriental medicine induces vomiting and diarrhea to rid a patient of fever, but this is too strong a method of discharging excess energy. Radish drink is preferable since it is a milder cure.

Children usually do not like the taste of this radish drink. They can be given apple juice or pickled apples instead. In autumn, apples can be pickled in rice bran.

Recipe II

1 cup juice from grated radish
1 cup water

Squeeze juice from grated radish. Combine juice and water in a saucepan. Place over a high flame; remove from flame at boiling point. Salt is not necessary.

This version of the radish drink is used generally for inducing urination. It is particularly beneficial for the kidneys (when the condition is Yang), and is equally good for alleviating body swelling, skin ulcers, and most skin diseases. Take once a day or once every other day. It need not be as hot as Recipe I. Drink two cups at a time when hungry, and eat nothing for at least an hour afterwards.

Because this remedy requires the taking of liquid in great volume, it cannot be used often. It is used mostly to treat constricted kidneys, a condition in which a small amount of water will have no effect. Continue

---

[1] The original recipe calls for the Oriental diakon radish, but the American red radish has been found to be equally effective.

taking it for one or two days; if the condition persists, allow a few days to pass and then try again.

Corn silk tea, pickled apples, and watermelon are also effective for Yang kidney disease.

RANSHIO

Ranshio is a very strong mixture; therefore it is most important to evaluate carefully the patient's condition and strength before administering it. In order to prevent a strong and sudden reaction in the organism, it is highly advisable to administer this mixture a little at a time, teaspoon by teaspoon. Nor should it be used too often; if regular treatment is needed, *egg oil* rather than ranshio is recommended. Ranshio can be used in extreme cases — for example, when a person's pupils rise, revealing the white of the eyes. This preparation will immediately restore the pupils to their normal position. Eyes turn upward because of extreme Yin present in the organism. The Yang ranshio produces a strong contraction which brings the patient back to normal.

Ranshio has only two ingredients: egg and soya sauce (in a ratio of 4 : 1 or 2 : 1).

Preparation:
fill ¼ an eggshell with soya sauce
mix thoroughly with the raw egg

This has been used with much success by persons with heart failure resulting from a weak condition. If symptoms indicate that the patient's condition is Yin (see "The Diagnosis"), ranshio may be given. However, if the person has been eating much animal food — especially just before the failure — ranshio is not advisable.[2]

RICE (*Brown*)

Brown rice has made its way into the American market. A few years ago it could be found only in health food stores, where it lay on the shelves and was treated as medicine. It was sold in small packages as if it were a food to be eaten once in a great while. Now it is being purchased by the 100-pound bag. It is a complete, staple food, rich in minerals and vitamins, indispensable to good health.

There are many ways to cook brown rice, but the most convenient is simmering. In using this method we retain more vitamins and minerals and obtain a better flavor.

Wash the pot and fill with the desired amount of rice and water. Try not to fill more than half the pot; otherwise the rice may fail to cook well or may even overflow. It may also burn because of insufficient water. Try using 1 cup of rice with 1⅔ cups of water.

Cover and set over a high flame. When the water reaches a rolling boil, lower flame to simmering point. Let cook for 50 minutes or so. It should then be done.

If the rice burns, it may be that the flame was too high during the simmering period or that there was not enough water. Lower the flame a bit next time. If the rice is too wet, or is uncooked, the flame may have been too low. If the rice is mushy, too much water was used. Do not remove cover while cooking. Leave it on until five minutes after the rice has finished cooking.

SOFT RICE

To make soft rice, use more water (1½ times more) than for regular rice. Simmer two hours.

Good for people with delicate stomach and intestines.

RICE CREAM

Rice cream sprinkled with sesame salt is excellent for breakfast, especially in winter. It is available in all health food stores. Be sure to buy it fresh; otherwise make it yourself in a flour mill or blender (do not grind it as thin as flour; it should be slightly coarse).

In case you want to grind the rice yourself, here is how to proceed: wash the rice, then rinse and toast it over a medium-high flame in a large cast-iron skillet. While toasting it, be careful to stir continually and fast enough to prevent burning. It should not take more than ten minutes to toast 1 cup of rice. Then grind.

Preparation (for 2–3 people):

5 tablespoons roasted ground rice
4 cups water
¼ teaspoon salt

Mix ground rice with cold water. Stir over high flame until mixture comes to a boil. Add salt, cover and simmer 30 minutes. Return two or three times to stir in order to prevent burning.

---

[2] There is another version of ranshio, in which only the egg yolk is used, mixed with almost an equal volume of soya sauce (a tablespoon or a bit less). This latter version is much stronger since it does not have the balancing influence of the egg white (Yin). As a rule, the recipe using the whole egg should be used. It is very effective; the egg white causes the salt to be retained.

RICE MILK

It is very easy to make rice milk. Simply cook rice with water 7 times its volume (1 cup rice, 7 cups water) for 2 hours over a low flame. When cooking, proceed as usual. When rice is finished cooking, place the solid rice grains in a cheesecloth and squeeze the liquid through by twisting the cheesecloth around the rice. Continue until no more liquid can be extracted and only pulp remains in the cheesecloth (this pulp can be used later in baking bread). After the juice has been separated from the pulp, it should be cooked again for from 10 minutes to 2 hours. For babies or very weak people, it should have a thin consistency; for stronger people it should be thicker. Rice milk may be fed to babies when the mother cannot produce enough milk.

Rice milk is an excellent remedy for gastric intestinal trouble. It is advisable to take this food exclusively in the event of severe trouble.

SALTED PLUM

Salted plums (*umeboshi* in Japanese) are plums which have been pickled in salt. They are pickled for more than two years in crocks, by a special acid bacterial process.

These very salty plums have many uses in the ancient Japanese pharmacopoeia. Their place in the kitchen is central. They enhance various dishes, sometimes serving as a dressing, replacing vinegar, sometimes as an alkalizer for some acid dish.

As medicine the umeboshi plum works miracles. Stomach aches, stomach cramps, migraines, certain types of headaches, and acidity are some of the minor pains these plums can relieve. They also counteract fatigue and act as a preventive against dysentery. Salted plums are usually sold packed in chiso (beefteak leaves), an herb high in calcium and an important in-

gredient in many of the herbal tea recipes. If the plums seem too dry, they can be soaked in water before being used. Salt plum juice, which is also a very effective medicine, can be found at the bottom of the crock, keg or jar.

Recipe

first
 100 pounds Japanese plums
  10 pounds sea salt

then
  10 pounds chiso leaves
   2 pounds sea salt
   1 cup umeboshi juice

In this country Japanese plums are becoming more and more popular. If you can get some, you should try making homemade umeboshi. This is an important thing to know how to do.

Get the plums when they are just beginning to turn from green to yellow. Wash them and put in a stone crock. Mix with sea salt. Then add pressure—a plate and a large rock, for instance—and allow to sit for one month.

After the month has passed, buy 10 pounds of purple chiso from a Japanese food store. Wash and knead with 2 pounds of sea salt. Squeeze the chiso and discard the dirty liquid which is expelled. Add the chiso to the crock and mix. Then add 1 cup of umeboshi juice from an old keg. At this point the chiso will turn a clear and beautiful purple color.

Now wait—one month at the very least. Three years is recommended. The older the better. Old umeboshi, aged 15 years or so, tastes very mild.

PLUM-SOY-GINGER-BANCHA DRINK

Preparation:

 ½ umeboshi plum
 5 drops ginger juice
 1 teaspoon soya sauce
 1 cup bancha tea (boiling)

Boil bancha tea; add salt plum, soya sauce, and ginger juice. Leave over low flame one minute or so. Drink it hot, but not too hot!

This drink may be taken for the following problems: fatigue, bad circulation, slow metabolism. It may be taken three times a day in the case of a duodenum ulcer. Good for intestinal digestion; initiates stomach activity and restores appetite.

This drink has the exceptional function of removing old salt from the organism and supplying new salt. Ginger (Yin) promotes good circulation; salt (Yang) strengthens the heart. Salt may prove bad for the heart when taken by itself; ginger may create acidity if taken raw; but the combination of both, if taken with soya sauce and bancha tea, constitutes a mild, highly effective drink. Soya sauce is an important ingredient, for salt alone will not be accepted by the cells. Oil—which is found in soya sauce—holds the salt inside the cells. Thus, old salt is discharged and this new salt, of a better quality than meat-salt, enters the cells.

SCALLIONS

For insomnia, eat raw scallions mixed with raw miso. Or, put diced scallion or onion on a plate next to your pillow at night. This often enables an insomniac to sleep well.

For a common cold or a headache, cook 6 grams of scallions (white part only) and 3 grams ginger in 1 cup of water, and drink.

For coughing, cut off the bulb of the scallion about 2 inches from the end and wrap in a cloth. Hold to the nose and inhale.

SEAWEED

Hijiki

This seaweed can be served many different ways: mixed with lotus root and carrots, plain, cold in salads (with lettuce), or warm as an accompaniment to other foods.

        3 ounces hijiki
        2 tablespoons corn or sesame oil
       10 tablespoons soya sauce
           water to cover

Rinse hijiki in a strainer with cold water. Soak 10 minutes. Rinse again. Do not discard water; it will be used later for cooking. Chop hijiki into one- or two-inch lengths. Heat oil in a large skillet and sauté the seaweed on a medium-high flame for 10 minutes. Remove from fire and put aside for a few minutes. Add soaking-water. Bring to a boil, add soya sauce, and simmer uncovered for 45 minutes to one hour, until most of the liquid has evaporated.

Hijiki-Lotus Root

        3 ounces hijiki
        8 ounces fresh lotus root
        2 tablespoons soya sauce
        1 tablespoon toasted sesame seeds

If you are using dried lotus root, soak it overnight. Wash and soak hijiki, then sauté. Dice lotus root and sauté in corn or sesame oil. Combine hijiki and lotus root in a saucepan with the water in which the hijiki was soaking. Bring to a boil, cover, and simmer 45 minutes. Uncover for the final 15 minutes. Add soya

sauce and sesame seeds once you have uncovered the saucepan.

Good for diabetes. Serve 2–3 tablespoons as an accompaniment to other foods.

Kombu

        1 sheet kombu
        4 cups water
        1 teaspoon salt
       12 tablespoons soya sauce

Break sheet of kombu into large pieces and soak in water for 10 minutes. The pieces will then be tender. Cut into one-inch squares. Boil water in which kombu was soaking. Add kombu and another 6 cups of water, then simmer 45 minutes. Add salt and soya sauce and simmer 15–20 minutes more. The juice can serve as soup stock. Serve kombu cool or warm, by itself or along with other foods. Kombu prepared in its juice this way keeps for days.

Wakame

Soak in water for 5 or 10 minutes. Drain, cut into 1/4-inch pieces and sauté in corn or sesame oil. Then add a little of the water in which the wakame was soaking, and cover. Add soya sauce before the end of cooking.

Wakame combines well with onions. Saute the onions first, then add the wakame.

Use wakame in miso soup (see this chapter).

MAKING SESAME SALT

SESAME SALT

Commonly known in Japan as *gomasio,* sesame salt is made as its name indicates—with sesame seeds (*goma*) and salt (*shio*).

Sesame salt serves many purposes. It is both a delicious table salt and a most helpful medicine. The salt is mixed with sesame seeds to prevent thirst. The oil from the crushed sesame seeds coats the salt, preventing it from causing an excessive attraction for water. Further, in coating the salt, the oil helps it enter the cells when necessary.

Sesame salt can be made using different proportions, from 1:5 to 1:10 (part salt to parts sesame seeds). Some people even use 1:12. First try 1:8 and see if it is too strong for you. You can change the proportions according to your taste and needs.

Use whole, unbleached sesame seeds from a health food store. First roast sea salt in a frying pan until a faint odor of chlorine rises from the salt. Then place salt in a suribachi. Wash seeds, rinse, and toast in a heavy cast-iron pan. Stir constantly with a wooden spatula until the seeds have "popped" about ten times; then they are done. To avoid an unpleasant aftertaste, be careful not to burn any of the seeds. Remove from fire and put in the suribachi (a special bowl for grinding) along with the salt. Place suribachi between your legs and rotate the wooden pestle with both hands. Don't use pressure. Your sesame salt is ready when most of the seeds have been crushed.

Sprinkle on rice cream, salad, rice and other grains. Keep in an airtight container.

To relieve headache or heartburn, take a teaspoon of sesame salt. Chew well, of course.

SHITAKE MUSHROOM

Shitake mushrooms are dried mushrooms used in Japan and China. It is possible that these mushrooms are growing somewhere in America. You can buy them now in most health food stores.

Preparation: boil or soak in water and sauté, or cook in soup, especially barley soup. This is an excellent medicine for the kidneys and is particularly effective in discharging animal protein.

SOYA SAUCE[3]

Soya sauce is a naturally fermented preparation made principally from soybeans. Other ingredients include water, salt and wheat. Soya sauce provides good quality vegetable protein that is easily digested. It is also very rich in minerals and vitamins.

Its uses are infinite. It can be added to soups, broths, sauces, sautéed and baked vegetables, fish, casseroles —almost anything that requires salt.

SOY-BANCHA

This is a most effective drink which can be taken for migraines and fatigue. It can be prepared in an instant.

Proportions:

1 cup bancha tea
1 teaspoon soya sauce

Heat the tea and stir in the soya sauce. Let simmer a few seconds. Take it hot, but not too hot.

WATERMELON DRINK

Squeeze the red pulp of the watermelon to extract the juice. Boil this liquid until thick. The resulting syrup is an excellent medicine for a Yang kidney condition (see Kidneys in "The Cure" and "The Organs"). Dilute 1 tablespoon of syrup in 1 cup of water and take 2 times a day at least 30 minutes before meals.

---

[3] This is not to be confused with the soya sauce sold in supermarkets which is aged artificially with chemicals and which contains sugar. Genuine soya sauce has a much richer taste and can be purchased in natural food stores.

USING
HERBS
AND TEAS

A Brief History of Herbal Medicine

ACCORDING TO LEGEND, Shinno, China's second emperor, was the first to teach agriculture and herbal medicine. Every day he would go to the fields to investigate the herbs and grasses, eating them if necessary. It is said that he poisoned himself eighty times a day. Other doctors tried experimenting in a like manner with the same and other herbs, but being less wise than the emperor they poisoned themselves and died.

It was an emperor's cook by the name of I-Yin who, 3500 years ago, was the first to serve the court a tea made of a combination of many herbs. The people of the court not only liked its taste but recognized its effectiveness as medicine. It is this I-Yin who is credited with developing Chinese classical herbal medicine.

Over 1800 years ago books on herbal medicine began to appear. The South of China specialized in the development of herbal medicine, whereas the North specialized in schools of acupuncture. *The Yellow Emperor's Classic of Internal Medicine* was compiled by the Chinese of the North.

The concept of the Yin-Yang relationship between body organs appeared approximately 3500 years ago. We may regard ourselves as being very modern and sophisticated, but we need only consider all the remedies utilized in the past by Chinese medicine to understand that we are far behind the accomplishments of the ancients. To this day herb teas prepared according to Chinese medicine are proving their worth to doctor and layman alike.

Shinno Honzokyo is an ancient herbal text which classifies herbs into three categories. It states that the best and safest medicine consists of a proper balanced diet accompanied occasionally by herbs. Second best is the use of special herbs which can be taken for an extended period of time without causing any harm. Third is the use of certain strong herbs for short periods of time, when sickness has advanced to a stage where it must be remedied rapidly. The latter approach is likely to produce side effects.

The *Shang Han Lun,* a famous work by Chang Chung Ching, known as the "Oriental Hippocrates," is an 1800-year-old text which is still very important today. Having been revised only slightly since its original publication, it is considered the classic Chinese book of herbal medicine. It describes about 120 kinds of teas and 90 types of herbs.

Pen Ts'ao Kang Mu, written 500 years ago by Li Shih Chin, lists approximately 1800 herbs, classified according to Yin and Yang. The smallest Chinese book of herbs lists 180 herbs, 60 roots, 20 seeds, 20 fruits, 10 leaves and flowers, 15 species of bark, 20 animals and 10 minerals, placing special emphasis on roots. This is different from European and other schools of herbology, which use mainly leaves.

Through the years Chinese medicine has discovered infinite possibilities for herb combinations. Over 30,000 herbs have been used. The question which naturally arises is how the Chinese could come up with such an extraordinary number of herbs and herb combinations. The answer lies simply in the size of their population and the long duration of their civilization. It was a common practice to busy oneself with herbal experiments. Down through the generations the most effective and amazing combinations developed. Nearly all the teas recommended in this chapter are at least as old as the *Shang Han Lun* (1800 years old), in which they are described; thus, their efficacy is born out by many centuries of empirical investigation. Only Oriental herbal combinations are recommended in this book. These herbs are available in the U.S. (see page 142). Recipes for all teas are listed alphabetically at the end of this chapter. There is also a glossary of Japanese herbal terms with their Latin and, whenever possible, English equivalents.

Curing Disease With Teas

In deciding which tea is the appropriate remedy for a particular illness, one must always consider the symptoms of that disease in conjunction with the patient's constitution and eating habits.

A tea which is administered for a particular ailment should also have a beneficial effect on the entire organism. This is why Oriental medicinal teas contain so many ingredients: it is not enough to treat only one organ. All parts of the body are interrelated. Only when the entire organism has been restored to balance can it be said that a true cure has been effected.

A tea composed of one ingredient works quickly and is appropriate for acute cases, whereas a tea composed of various herbs works more slowly and is appropriate for chronic cases. If a tea of 100 herbs could be made, it would work very slowly and would therefore be completely safe and require no prolonged diagnosis. It would not, however, be very effective.

A tea is always prescribed in relation not only to the symptoms but to the individual. Two people with the same disease will often be given different teas, according to the differences in their basic constitutions.

From what has just been said, it might seem that if one thousand people were sick, one thousand different teas would be required to treat each individual condition. However, we need not be so literal. Many people have conditions and symptoms similar enough so that we can identify the common nature of their illnesses and arrive at a single tea containing the necessary major ingredients. For headaches alone there are as many as 27 different teas; for stomachaches, 41 teas. Yet within each group many of the teas have several common ingredients and are similar in composition; furthermore, many of the teas are common to both groups.

The specific combination of herbs is very important. After all, the body is not a simple machine to be repaired one part at a time. It needs a combination of several different herbs so that the treatment will be effective on all levels. The same herb prepared in different proportions with other herbs produces totally different effects. For example, Cinnamon Tea is for the Yang stage of disease. But if we should increase by two grams one of its components, the peony root, we no longer have Cinnamon Tea but Keishikashakuyakuto, which is good for Yin people.

Some herbs are strongly Yin or strongly Yang. They can be mixed together to produce either a more gentle or a more violent effect. By mixing one herb with another we embrace the effects of both, at the same time creating balance between their respective Yin and Yang qualities.

Herbs may be taken for six months—even for a year—without harming the body as pills do. Japanese doctors of herbal medicine are not required to be licensed because it is recognized that herbs are not hazardous to the health. If the herbs one chooses prove ineffective, at least one will not suffer the side effects that drugs often produce. Nevertheless, whenever one is unsure of an herb it is advisable to take less than the normal amount.

One guideline to follow in choosing a treatment is that if a tea smells and tastes bad to you, it is not suitable for your condition. However, if it has a pleasant smell but tastes bad, you may try it.

Choosing a Tea

There are three fundamental teas corresponding to the three basic physical types. Cinnamon Tea is for a person with a relatively weak (Yin) constitution. Mao Tea is usually given to a person with a strong (Yang) constitution. For the in-between person, whose body is neither extremely Yin nor extremely Yang, Kuzu Root Herb Tea is recommended.

Someone who sweats when he has a high fever is of a Yin constitution. For him, Cinnamon Tea would be recommended. Someone who never sweats, even when he has a fever, should try Mao Tea, which is more Yin than Cinnamon Tea. Kuzu Root Tea is recommended for someone who does not sweat but whose body is not so strong. These teas are very effective in combating colds or fever.

Most Americans have an overly Yang constitution and would benefit from Mao Tea. Kuzu Root Tea has a wider application in Japan, where the middle body-type predominates. Only about ten percent of all Americans have a basically Yin constitution. Of these, some are not extremely Yin and would benefit from Cinnamon Tea. The rest are very Yin and would require a more Yang remedy.

Cinnamon Tea, Kuzu Root Tea and Mao Tea are highly effective when the three stages of Yang disease [1] are developing.

Cinnamon Tea

This tea is made from cinnamon bark, peony root, dates, ginger and licorice. As has already been mentioned, it is recommended for people who sweat often. Sweating is "a little Yin in a Yang disease," which means that the body has enough energy to produce perspiration. Cinnamon is good for the skin, both in closing pores which are too large and in opening pores which are too small.

---

[1] See "On Understanding Disease."

Only the cinnamon bark is used, never the roots. It should be kept in mind that the quality of cinnamon varies according to the condition of the soil, the climate, and other factors. Cinnamon Tea has no side effects and therefore can be used over a long period of time. There is another version of this tea with only one additional ingredient, a kind of candy made from fermented barley and rice, containing no sugar at all (it is very sweet, but not as much so as regular candy). If 20 grams of this candy [2] and 2 more grams of peony root are added to Cinnamon Tea, it becomes a tea called Small Kenchuto, which can be used by both Yin people and Yang children who bedwet. It is also effective for a hernia. This tea is very helpful, regardless of what diet one may be following. Further, by adding 4 grams of ohgi to this mixture we get yet another tea, Ohgi-Kenchuto, which helps cure peritonitis.

Mao Tea [3]

This tea is usually given only to strong people since it has some side effects. It can, for example, cause insomnia, lack of appetite and excessive sweating. If any of these symptoms results, especially the sweating, the tea is too strong for the individual. Kuzu Root Tea would quite likely work better.

Mao (*efedra*) is a wild grass found in Mongolia. It has no leaves and looks something like horsetail. Only the joints are discarded. The top (Yin) part of the plant induces sweating, whereas the root (Yang) prevents it.

* *

Mr. Muramoto told us about some ideas he had in Japan before leaving for America: "I had read that many Americans were red and fat and troubled by heart disorders, and that great numbers suffered from constipation and coughing. So I decided to come prepared. I brought along sizeable quantities of daio, Mao Tea, Sage's Path Tea and kanten. The Sage's Path Tea and the kanten [sea gelatin] were for the red, fat people with high blood pressure and other heart troubles. Mao Tea is excellent for strong, Yang-type people who have coughs or colds. Daio is an herbal laxative, a major ingredient in the Jokito and Saiko teas.

"I certainly guessed right; they all proved very useful. I only wish I had brought along a large quantity of Nine Taste Tea—I have met many people who have vitamin B deficiency!"

Note: Further information and recipes for all these teas can be found in this chapter, except for Sage's Path Tea, which comes pre-blended since the process for making it is quite complex.

* *

About forty years ago a Western doctor extracted efedrine from Mao and gave it in both pill and injection form as a treatment for coughing and asthma. It provided a very effective and rapid cure; however, several days or weeks after the treatment was administered the sickness would return, requiring an increasing number of injections or pills. This doctor became quite rich from his discovery!

Western medicine will extract a certain component from a plant. On the other hand, Oriental medicine is aware that there are many active components in any one herb (Mao grass has 20). Oriental medicine will always use the plant in an unrefined state rather than extract the most effective part. Mao Tea does not cure a cough suddenly. It will eventually cure it, but not for one or two days. If it does not relieve the cough, this simply means more tea is needed.

Mao Tea contains apricot seeds, cinnamon, licorice and mao. As we have mentioned, it is for Yang people and Yang diseases, and is an excellent remedy for headache, asthma, coughs and excessive urination.

Kuzu Root Tea

Kuzu Root Tea contains kuzu root, mao, cinnamon, dates, ginger, licorice and peony root. It is a mixture of Mao and Cinnamon teas, excluding only the apricot seeds and introducing the kuzu root. Apricot seeds are Yin as compared to kuzu, which is a deep root from the mountains. Kuzu Root Tea is for the more balanced type of body and is generally effective for all Yang diseases.

Kuzu Root Tea is the medicinal tea most commonly used in Japan. It is especially appropriate for the medium type of body, and is effective for almost all diseases that type of body develops. As has been said, Americans are more Yang than the Japanese, thus Mao is better for them. Many Americans cough, have stiff shoulders and experience body pain—all Yang symptoms. Mao works very well for these specific ailments. But for those suffering from chronic headaches, kuzu is advised. Kuzu is also very good for the stomach and intestines. Another tea containing kuzu root, Kuzu-Safflower Tea, is taken by people with an enlarged heart. This tea has four other ingredients besides kuzu root and safflower.

Licorice

The three basic teas mentioned previously have a common ingredient, licorice, which is an important component not only in these teas but in many other

---

[2] This Japanese candy is sold in America under the name of "Yinnies." Some natural food stores carry it.
[3] See preparation further on in this chapter.

teas as well. It gives the tea a pleasant taste and makes it more Yang. German researchers have recognized licorice as an excellent remedy for gastric ulcers. In the Orient, however, it is believed that licorice is most beneficial to the liver. By aiding the liver in discharging the poisons it filters from food, the licorice allows the kidneys to filter in turn and to eject these poisons from the blood once they have been released by the liver.

The special property of licorice is difficult to explain. It tastes sweet at first, usually at the back of the tongue (although something sweet is normally tasted at the tip of the tongue), but its aftertaste is bitter. For a person with body swelling, licorice is not beneficial; scientists have discovered that it causes the body cells to retain water. A person who is thin and dehydrated should take licorice to help his body retain liquid.

* *

A Misunderstanding

An old man in Los Angeles who complained of frequent urination at night was given Hachimigan Tea, which contains bushi. After taking this tea for one week, he felt better and bought a month's supply of it—a fairly generous amount for effecting a cure. This man was about 65. In the same house lived his sister who was about 43, a woman of a very Yang type. She started taking her brother's tea and began to experience sharp headaches. Then she came to me, saying that she was afraid she would die from all the pain. I told her that the tea she had been taking was not good for her. "Bushi is Yang and you are Yang!" The woman had misunderstood a lecture I had given concerning herbs and teas, thinking that any tea could be taken without fear of toxic effects. She did not realize the basic difference in teas, that Yin teas are for Yang people and Yang teas for Yin people.

I told her to cook 30 grams of black beans and 15 grams of licorice with 1 quart of water and drink as much as possible. Soon the bad reactions ceased.

* *

A remarkable tea which also contains licorice is *Kambakudaisoto*. This tea also contains chopped dates (pits and all), but its major ingredient is whole grain wheat! It is used to treat hysteria and other mental disorders, and also in cases where physical damage has been done to the head (for case history, see page 110). However, this tea seems to be effective only for women and children. It does not work on post-puberty males. For them, *Sanoshashinto* is recommended.

Kambakudaisoto can also be given to babies who cry too vigorously and too often.

Once a young married couple in San Francisco invited me to stay with them for a while. Their baby cried a lot, and very loudly too. Sleep was impossible for all of us. When the baby was given Kambakudaisoto, the problem was soon solved.

Another tea which utilizes licorice and a grain is *White Tiger*. This time the grain is brown rice. The other ingredients are sekko (gypsum) and chimo. This tea is noted for its effectiveness in reducing fever.

Licorice is also used to stop pain. It dispels pain rapidly and effectively, generally after ten to fifteen minutes. For sharp pain, a mixture of 6 grams of licorice and 4 grams of peony root is helpful. However, if the pain is not sharp this mixture won't be effective. One would think that what works for intense pain would also work for minor pain. But this is not always so, and it is not the case with the licorice and peony mixture.

The peony has always been very popular in the Orient because of its large, beautiful flowers. The tea recipes in this book include two kinds of peony: the root of peony, and botanpi, which is called "tree peony." With the latter, the bark of the root is used. Keishibukuryogan Tea contains both kinds of peony. This famous tea, known appropriately enough as Two Peony Tea, also contains cinnamon, peach seeds, and bukuryo mushroom (in equal amounts). It purifies the blood and is said to cure hemorrhoids and intestinal cramps, but is best known for its positive effect on the skin. Used both medicinally and cosmetically, it is also said to be beneficial for the ovaries and uterus.

Daio and Bushi

The most dramatic representatives of Yin and Yang in the plant kingdom are *daio* and *bushi*. Daio is probably one of the most Yin medicinal herbs, and bushi the most Yang.

Daio is a kind of wild Chinese rhubarb, the root of which is used medicinally. A natural laxative, it is very effective in cases of constipation. But one must be strong enough to withstand its powerful effects, since it is very Yin.

Sanmishakosaito, known as *Three Taste Tea*, is one of the teas that contain daio and is highly effective in expelling worms and parasites. Its other two ingredients are shakosai, a kind of seaweed, and licorice. The shakosai weakens the parasites, and the daio flushes them out.

Daio is good for the stomach as well as for the intestines. It makes the feces soft. One might be required to take it for a month or so, after which the intestines would work naturally. Daio Tea is far superior to Senna Tea. The latter becomes habit-forming; when the patient stops taking it, the constipation returns. An insufficient amount of daio (1 gram, for example) taken for constipation or any other ailment will not be effective. However, it is still advisable to take only a little in the beginning to avoid possible trouble. The amount may be increased gradually. Daio is never taken by itself. Both the Jokito and the Saikoto teas contain daio as a major ingredient. One or the other of these teas is usually appropriate for constipation, depending upon the individual's condition.

Bushi is made from aconite, a strong poison when in raw form. A wild flower of a violet color, aconite is also found in America under the name of "monkshood," a member of the Crowfoot family. The root is the part that is used; it is the most toxic part of the plant. In the production of bushi, the aconite is first dipped in salt, then dried, and then roasted. This process changes a dangerously Yin ingredient into a valuable Yang one. "Poison" is a misleading word. Knowledge and proper technique can change the extreme nature of any plant.

Bushi is most effective for Yin, weak people. It is very beneficial for the heart and small intestines. In many instances it has worked well in increasing sexual appetite, even in old men. As a replacement for the now-famous ginseng, bushi is a less expensive and much more effective cure for impotency. However, it should not be taken alone but always in combination with other herbs. Furthermore, the dosage must be discontinued as soon as the disease symptoms have disappeared.

One very useful tea containing bushi is *Hachimigan*. This tea has seven additional ingredients. It is used for weakness in the area of the lower organs and has been effective in cases of high blood pressure, cataracts, diabetes, nephritis, hypertrophe of the prostate gland, and all problems related to urination.

There are several Yang-quality teas containing bushi which are used to counter the three stages of Yin disease. These teas are all quite similar. *Shigyakuto* contains licorice, steamed ginger and bushi. Shinbuto, or *Black Warrior Tea,* contains bukuryo mushroom, peony root, ginger, jutsu and bushi. *Bushi Tea* has the same ingredients as Black Warrior Tea, plus ginseng. However, *Ginseng Herb Tea,* which is also used for Yin diseases, does not contain any bushi. It contains ginseng root, licorice, jutsu, and steamed ginger.

All four of these teas are quite similar in composition and quality. Each is appropriate for all the Yin stages of disease.

Ginseng is a very important herb which in the last decade alone has known immense success in the Occident. Europeans and Americans cannot understand why it should increase sexual potency; nevertheless, everyone wants it because its price goes up each year. Ginseng is very effective for Yin people. With Yang people it will either be ineffective or cause high blood pressure.

Ginseng contains germanium, which has recently been discovered to be effective in curing cancer. Some ginseng is shaped like a man; this characteristic is said by the Chinese to be the sign of the highest quality ginseng. Korean ginseng is of very good quality; Korean soil is high in germanium.

When the heart or the digestive organs become weak, ginseng can be used. It is also effective in cases of anemia, thin urine and cold feet. However, it is rarely used alone and preferably should be mixed with some other herb—a Yin herb, of course.

Shigyakuto is very effective in treating diarrhea or a Yin kidney condition in which the body is unable to retain liquid. Black Warrior Tea is also effective for diarrhea and for cases of heart palpitation. Bushi Tea is very strong; it produces much warmth. Extremely effective in relieving severe coldness and sharp pain such as accompanies arthritis and rheumatism, it can also be very beneficial for the heart and intestines.

If Bushi Tea should cause bad after-effects, the following preparation should be given:

Combine 30 grams of black beans and 15 grams of licorice in 5 to 6 cups of water. Cook over a high flame for 20 minutes. Drink as much as possible.

Should Daio Tea produce diarrhea, give Bushi Tea or another tea containing bushi, such as Black Warrior or Shigyakuto. The intestinal trouble will abate.

Bushi should not, of course, be used by Yang people, since it does not always agree with their temperament. However, bushi combined with daio is a good remedy for gout. This combination causes the body to "shake," discharging both Yin and Yang poisons. Before advising such a treatment, one must determine whether the patient can withstand the strong effects. If so, one tea to recommend is *Daiobushito*. This tea contains saishin (a kind of wild ginger) in addition to daio and bushi. Another tea, *Shakkanoshinbuto,* is used even more widely. It consists of Daiobushito plus licorice and peony root which, as we have said, are effective pain relievers and blood purifiers. Both of these teas are used for arthritis, rheumatism and similar afflictions, as well as for gout.

The *Jokito* teas also contain daio. All of them are Yin teas and should not be taken by Yin people. *Big Jokito* is the most Yin and is to be used only by the most Yang people. *Tokaku Jokito* is the fundamental tea for blood disease. It is strong and sometimes causes diarrhea. It is mostly for Yang people suffering from headaches, bladder trouble, hemorrhoids, nose pain and certain stomach pains. Particularly beneficial for women's sexual organs, it is used to treat internal tumors and diseased ovaries. This tea has gained a reputation as a cure for skin ulcers. In one case ulcers disappeared after three or four days (an indication that the ulcers in this particular case were the result of excess Yang, probably animal food—for another case history, see page 133).

Tokaku Jokito Tea is effective in treating diseases created by blood stagnation. It breaks up blood clots, thus eliminating old blood and improving circulation. The entire body is affected by this tea. Its ingredients are daio, bosho, licorice, cinnamon, and peach seeds.

Choi Jokito is less Yin than Tokaku Jokito. It is effective in cases of constipation and other intestinal problems.

Small Jokito is the least Yin of the Jokito teas and therefore is recommended for people whose condition is basically Yang, but only slightly so. This tea contains daio, koboku (magnolia bark) and kijitsu (green orange). Magnolia bark is an herb that has a soothing effect on the nervous system. Accordingly, it is helpful in cases of stomach and intestinal disorders, muscle spasms and cramps, and is said to produce a more peaceful frame of mind. Small Jokito is advisable for the treatment of Parkinson's Disease, but in this case the quantity of magnolia bark is increased from 3 grams to 10.

Some of the Saiko teas also contain daio. All of them are appropriate for the "Small Yang" stage of disease.[4] The Jokito teas may be used during the "Clear Yang" stage. The four Saikotos are Big Saikoto, Small Saikoto, Saikokeishito, and Saikokaryukotsuboreito. Which one should be used depends on both the condition and the constitution of the individual.

Big Saikoto is the most Yin of the four. It is effective in the Clear Yang as well as in the Small Yang stage of disease, for it reduces the excess energy that is being generated at these times. It is especially effective for heavy people with a strong, Yang condition and for all those with high blood pressure, cataracts, and asthma caused by heart trouble. For such people, Big Saikoto has a positive effect on the entire body. It is said to be beneficial for the eyes, nose, throat, scalp, heart, stomach, intestines, liver, gall bladder, bladder, kidneys and sex organs.

Saikokeishito is the least Yin of the four Saikoto teas, but all four are similar in quality, and Saikokeishito is still a Yin tea. It is used by people whose condition is Yang, but only slightly so. It is effective for colds, stomach ulcers, bedwetting and gall stones.

Small Saikoto is recommended for people with bronchitis, tuberculosis and other respiratory diseases. It may be taken as a tonic for an extended period of time, especially by people who suffer from weakness or loss of appetite.

* *

22 Years Epileptic, Cured in 2 Months —Cheap at Twice the Price!

A woman I met in Seattle had suffered epileptic attacks for 22 years, ever since injuring her spine in a fall at the age of 13. She had become very thin; thus, fasting, which is usually an effective remedy, could not be advised. I gave her Day Lily Tea (Saikokaryukotsuboreito), which is excellent for the nervous system. She took it for 60 days, and now she is cured. She no longer takes the medicine the doctor gave her, and she has suffered no recurrence of the attacks.

When teas are used to cure a chronic disease, they usually must be taken over a longer period of time. Day Lily Tea happens to be somewhat more expensive than most, for it contains ginseng. To cure such a lengthy illness it is necessary that this tea be taken for at least two months, at a cost of one hundred dollars. This may seem like a lot of money, but one hundred dollars to cure a long history of epilepsy? That's really quite cheap!

* *

Saikokaryukotsuboreito (*Day Lily Tea*) is excellent for the nervous system. In terms of Yin and Yang, it is in between Big Saikoto and Small Saikoto. It is a good treatment for mental disease as well as for lack of sexual appetite, falling hair, and, sometimes, epilepsy, all of which are diseases related to the nervous system. This tea is also very good for burns. Day Lily Tea contains 10 ingredients. In addition, chodoko may be added in case of mental illness.

Saikokaryukotsuboreito has ten ingredients, Saikokeishito has nine, Big Saikoto has eight and Small Saikoto has seven. Saiko and hange are the two major ingredients in all of them; ginger and chopped dates are also contained in all four, but in smaller amounts; ginseng is present in all but Big Saikoto; Big Saikoto and Saikokaryukotsuboreito (Day Lily Tea) contain the famous daio.

Hange is a species of thoroughwax. The root is used medicinally; it has a very egui, potassic taste. Hange is an herb that is used often in Oriental medicine. It is excellent for morning sickness. *Small Hangebukuryoto,* which contains hange, bukuryo mushroom and ginger, is especially recommended for that malady. A similar tea, *Hangekobokuto,* contains the same ingredients along with magnolia bark (koboku) and beefteak (chiso) leaves. This is the fundamental tea for treating Ki disease (see "On Understanding Disease"). It is particularly effective for people who are bothered by stomach/intestinal gas. Both of these Hange teas are recommended for a sore throat.

Two other teas whose major ingredient is hange are *Karoto* and *Rikakuto.* Karoto also contains white scallion, chopped roasted green orange, ginger and karojitsu (a Japanese seed). It is said to be very helpful in case of heart attack. Rikakuto is used for trouble in the upper stomach (which is usually the result of excessive consumption of sugar). It contains gardenia seeds and bushi in addition to hange. Gardenia seeds are an important ingredient in many herb teas. The most famous is *Inchinkoto.* Inchinko is a species of mugwort. Inchinkoto, sometimes called Gardenia Herb Tea, also contains daio. It is useful in dealing with all problems of the liver—gall bladder—spleen area. Best known as a highly effective remedy for jaundice (for case history, see section on jaundice in "The Cure") and hepatitis, it is also helpful in cases of food poisoning, especially from fish.

Two other teas containing gardenia seeds as a major ingredient are Shishihakuhito and Shishikanrento.

Shishikanrento is excellent for duodenum and gastric ulcers, stomachaches and headaches. It contains gardenia seeds, licorice and ohren (known in this country as "goldthread"). Shishilhakuhito is similar, except that it contains obaku bark instead of goldthread. It

---

[4] See "On Understanding Disease" for an explanation of the different stages of disease.

is also used for stomach ailments and headaches, since it is an effective neutralizer of stomach acidity.

Here is a case history where Shishikanrento was used effectively:

A girl could not understand why her feces were so black. We have already learned that dark brown, nearly black, is a Yang color and indicates animal food. We have also learned that yellow, greenish and thin feces indicate a Yin food intake. However, very dark, almost black feces are often indicative of internal (stomach or duodenum) bleeding. In this particular case the blood had probably remained in the body for a long time. When the bleeding is in the large intestine, near the anus, the feces are red. The deeper in the body the bleeding occurs and the older the blood is, the darker the feces will be.

The trouble was diagnosed as gastric ulcer. The girl was advised to take Shishikanrento and was cured rapidly (for another case history, see section on stomach trouble in "The Cure").

Bukuryo and Goshuyu

Bukuryo mushroom (*Pachyma cocos*) has special medicinal properties. Its importance is attested to by the fact that it is included in Black Warrior and Bushi Tea, Hachimigan Tea, Hangebukuryoto and Hangekobokuto, Day Lily and Two Peony Tea. It is very Yin in quality, five times more so than the shitake mushroom, which itself has the reputation of being a Yin mushroom (as well as being both delicious and effective for certain kidney problems). Mushrooms in general are very good for kidney ailments or for any problem involving liquid retention. Plants that grow in watery regions are also good for this purpose. Why is this so? Because plants that grow in watery regions shed water, while plants from dry regions retain as much water as possible. Mushrooms, since they grow in humid climates, are effective in repelling excess water. Bukuryo mushroom is one of the most effective. The fundamental tea for all water diseases is *Goreisan*. It contains bukuryo and chorei, takusha and jutsu, and cinnamon. The first two ingredients are mushrooms while the second two are water plants, the roots of which are used medicinally. Goreisan can be taken for nearly all kidney ailments and is especially effective for body swelling.

CASE HISTORY

In Japan I was once called on to treat a six year old boy whose body was so swollen he couldn't walk. His face was like a watermelon! It turned out that he had been hospitalized for a skin disease the previous year. "The treatment was successful, but . . . ."—after that his body began to swell. He underwent many hos-

pital treatments, but to no avail; his condition grew worse. The swelling was gradual, but almost constant. The hospital doctor said that there was no cure, that the boy might die soon. At this point, even though it was not my responsibility I was obligated to try to help.

First the skin disease and then the swelling. The source of the boy's problem was obviously malfunctioning kidneys. I discovered that he was passing only about 1 cup of urine a day (the average is 5 to 7 cups). I gave him Goreisan Tea and applied an albi plaster to the back on the kidney area. After two days his urination began to increase. The treatment was continued and in two weeks the swelling had receded to the point where the boy could walk. Soon his kidneys were functioning normally.

Chorei (Mushroom) *Tea*, which contains bukuryo, chorei, takusha, and kasseki, a kind of mineral, is used in cases of bladder trouble and gonorrhea; however, inchinko mugwort must be added to it. *Jyumihaidokuto* and *Kagawagedokuto*, two teas used for curing syphilis, also contain bukuryo mushroom. So does *Ryokeijutsukanto*, which is good for visual problems (see section on eye trouble in "The Cure") and whose other ingredients are the water plant jutsu, steamed ginger and licorice.

A person with a strong, Yang-type constitution who has a headache may take *Goreisan Tea*. However, a Yin-type person with the same problem should take *Goshuyu Tea* instead. The main ingredient of Goreisan Tea is bukuryo mushroom, which has a very Yin quality. Goshuyu Tea, on the other hand, is quite Yang. This contrast is made strikingly clear in the recipe for *Kumibinroto*. Kumibinroto, or Nine Taste Tea, is extraordinarily effective in cases of vitamin B deficiency. This tea contains virtually no vitamin B, however. It works by stimulating the growth of intestinal flora (for more information and a case history, see section on vitamin B deficiency in "The Cure"). The nine ingredients are binroji (betelnut seeds), koboku (magnolia bark), kippi (a fruit), cinnamon, chiso leaves, daio, mokko (a root), licorice and ginger. But one more herb must be added: 3 grams of bukuryo mushroom (Yin) for Yang people, or 1 gram of goshuyu (Yang) for Yin people. According to Mr. Muramoto, here in America bukuryo should be used in nearly every case.

There are two teas containing goshuyu: Goshuyu Tea and—take a deep breath—*Tokishigyakukagoshuyushokyoto* (fortunately, there is an English name —*Heavenly Root Tea*). These two teas are similar and both are for Yin people. Goshuyu Tea contains dates, ginger and ginseng, in addition to goshuyu. Heavenly Root Tea has nine ingredients (but no ginseng): goshuyu, dates, ginger, toki (*Angelica polymorpha*), cinnamon, peony root, licorice, mokutsu (virgin's-bower) and saishin (a kind of wild ginger).

Both teas are effective for severe headaches and poor circulation. When winter comes along they serve as an excellent aid for Yin people, for they produce warmth by activating the circulation. When the hands and feet are cold and when the nose and fingers swell from the cold, these teas will be very useful. Heavenly Root Tea is also said to be beneficial for the nervous and glandular systems and for increasing sexual vigor in men and sensitivity in women.

What you have read thus far about herbs and teas is sufficient to acquaint you with the medicinal values of this ancient healing method. Truly a whole book should be devoted to herbs, a book which would analyze each tea, herb by herb, giving the apprentice herbalist the opportunity to learn in depth about the combinations and their possibilities. Such a book will probably be written in the near future. Until then, the present one will supply you with enough material to develop the self confidence you will need to practice this natural medicine.

* *

How To Prepare an Herbal Tea

Usually, making a tea involves the following simple preparation:

Mix the prescribed amount of herbs in 3 cups of water. Bring to a boil and leave over a medium flame for approximately one hour, until the water has evaporated by half. Sometimes the consistency will be a bit soupy. Earthenware is best for the preparation of teas. However, glass or almite will do. Do not use pots made of aluminum or iron, for these metals seep into the tea, drastically changing its precious qualities.

Of course, there are cases where the cooking directions are different. In such instances these "unusual" directions will always be pointed out.

Take one-half cup of the tea three times a day, usually thirty minutes before each meal. There is no set rule for the length of time a tea should be taken. This depends on the individual and on the nature of the disease. As soon as the symptoms disappear, the use of the tea should be discontinued. If no positive effects are noticed after three days, you are probably taking the wrong tea.

A general guideline is that acute ailments will be cured or at least improved noticeably after three days, while chronic illnesses or illnesses that take a long time to develop before they manifest symptoms will probably require weeks or even many months of treatment. Blood diseases such as syphilis usually require ten days to three months.

A child should be given a smaller quantity of herbs than an adult. The proper quantity is determined by the patient's weight. For example, a child of 70 pounds should take half the amount of herbs that a 140 pound adult would take, while a heavier person of 210 pounds should increase the quantity proportionally, taking 1½ times the amounts listed in these pages.

A glossary of herbs follows the tea recipes.

* *

Tea Recipes

MONKSHOOD (BUSHI)

BIG JOKITO (*see* JOKITO)

BIG SAIKOTO (*see* SAIKOTO)

BLACK WARRIOR TEA (*Shinbuto*)

    5 grams bukuryo
    3 grams peony root
    3 grams ginger
    3 grams jutsu
    0.5 grams bushi (0.5 gr→2 gr) [5]

May be used for all Yin-type diseases in general. Especially effective against diarrhea and other intestinal problems. Beneficial for those with low blood pressure (see page 96).

BOFUTSUSHOSHAN (*see* SAGE'S PATH TEA)

BUSHI TEA

    4 grams bukuryo
    4 grams peony root
    5 grams jutsu
    3 grams ginseng
    0.5 grams bushi (0.5 gr→1 gr) [6]

Good for weak people. Especially beneficial for heart and small intestines. Can increase sexual potency more effectively than ginseng alone (see page 96).

for *Bushi Poisoning*

    15 grams licorice
    30 grams black beans

Cook mixture in 5 to 6 cups of water over a high flame for 20 minutes. Drink as much as possible.

[5] See box, page 100.   [6] ibid.

CHOREI TEA

3 grams chorei
3 grams bukuryo
3 grams kasseki
3 grams takusha

For gonorrhea, bladder and uterus trouble.

* *

IMPORTANT

bushi — In recipes that call for bushi, the smallest amount mentioned should be used at first. It may be increased gradually every few days.

ginger — Fresh is better than dried. When a recipe calls for a large quantity of ginger, fresh ginger is implied, while small quantities (0.5-2.0 g) imply dried. Five grams of fresh ginger equals 2 grams dried; 4 grams fresh equals 1.5 dried; 3 grams fresh equals 1 gram dried. Ginger is used raw unless indicated otherwise. "Steamed ginger" is prepared by steaming the ginger for 1 hour, then cutting and drying it.

dates — Whole dates, including pits, chopped very finely.

peach/apricot seeds — Chopped.

green orange (*kijitsu*) — Roasted and chopped.

For the method of preparing teas and instructions as to how long, how often and in what quantities they should be taken, see page 99.

* *

CINNAMON HERB TEA

4 grams cinnamon
4 grams peony root
4 grams dates
4 grams ginger
2 grams licorice

LICORICE

Very good for fevers and colds, especially for people who sweat excessively during fever (see page 93). One-half hour after drinking tea, eat a bowl of soft brown rice (rice cooked with extra water).

DAIOBOTANPITO

6 grams kashi
4 grams bosho
4 grams peach seeds (tonin)
4 grams botanpi (tree peony)
2 grams daio

Good for problems in lower part of abdomen. Effective against appendicitis and dysentery; also a laxative for constipation.

DAIO-BUSHI TEA

1 gram daio
0.5 gram bushi
2 grams saishin (a kind of wild ginger)

A helpful remedy for gout and similar ailments (see page 96).

DANDELION HERB TEA

8 grams dandelion root
6 grams toki
3 grams kobushi
3 grams tree peony
4 grams sanyaku (jinenjo)

For mothers who have trouble producing milk and for stomach troubles.

DAY LILY TEA (*see* SAIKOKARYUKOTSUBOREITO)

* *

Dragon's Bone Tea

Here is a unique tea, famous in Oriental medicine. It is an old remedy, made from fossilized "dragon's" bones, more probably from the bone of the ancient mammoth. The fossilized bone is pulverized and used as an ingredient in the following recipe:

4 grams bukuryo mushroom
3 grams dragon bone
3 grams oyster shell
3 grams cinnamon
3 grams ohgi
3 grams bukumonto
1.5 grams licorice
1 gram ginger

This tea is very beneficial for the nervous system. It is effective for overpalpitation, sleeplessness, agrypnia or phrenitis. I do not know where you can buy "dragon's bone" . . . except in a Chinese pharmacy. If you should find any in America you may use it to make this tea.

* *

DRAGON TEA

6 grams hange
3 grams mao
3 grams peony root
3 grams steamed ginger
3 grams licorice
3 grams cinnamon
3 grams saishin
3 grams gomishi

For asthma, bronchitis, whooping cough and other respiratory ailments.

GARDENIA HERB TEA (*Inchinkoto*)

4 grams inchinko (a kind of mugwort)
3 grams gardenia seeds
1 gram daio

For all liver and gall bladder diseases, such as hepatitis. Highly effective in treating jaundice (green vegetable soup should be taken a half hour after tea if patient is hungry). Good for food poisoning, especially poisoning from fish.

GINSENG

GINSENG HERB TEA

3 grams ginseng
3 grams licorice
3 grams jutsu
3 grams steamed ginger

For weak people, especially those with problems in the digestive organs (and heart). Is used for all Yin diseases in general, as are Bushi Tea and Black Warrior Tea; all three are similar. Shigyakuto (page 96) may also be used for Yin diseases.

GOREISAN TEA

5 grams takusha
3 grams chorei
3 grams bukuryo
3 grams jutsu
2 grams cinnamon

Good for kidney problems, swelling, and all manifestations of water disease. Also good for headaches in Yang people. When 4 grams of inchinko are added, this tea becomes an effective treatment for kidney and liver trouble.

GINGER

GOSHUYU TEA

4 grams dates
4 grams ginger
3 grams goshuyu
2 grams ginseng

Good for headaches in Yin-type people. Also improves circulation (page 98).

HACHIMIGAN TEA

5 grams jio
3 grams sanshuyu
3 grams sanyaku
3 grams takusha
3 grams bukuryo
3 grams tree peony
1 gram cinnamon
1 gram bushi [7]

For weakness in lower abdominal / lower back area, problems with urination, whether of excess or of deficiency, bedwetting and bladder trouble, hypertrophe of prostate gland, nephritis. Also effective for high blood pressure, cataracts, lack of sexual appetite, and diabetes (see page 96).

HANGEBUKURYOTO (*Small Hange Tea*)

5 grams hange
5 grams bukuryo
5 grams ginger

Excellent for morning sickness. Can be used for sore throat.

HANGEBOKUTO

6 grams hange
5 grams bukuryo
4 grams ginger
3 grams magnolia bark (koboku)
2 grams chiso

For inflamed throat, stomach and intestinal gas, and all Ki diseases.

HEAVENLY ROOT TEA
(*Tokishigyakukagoshuyoshokyoto*)

5 grams dates
2 grams goshuyu
4 grams ginger
3 grams toki
3 grams cinnamon
3 grams peony root
3 grams ground clematis (virgin's-bower)
2 grams saishin
2 grams licorice

For relieving headaches in Yin people. Improves blood circulation, generates warmth. Good for nervous and glandular systems. Is said to increase sexual vigor in men and sensitivity in women.

INCHINKOTO (*see* GARDENIA HERB TEA)

JEWEL'S TEA (*Renju-in*)

6 grams bukuryo
4 grams cinnamon
4 grams licorice
3 grams jutsu
3 grams jio
3 grams senkyo
3 grams peony root
3 grams toki

For worms and anemia. Helps build blood and strengthen the intestines.

---

[7] See box, page 100.

JOKITO (*listed from Yin to Yang*)

All the Jokitos are quite similar. Thus, Small Jokito, the most Yang, is still a Yin tea and is suitable for slightly Yang people. Big Jokito, on the other hand, is used for those who are very Yang. Choi Jokito is in the middle. All contain daio and thus can function as laxatives in case of constipation.

BIG JOKITO

5 grams magnolia bark	2 grams green orange
2 grams daio	2 grams bosho

For very Yang people afflicted with constipation, obesity, high blood pressure, food poisoning.

TOKAKU JOKITO

5 grams peach seeds	1.5 grams licorice
3 grams daio	4 grams cinnamon
2 grams bosho	

For all blood diseases caused by blood stagnation—hemorrhoids, pyorrhea, headache, uterine tumor, irregular menstruation, etc. (see page 96).

CHOI JOKITO

2 grams daio
1 gram bosho
1 gram licorice

For stomach and intestinal problems. In terms of strength, this tea falls between Big Jokito and Small Jokito.

SMALL JOKITO

3 grams magnolia bark
2 grams green orange
2 grams daio

A slightly Yin tea. Good for constipation and other stomach and intestinal problems. If you increase the amount of magnolia bark to 10 grams, you will have an effective treatment for Parkinson's Disease.

JYUMIHAIDOKUTO

2.5 grams saiko	2.5 grams bofu
2.5 grams cherry bark	1.5 grams dokkatsu
2.5 grams kikyo	1 gram ginger
2.5 grams senkyiu	1 gram licorice
2.5 grams bukuryo	1 gram keigai

This tea, composed mostly of Yin herbs, is good for problems of skin discharge: psoriasis, syphilis, leucorrhea, etc.

KAKKONTO (*see* KUZU ROOT HERB TEA)

KAMBAKUDAISOTO

20 grams wheat
6 grams dates (diced, including pits)
5 grams licorice

For babies who cry too strongly, give 1 or 2 teaspoons, 3 times a day for 1 or 2 days. For hysteria and similar mental problems in women and children, it may be taken for 10 days to 2 months. In case of accidental brain damage, the tea may be taken for as long as a year. This tea is not effective with adult men, who should take Sanoshashinto instead.

KAGAWAGEDOKUTO

5 grams bukuryo	1 gram daio
4 grams mokutsu	2 grams keigai
3 grams senkyio	3 grams bofu
3 grams nindo	3 grams renjyo
1 gram licorice	

For syphilis.

KAROKIJITSU TEA

No recipe—too complicated to prepare. Purchase ready-made.

For angina pectoris

KAROTO

6 grams hange	2 grams green orange
4 grams white scallion	2 grams ginger
3 grams korojitsu	

For heart attack.

KEISHIBUKURYOGAN (*see* TWO PEONY TEA)

KEISHISHAKUYAKUTO

Add 2 grams peony root to Cinnamon Tea. A Yang tea for Yin people.

KENCHUTO

SMALL KENCHUTO

20 grams Yinnies (about 2 Yinnies) [8]
2 grams peony root
Cinnamon Tea

Good for general weakness, hernias, and Yang children who bedwet.

OHGIKENCHUTO

Add 4 grams ohgi to Small Kenchuto. A treatment for peritonitis.

KIKYO TEA

2 grams kikyo
3 grams licorice

For sore throat.

KUMIBINROTO TEA
(*see* NINE TASTE TEA)

CREEPING BELLFLOWER

CLUSTERED BELLFLOWER

---

[8] If you are unable to obtain Yinnies, the best substitute is dark honey.

KUZU ROOT HERB TEA (*Kakkonto*)

This tea is a mixture of Mao and Cinnamon teas plus kuzu root and minus the apricot seeds.

    8 grams kuzu root
    4 grams mao
    3 grams cinnamon
    4 grams dates
    4 grams ginger
    2 grams licorice
    3 grams peony root

For stomach and intestinal upset, colitis, general body stiffness and pain. Generally effective against nearly all diseases in people of average constitution (see page 94). Especially effective for those suffering from chronic headaches.

KUZU-SAFFLOWER TEA

    3 grams kuzu root
    3 grams peony
    3 grams jio
    1.5 grams safflower
    1.5 grams gardenia seeds
    1.5 grams goldthread
    1 gram licorice

Good for enlarged hearts—especially if the person has a large red nose.

MAO TEA

    5 grams apricot seeds
    4 grams cinnamon
    1.5 grams licorice
    5 grams mao

For Yang people and Yang diseases. Excellent for headaches, coughing, high fever (strong pulse), and excessive urination. Good for asthma and typhoid fever (see page 94).

MOKUBOI TEA

    4 grams mokuboi
    3 grams sekko
    3 grams cinnamon
    3 grams ginseng

For asthma resulting from heart trouble.

MU TEA

For coughs (wheezing type) and other respiratory trouble where there is difficulty in breathing. Commercially available in natural food stores.

GOLDTHREAD

NINE TASTE TEA (*Kumibinroto*)

    4 grams binroji   1 gram daio
    3 grams magnolia bark   1 gram mokko
    3 grams kippi   1 gram licorice
    3 grams cinnamon   1 gram ginger
    1.5 grams chiso leaves

{ 1 gram goshuyu (for Yin people)
{ 3 grams bukuryo (for Yang people)
(In America, it is almost always proper to use bukuryo.)

For vitamin B deficiency; reestablishes functioning of intestinal flora.

OHGIKENCHUTO (*see* KENCHUTO)

RENJU-IN (*see* JEWEL'S TEA)

RIKAKUTO

    8 grams hange
    3 grams gardenia seeds
    0.5 grams bushi [9]

For trouble in upper stomach (which usually results from excessive intake of Yin food.)

RIKKOSAN TEA

    2 grams saishin
    2 grams shoma
    2 grams bofu
    1.5 grams licorice
    1 gram ryutan

Relieves toothache.

FRINGED GENTIAN

RYOKEIJUTSUKANTO

    6 grams bukuryo
    3 grams jutsu
    4 grams cinnamon
    2 grams licorice

For eye and vision problems: nearsightedness, farsightedness, astigmatism, etc. (see page 123).

RYOTANSHAKANTO

    5 grams toki
    5 grams ground clematis (virgin's-bower)
    5 grams jio
    3 grams plantain seeds
    3 grams ohgon
    3 grams takusha
    1.5 grams gardenia seeds
    1.5 grams gentian root
    1.5 grams licorice

Good for bladder trouble, gonorrhea, and similar diseases in which the problem remains internal. Also effective against syphilis; but in cases where there is an active discharge, Jyomihaidokuto is recommended.

---

[9] See box, page 100.

SAGE'S PATH TEA (*Bofutsushoshan*)

No recipe; too complicated. Order by name.

Used by people whose body quality is very Yang and who need to lose weight. Is also effective with related problems such as high blood pressure and intestinal, kidney and skin diseases.

SAIKOTO

All the Saikoto teas are fairly Yin and can be used to treat Yang stages of disease,[10] especially the Small Yang stage. Big Saikoto is the most Yin of the Saikoto teas and can be used effectively for Clear Yang disease. Saikokeishito is the most Yang of the Saikoto teas, but is nevertheless a Yin tea. It is suitable for sick people whose body quality is basically balanced or who lean slightly to the Yin side.

BIG SAIKOTO

6 grams saiko	3 grams peony root
4 grams hange	3 grams dates
4 grams raw ginger	2 grams green orange
3 grams ohgon	1 gram daio

Used for Clear Yang disease. Very good for heavy people with problems such as high blood pressure, stomachache, and asthma, and for all those troubled with liver and gall bladder problems.

SAIKOKARYUKOTSUBOREITO (*Day Lily Tea*)

5 grams saiko	2.5 grams bukuryo
4 grams hange	2.5 grams dates
2.5 grams ryukotsu	2.5 grams ginger
2.5 grams borei	2.5 grams ginseng
2.5 grams cinnamon	1 gram daio

Good for diseases of the nervous system and related problems such as loss of hair, loss of sexual appetite, and epilepsy. Also effective for burns.

Can be used for mental illness if 3 grams of chodoko are added.

SMALL SAIKOTO

7 grams saiko	3 grams dates
5 grams hange	3 grams ginseng
4 grams ginger	2 grams licorice
3 grams ohgon	

Can be taken as a tonic for an extended period of time, especially by people who suffer from weakness or loss of appetite. Also good for bronchitis, tuberculosis, and other respiratory diseases.

SAIKOKEISHITO

5 grams saiko	2 grams peony root
4 grams hange	2 grams ginger
2.5 grams cinnamon	2 grams dates
2 grams ohgon	1.5 grams licorice
2 grams ginseng	

A more Yang tea for less Yang people. Effective for colds, stomach ulcers, gall stones, bedwetting and hernias.

SANMESHAKOSAITO (*see* THREE TASTE TEA)

SANOSHASHINTO

1 gram ohren
1 gram ohgon
1 gram daio

For epilepsy, convulsions, insanity, etc. (whenever there is too much blood in the brain). May also help stop internal bleeding (tuberculosis, stomach ulcers, etc.).

Boil in water for 3 or 4 minutes and let cool. *Do not drink it hot!*

SHAKKANOSHINBUTO

3 grams peony root
3 grams licorice
2 grams saishin
1 gram daio
0.5 grams bushi (0.5→2.0 gr) [11]

Has both strong Yang (bushi) and strong Yin (daio) herbs. Excellent for relieving pain and removing deep-rooted toxins which result from extreme Yin and Yang foods taken over a long period of time, as in arthritis, rheumatism, gout, etc. Start with a small quantity of bushi and increase weekly if there is no noticeable improvement.

SHAKUYOKOKANZOTO

6 grams licorice
4 grams peony root

For sharp pain only. For minor pain, use licorice alone.

SHIGYAKUTO

3 grams licorice
2 grams steamed ginger
0.5 grams bushi (0.5→2.0 gr) [12]

For Yin kidney condition (when body cannot retain liquid) and Yin diarrhea. Effective with Yin-type diseases in general.

SHINBUTO (*see* BLACK WARRIOR TEA)

SHISHIHAKAHITO

3 grams gardenia seeds
2 grams licorice
2 grams obaku bark

Neutralizes stomach acid; relieves headache and stomachache.

SHISHIKANRENTO

3 grams gardenia seeds
4 grams licorice
1 gram goldthread

Good for gastric and duodenum ulcers, indigestion, headache and stomachache, and other stomach problems.

---

[10] See "On Understanding Disease."
[11] See box, page 100.
[12] See box, page 100.

SHITEITO

     5 grams persimmon stem
     4 grams ginger
     1.5 grams choko

For hiccups.

SMALL HANGE
(*see* HANGEBUKURYOTO)

SMALL JOKITO (*see* JOKITO)

SMALL KENCHUTO
(*see* KENCHUTO)

SMALL SAIKOTO (*see* SAIKO)

PERSIMMON

THREE TASTE TEA (*Sanmeshakosaito*)

     4 grams shakosai
     1.5 grams licorice
     1.5 grams daio

Very effective in eliminating worms and other parasites from the intestines. May be effective for anemia, a disease in which parasites are often present (see page 95).

TOKAKU JOKITO (*see* JOKITO)

TOKISHIGYAKUKAGOSHUYUSHOKYOTO
(*see* HEAVENLY ROOT TEA)

TWO PEONY TEA (*Keishibukuryogan*)

     3 grams peony root
     3 grams tree peony
     3 grams bukuryo
     3 grams cinnamon
     3 grams peach seeds

Very effective in cleansing the skin and purifying the blood, although not as strong as Tokaku Jokito. Good for hemorrhoids. Add 2 grams baimo and you will have a very effective treatment for draining pus from skin infections. This tea is used by women to relieve cramps and as a tonic for frigidity and sterility. As a beauty aid it may be taken over a period of several months.

WHITE TIGER TEA

     5 grams chimo
     8 grams brown rice
     15 grams gypsum
     2 grams licorice

For reducing fever.

WILD BARLEY HERB TEA
(*Hatomugito or Yokuininto*)

     8 grams wild barley
     4 grams mao
     4 grams toki
     4 grams jutsu
     3 grams cinnamon
     3 grams peony root
     2 grams licorice

Good for rheumatism, arthritis, gout, etc.

For information on obtaining any of these teas, see page 142.

HERB GLOSSARY

baimo — *Frutillaria thunbergii — root*

binroji — *betelnut seed*

bofu — *Ledebouriella seseloides — root*

borei — *oyster shell*

bosho — *sodium sulphate and water ($Na_2SO_4 \cdot nH_2O$)*

botanpi — *tree peony — bark of root*

bukuryo — *Pachyma cocos — mushroom*

bushi — *salted, dried, roasted aconite (monkshood — crowfoot family) — root*

chimo — *Anemarrhena asphodeloides — root*

chiso — *beefteak leaves*

chodoko — *species of fathead tree — twig*

choko — *Eugenia caryophyllata — berry*

chorei — *Grifola umbellata — mushroom*

daio — *Chinese rhubarb — root*

dokkatsu — *Aralia continentalis (wild Oriental asparagus — sasparilla family) — root*

gomishi — *Schizandra chinensis — berry*

goshuyu — *Evodia rutaecarpa benth — berry*

hange — *Pinellia tuberifera (egui-potassium taste) — root*

hato — *Job's tears (wild barley)*

inchinko — *Artemsia capillaris (a species of mugwort)*

jio — *Rehmania glutinosa libosch — root*

jutsu — *Atractylis ovata (a water plant) — root*

kakkon — *kuzu root*

karojitsu — *Trichosanthes japonica reget — seed*

kashi — *Terminalia chebula — fruit*

kasseki — *a mineral*

keigei — *Saphoria augustifolia — berry*

kijitsu — *chopped, roasted green orange*

kikyo — *Chinese bellflower (dark violet) — root*

kippi — *Citrus leiocarpa hort — fruit*

koboku — *Magnolia officinalis*

kobushi — *Cyperus rotundus — root*

mokko — *Aristolochia debilis sieb — root*

mokuboi — *Cocculus trilobus — root*

mokutsu — *ground clematis (virgin's-bower — crowfoot family) — stem*

nindo — *a species of honeysuckle*

ohgi — *Astraganshoantschy hoan — root*

ohgon — *Scutellaria baicalensis — root*

ohren — *Coptis sinensis (goldthread — crowfoot family) — root*

rengyo — *a species of forsythea — berry*

ryutan — *gentian root*

saiko — *a species of thoroughwax — root*

saishin — *Asarium sieboldi migo (a species of wild ginger) — root, and sometimes leaves*

sanshuyu — *Cornus officinalis — berry*

sanyaku — *jinenjo root (Japanese vegetable, tastes similar to potato)*

sekko — *gypsum*

senkyu — *Enidium officinale — root*

shakosai — *a kind of seaweed*

shin-i — *Magnolia denudata — flower pod (whole)*

shoma — *Cimicifuga simplex (bugbane family) — root*

takusha — *Alisma plantago aquatica (a kind of water flower — arrowhead family) — root*

toki — *Angelica polymorpha — root*

tonin — *peach seeds (inside pit)*

yokuinin — *see "hato"*

EXTERNAL
TREATMENTS

EXTERNAL AND INTERNAL TREATMENTS differ in their respective functions.

An internal treatment such as an herb tea works in multiple ways. It changes the entire body. Depending on the individual, it may either alkalize or acidify, reduce energy or increase it.

An external treatment, however, has a very simple role: to drain out that which is causing pain, using the skin pores as little exits from which the various types of waste can be eliminated.

External treatments are effective in their place, but by themselves they do not constitute a complete cure. A corresponding internal treatment is needed—that is, of course, a proper diet. The body must constantly be "treated" with good food in order to maintain health. There is not a more effective treatment for the body. It is when we disregard this aspect of medicine that we end up turning to symptomatic treatments such as aspirin, penicillin and other drugs. And when these fail, we either go to a surgeon to have the "waste" removed, or resort to some other radical solution—for by now we are in serious trouble.

The best method is twofold: a proper diet supplemented by external treatment, both of which in their respective ways will help cure the disease. A balanced way of eating—which implies the avoidance of excess—will relax bodily tension and help eliminate that which the external treatment is working to drain out. Once the external remedy has succeeded, a good diet should be maintained; this will complete the cure by uprooting the original cause of the problem.

The external treatment generally works as a "magnet" to draw out that which is causing the suffering. But there are exceptions, in which case its function is simply to work as a balm.

The most typical external treatment (preparation will be given in this chapter) is the *plaster,* especially the *albi plaster,* whose Yin quality produces activity (Yang) in the painful area. This activity in turn draws out whatever waste is behind the skin. We shall learn that in order to encourage that particular activity, we use a hot compress on the painful area, usually a ginger compress. The ginger compress prepares the area so that the albi plaster can work under the best possible conditions. It works as a catalyst by loosening the diseased area.

When a plaster is applied, pain, pressure or other strange sensations may be experienced. This should be regarded as a good sign. It means that the plaster is doing its job; the waste is breaking up and will soon appear on the surface of the skin.

The Plasters

Albi Plaster

Albi is a vegetable that looks somewhat like a potato. In America it is known as the "taro." Puerto Ricans call it "yuca" or "iya otiya." Albi is also used as food.

When purchasing albi one should choose those that are small, young, fresh, and light in color (like a white potato). It is advisable to peel off the brown outside skin.

The albi plaster is used for various complaints and can be applied to various parts of the body, front and back: over the eye (for eye trouble), behind the ear (for ear trouble), on the face, throat, arms, and legs—everywhere.

CASE HISTORY

One evening I received an emergency phone call from a woman. Her husband was suffering from swollen testicles and he was in great pain.

I went to their home immediately. The man's legs were swollen, his testicles were the size of a cow's udder! He was moaning from the pain.

The previous day the man had eaten a large quantity of sukiyaki and beer, and had not urinated since then. He was 35 years old.

I quickly made an albi plaster and tried to apply it from underneath, but the testicles were so large that I had to make a bigger plaster. At midnight I gave him Goreisan Tea.

I spent the night at the man's house. When I saw him in the morning, the pain had abated but the swelling was still there. I applied a fresh albi plaster. Thirty minutes later the man passed urine, but in a huge quantity—like a horse! This happened again one hour later, and two more times at exact one-hour intervals. The testicles shrank rapidly. I gave him the tea again and returned home. When I called the next morning, he was almost completely well. His legs were back to normal and he could walk.

His condition had been potentially very dangerous, but prompt and proper treatment averted the danger quickly.

The appropriate mixture for an albi plaster varies, depending on the water content of the albi.

1) One mixture contains 50% grated albi, 5% grated ginger and 45% flour (white flour is best for plasters because it is the most glutinous).

This combination is used whenever a harder consistency is desired.

2) Another mixture might have the following composition: 70% albi, 20% flour, 10% ginger.

ALBI PLASTER

How to Prepare an Albi Plaster

Albi exists in powder form, but the fresh vegetable is preferable. The volume you will need depends on the area you wish to cover. If the tender area is, for exam-

ple, 5″ by 3″, then the mixture will be at least the size of that surface. The cotton cloth on which the mixture is spread should be big enough so that when the plaster is tied in place, the mixture will not escape from the sides. The consistency of the mixture should be neither watery nor solid. Rather, it should be an easily spreadable paste. The thickness should be between ¼ and ½ inch. If in the process of mixing the ingredients you should find that the consistency is too thick, you may use less wheat flour.

Use a cotton cloth to hold the albi mixture over the affected area. Do not use plastic or oil paper; these prevent the area from breathing and thus may cause skin disease. For the eyes, use one thickness of gauze between eyes and plaster.

Wear the plaster for at least four hours (changing to a fresh plaster after two hours). The first one will become saturated with poisons from the skin.

For internal bleeding, apply plaster as soon as possible. Blood clots within 48 hours.

For cancer tumors and cancer in general, apply first a ginger compress (see preparation further on in this chapter), then the albi plaster. Next put roasted salt in a cloth bag and apply on top of the plaster. This treatment is especially effective for diseases of the abdomen and other diseases close to the surface of the body.

Ideally the plaster should be changed every four hours. However, you may sleep with the plaster overnight, since changing it during the night would be too much trouble and would prevent a good night's sleep. Should the plaster cause a skin irritation, cover the inflamed area with sesame oil.

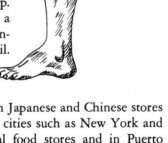

Albi may be obtained in Japanese and Chinese stores (for people living in large cities such as New York and San Francisco), in natural food stores and in Puerto Rican stores. Some supermarkets are now beginning to sell it.

Chlorophyll Plaster

This plaster may be used as a substitute for the albi plaster when albi is not available. It is a very easy plaster to prepare. When you become an expert you will be able to go to the field and select the best-suited greens.

Until then, here is a simple preparation which does not require much expertise. Use fresh green plant leaves. Radish tops, for example, are very good; the same goes for carrot tops, swiss chard, watercress, parsley, spinach, etc. Many wild grasses are also suitable. Vegetables such as cabbage and lettuce are not so green; they are considered white.

Preparation:

Cut leaves and crush in a suribachi, the same instrument in which sesame salt and mochi are made. The mixture should be 80% leaves, 10% dried peppermint leaves (20% if fresh), and 10% flour (preferably white flour). No water is necessary, since fresh leaves contain moisture. Apply on afflicted area for a few hours; renew if necessary.

* *

CASE HISTORY

Tim was a middle-aged bachelor employed by a small independent publishing company in San Francisc. For several years he had eaten rather well— that is, not too much animal food, not too much sugar and sweetened food. Still he suffered from extreme stiffness and pain in the lower back. I met him in August of 1971. At that time he had been receiving treatment from a chiropractor every day for two months. He was unable to work, to stand straight or bend over very far. After a consultation I began treatment with chlorophyll plasters at night; albi was unavailable. The next day he felt very comfortable but mentioned that he had experienced strange sensations in his back the previous night. While these sensations were not particularly painful, they did prevent him from sleeping. Though he was grateful for his improvement, he did have one complaint—the sheets and bed clothes were soiled from the plaster. I told him, "Bed clothes are inexpensive and are easily cleaned or replaced. Your body is not."

From the following night on, he slept well. For four consecutive nights the plaster was applied, after which time the pain had disappeared almost completely and he could move and work. The morning after the fourth night he told me that he felt sexually invigorated. This surprised him somewhat, since it had not occurred for a very long time. I reassured him by telling him that in the Orient it is considered a sign of good health.

* *

Tofu Plaster

This type of plaster is best for head wounds, concussions, headache and earache, and cerebral hemorrhage, although for certain problems chlorophyll and albi plasters may be used with the same effectiveness.

This treatment is 100% effective for cerebral hemorrhage, if applied within 48 hours of the time the injury occurs. After that time, a blood clot will most likely have formed, making the cure extremely difficult. In such a case, cut the hair close to the scalp and apply tofu plaster. If paralysis has set in on one side, apply the plaster to the alternate side of the head. If blindness has set in, apply plaster to both sides. This may be somewhat effective. For cerebral hemorrhages and other very serious accidents, change the plaster every thirty minutes. It should be maintained constantly for a period of at least one week. Tofu is recommended because it is slow to harden and is thus best for healing internal bleeding.

Preparation:

Tofu can be purchased at any Japanese store or in Chinatown. Put the tofu squares in a clean cloth and squeeze out the liquid. Next, place the squeezed tofu in a bowl and add 10% flour. Mix thoroughly. Put the mixture on a clean cloth, spreading it evenly.

When tofu is not available, use ground soaked soya beans (from which tofu is produced).

* *

CASE HISTORY

One of the first cases I had in this country involved a baby girl who had fallen on her head at age 10 months. Her parents had taken her to the hospital where she was kept for one month, but the doctors couldn't help her and offered no hope of her every growing normally.

I first saw her 11 months after the accident. Her right hand and right foot were paralyzed. The middle finger on her right hand and the second and third toes on her right foot were bent inwards. Her left eye wouldn't close and the pupil was enlarged (the left side of the brain controls the right side of the body).

I ordered the little girl's head to be shaved, which the parents thought strange. They objected at first, but later agreed. The shaving revealed a big red bruise, a sign of cerebral hemorrhage. Tofu plasters were applied to the spot for 10 days. The first night the baby cried continually until morning, but at the end of the 10 days she was able to move her hands and feet—this despite the fact that the hemorrhage had been present for nearly a year.

The condition of her eye remained the same, however. For this I recommended a tea, Kambakudaisoto (for more about this tea, see page 95). One mouth later her eye was able to close and her teeth started coming in. The bruise was completely gone.

She began to grow, but not enough. It turned out that her case was complicated by intestinal worms, which were hampering her growth. The latter problem was cured with Three Taste Tea (see page 95). Today, one year after I first saw her, the little girl's condition is still improving. There certainly is hope. She is still taking Kambakudaisoto.

* *

The Ginger Compress

The ginger compress is the typical symbol of "clean" medicine. It makes few demands of its user and takes only a few minutes to prepare. It is painless and even rather pleasant, costs little—the price of a few pounds of ginger—and accomplishes a lot. In fact, one could write a book simply recording case histories of its successes. You will find it helpful in times of uncertainty as to the proper procedure for treating an especially stubborn disease. A practical solution to various problems, it is an excellent pain reliever and a good antidote for inflammations. With its help, a cancer tumor will shrink and eventually disappear. Even internal organs and the body's internal condition in general will benefit from this treatment. The ginger compress will become a friend on which you can always depend. Here is the preparation:

2 quarts of water   } can be doubled
5 ounces grated ginger } if necessary

Heat water to 158 degrees Fahrenheit (70 degrees Centigrade). Do not boil! Boiling will destroy the ginger's value.

GINGER COMPRESS

Grate ginger and place it in a cloth (preferably cheesecloth). Wrap it and tie in a bag with a string; put the cloth containing the ginger into the warm water. Cook until the water is pale yellow. Then, while it is still sitting in the water, crush the bag slightly with your hand to squeeze out the ginger. Soak a towel in that water, squeeze out some of the liquid, and place on the afflicted area. The water should be as hot as the patient can tolerate. Always keep changing the towel to maintain a constant temperature on the skin. The same water may be used for 24 hours.

Eventually the skin should become red. When this happens the compress is no longer necessary. People with strong constitutions will redden in about ten minutes, whereas weaker patients will redden after twenty to thirty minutes of compress application. For weaker patients, it is better to heat the water once or twice, being careful, of course, not to bring it to a boil. Red skin indicates that good circulation has been promoted; the excess fat or oil is melting away.

Bedridden people will usually need repeated treatment. For a serious problem, use the ginger compress followed by an albi plaster, four to five times a day, changing after four hours. The pain will be relieved as the blood starts flowing through the vessels and efficient circulation is established.

Compared to deeper problems such as stomach or uterus pain, surface problems are very easy to cure. Asthma, arthritis and nervous pain can also be cured relatively easily.

GINGER BATH

Ginger Bath (*for the feet*)

The function of the ginger bath is to promote good circulation. When the feet become hot and red, the entire body circulation improves.

Seriously ill patients who are too weak to stand or sit can remain on their backs and place their feet in the bowl containing the ginger mixture. Preparation is the same as for the ginger compress.

Ginger Bath (*for the body*)

This bath has always proved very helpful for arthritic people with pain in different parts of the body. It is also good for gout and bursitis (calcification of the joints). The preparation is the same as for the ginger compress, except that it requires a larger volume of water and, consequently, more ginger. For a gallon of water, use two pounds of grated ginger.

Ginger Oil

This is a very helpful remedy for headaches, pain in the spine or joints, earache, and scalp diseases resulting in dandruff or baldness.

Ingredients:

> juice from grated ginger
> an equal amount of sesame oil

Mix ingredients and massage into the skin for pain in muscles or spine. The effect is equal to that of a ginger compress, and sometimes even more so.

In case of earache, place two or three drops of the mixture on a piece of cotton and press into the aching ear, keeping the head tipped sideways for a while until the mixture has penetrated the ear. Keep the used piece of cotton in the ear hole for a few hours.

For dandruff, make enough of this mixture to rub on the entire skull. Apply at night so that it can be kept on for at least 8 hours. It is even better to keep the mixture on throughout the following day and then wash with an herbal shampoo. Try this a few times— twice a week, for example.

* *

CASE HISTORY

For some people the ginger oil treatment works very quickly. A curved spine soon becomes straight. Other people have to try several times (i.e. taking the treatment for one week, then skipping a week, then taking the treatment for another week, etc.). Sometimes even that is ineffective. If the ginger oil does not work, one should then try "Moshio," which is carbonized salted kombu (sold by Chico San). Mix with just enough water to form a paste.

One woman, Mrs. M., was patient enough to try the ginger oil treatment every other week for six months, for her son. After six months she and her son came to see me. The spine had become completely straight. To my knowledge, this is the longest experiment ever made with the ginger oil treatment.

I was deeply moved by the mother's love.

* *

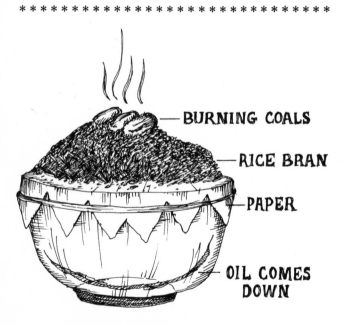

MAKING RICE OIL

Rice Oil

Cover a large bowl with a layer of very thin paper. Make needle holes in the paper; then cover the paper with rice bran. Over the rice bran put burning char-

coals. The oil from the rice bran will drip down into the bowl. This oil can be applied directly to diseased skin, especially to the skin rash between the legs which is so common to athletes.

Salt-Bancha (*salted at 1%*)

Ingredients: salt and bancha tea

Heat one cup of bancha tea and add a pinch of salt (1% of the volume of tea).

This simple preparation can prove very helpful when used as a substitute for the ginger compress. Sometimes a ginger compress is too strong for a tender area, such as the eye.

Let us take a case where the eyes hurt. To relieve the pain, put lukewarm salt-bancha in an eye glass and let the painful eye (leave the eyes open!) bathe in the salty liquid for a few seconds. Renew the liquid and repeat a few more times.

To help cure either nearsightedness or farsightedness, this treatment should be followed by the application of an albi plaster every night for a week (one layer of gauze between plaster and eye). Ryokeijutsukanto may also be taken.

Salt-Bancha (*salted at 3%*)

Ingredients: salt and bancha

Proceed as above, but this time add a little more salt. This is almost the same as the proportion of salt found in sea water.

Usage: In case of internal nose trouble, rinse the nasal passages with this liquid to cleanse them and remove mucus. Use a nose dropper or a nasal douche. Nose trouble is indicated by yellow, green or blue mucus. If mucus membrane is swollen, use a lotus root pipe.

Carp Plaster

Buy a whole carp from a fish market. Make an incision in the head from eye to eye. Drain one tablespoon of blood from the incision and have the patient drink this. Next remove the organs and discard them. Then chop the meat into small pieces. Spread the chopped meat on the patient's chest. Keep a constant check on the body temperature. When the temperature reaches 98.6° remove the plaster. If carp is not available, horse meat may be substituted. Cow's meat is not effective, however.

Carp plaster is an effective treatment for pneumonia.

POISON OAK

In the beginning of my camp session in the redwood forests of Northern California, many people had problems with poison oak. They asked me for a cure. I told them that for every problem she gives us, Nature also provides the cure. Since there were many oak trees in the area where the poison oak abounded —as is usually the case—I reasoned that there must be a healing relationship. I set out to discover it. I gathered leaves and bark from the oak trees; then I picked some poison oak and rubbed it on my body until my skin broke out in a rash. I experimented. Sure enough—if you cook oak leaves in water and make a plaster, this plaster will heal the rash caused by poison oak.

To develop an immunity to poison oak, eat it! Pick it by the stem and swallow a small leaf. Eat some bread or a rice ball afterwards, and don't *lick your lips.*

Enemas

Enemas are mentioned here only reluctantly. In certain cases they serve a good purpose, but it is advisable not to develop a dependence on them. Sometimes eating raw vegetables can be equally effective; fruits and even grains can, in the long run, take care of constipation.

In other words, it is better to cure constipation with a more natural method. Daio is a good remedy for people suffering from constricted intestines. It has a laxative effect that is preferable to the one caused by the enema. However, daio is suitable only for people with strong constitutions. It can prove harmful for those in delicate health.[1]

In Japan, an enema usually consists of soap and water, or slightly salted water. *For people with strong constitutions,* an enema may be taken for an acute condition such as high blood pressure or cerebral hemorrhage. In such cases, excreting old feces is not dangerous. However, it should not be done more than once or twice, whether or not it is successful. People in delicate health, as has been mentioned, should try to avoid the use of enemas, for the reaction can be quite violent when the feces are eliminated. In any case, this method is usually not advisable, for it causes one to rely on its immediate benefit as if it were another pill or drug.

LOTUS ROOT PIPE

Lotus Pipe

This is a very effective treatment for a blocked nasal passage resulting from a swollen mucus membrane. A swollen mucus membrane prevents oxygen from reaching the brain, whose function is thus impaired.

Buy a lotus root and cut out a round length around one of the lotus holes to form a tube (or pipe). Place the tube inside the blocked nostril and breathe through it. It works!

---

[1] However, there are several mild herbal teas which are still effective as laxatives. For the names of both strong and weak ones, see the section on constipation in the chapter "The Cure."

First Aid

Here are a few tips which can be of great help in case of car accidents, burns, broken bones, etc.

Burns

Apply cucumber juice, soya sauce, miso, sesame oil, tofu or ice cold water.

Green persimmon is another possible remedy. To prepare, crush the persimmon and take the juice. Apply some of the juice to the burn and keep the remainder in an airtight jar.

Cucumber juice (applied externally) is the best treatment for burns. Saikokaryukotsuboreito tea is also good when taken three times a day. The combination of cucumber juice externally and tea internally is an effective remedy.

Car accidents

Car accidents or falls from high places may cause injuries which result in bleeding. In some cases the bleeding has to be stopped immediately. If this is the case, and the bleeding is on the arms or legs, tie the wound with cotton gauze. If this does not stop the bleeding, tie a tourniquet around the area on the side of the wound nearest the heart. The tourniquet must be loosened every thirty minutes so that the blood supply will not be cut off completely. Firmly pressing the artery with the finger will also help stop the bleeding.

In case of injuries to chest or abdomen, or in case of poor blood coagulation, feed the patient one teaspoon of sesame salt. The worst thing you can do is to give water or any other liquid (cold or warm) to the wounded person. Liquids will prolong the bleeding. Remember that many injuries cause thirst; the patient may ask for something to drink. However, drinking may prove fatal. It is always better to wait until the bleeding stops.

Blood coagulates by oxidation. Therefore, washing or rubbing the wounded area is not a good idea. Washing with hydrogen peroxide is even worse.

Any internal hemorrhage should be taken very seriously. An injury or wound inside the brain needs quick treatment, even though there may be no evidence of bleeding. Delayed treatment may cause mental retardation, if not death. Internal bleeding begins to coagulate within 48 hours. The treatment must therefore be given before the coagulating process starts. In the hospital an examination of the wound, such as an X-ray, often takes much time—enough to be fatal to the wounded person.

Apply *tofu plaster* to the head and *chlorophyll plaster* or *albi plaster* to other areas in the event of internal hemorrhage. If the location of the injury cannot be detected, apply plasters all over the body. This will prevent the blood from coagulating.

Bone Fracture

In the event of an accident, the possibility of bone fractures must be examined carefully. If there is a bone fracture, apply the plaster to the broken area. Then tie a piece of wood to the area to keep the bones in place.

If there is joint pain, dislocation may have occurred. Apply albi or chlorophyll plaster. In this special case it is wise to consult a chiropractor or surgeon.

Minor Injuries

If the injury is external, the cure is easy. In this case wash with towel dipped in hot water; then apply dark sesame oil soaked in gauze. Dentie may be applied as well, for it is very effective in stopping bleeding and closing the wound. However, since its black color will remain for a while, it need not be applied to exposed areas.

Sharp cuts will heal easily. Cuts from glass, porcelain, or any material with dull edges may take time to heal and may leave a scar. Therefore, the treatment must be administered carefully—as, for example, in the case of a wide cut, which if not kept closed will leave a scar.

Follow these simple directions. Wash the cut, dry the area around it and close with a Band-Aid. To close the cut properly, first stick one end of the Band-Aid on one side of the cut; pull gently until the two sides meet; then secure the other end of the Band-Aid. There will be no scar.

The Problem of Suppuration

Suppuration from bacteria does not occur as long as one follows a diet relatively free of sugar, meat and chemical additives. The condition could possibly develop even in a person who is on a good diet, but only if that person has just begun to acquire proper eating habits.

In any case, one should not eat any animal food in time of injury. Sometimes the consumption of animal food may cause discomfort from an old wound. Even old injuries may be cured with albi or tofu plasters.

Japanese folk medicine recommends a loach (fish) plaster to relieve severe pain. Prepare it thus: cut the loach in half lengthwise, take out the bones, and apply the fish, skin down, to the affected area.

THE CURE

Healing Ourselves on Our Own

The Nature of Disease and Its Cure

I T IS OUR RESPONSIBILITY to heal ourselves. After all, we choose our sickness when, through neglect or ignorance, we allow it to spread within us. Not until the disease has already assumed great proportions do we frantically try all sorts of symptomatic remedies, which have but a small effect on the advance of the disease. With this attitude we are likely to make mistakes, for in our fear of dying we rashly accept all kinds of cures, being unable ourselves to judge which one we should adhere to. As a teacher I can help only a little— enough to give the sick the assurance that the cure is at hand and to give some advice as to how it might be effected. I try my best to help others, but I cannot guarantee a cure. No man is infallible; we are human beings, not angels.

Although our body builds millions of cells naturally, we cannot will even a single one into existence. It is the desire of the body to renew itself, but in taking bad quality food we interfere with that renewal of life, thereby inviting premature death. Nature always gives the best treatment; our job is to try to understand its ways and conduct our lives accordingly. We can accomplish this only by improving our judgment. There is no one rigid and absolute cure for any given illness. Will is an important component of cure, but will alone is not sufficient. The same is true of Ki. The spiritual and the physical must be combined. Food alone or thinking alone is useless.

Oriental medicine offers all types of cures, from the fundamental to the symptomatic. It reveals the cause of the disease and its effect, and leaves everyone to choose his own cure. As was mentioned previously, although the environment, condition, and constitutional weakness of the individual determine the form his disease will take, these factors are not the primary cause of illness. Just as wrong food is the cause of disease, so good food is the best medicine, for proper eating is responsible for the maintenance of good Ki and good blood in the organism. In order to understand this, we have no choice but to study food, for today we are out of touch with this realm. Good food, well-prepared and properly eaten, gives us the ability to continually prevent disease from overwhelming us. Understanding and judgment will follow naturally as we seek methodically a way of life compatible with our internal physiological development.

Oriental herbal tea remedies are also recommended in this chapter. The herbal tea method is sometimes quicker, and may be used by those people who are not so careful with their diet. The Oriental method of using herbs for medicine differs greatly from all other medicines. Healing ourselves with food is a slower, but surer and more lasting cure. The use of herbal teas is a system of medicine in its own right, as well as an excellent complement to the benefits of proper diet.

In the following chapter the reader will find many of the most common diseases, listed in alphabetical order. We are well aware that this list is by no means complete, and that the diseases mentioned here can be cured by several other methods. However, for the sake of simplification and clarity we have chosen to set forth that which is most essential for the student to know: a method which, by elevating the understanding, opens the door to an infinite number of ways to treat any disease.

It should be made clear that this approach—the alphabetical listing of a number of diseases, each having its own set of symptoms and treatments—is quite foreign to the usual Oriental medicine. The Eastern approach to medicine is philosophic, as compared to the Western scientific method. The last three hundred years have seen dramatic changes in Western medical knowledge and tradition. There is now a catalog of 1800 different diseases; and new ways to treat them are constantly being demanded and pursued. In contrast, traditional Eastern medicine has changed very little. In the second century, about one hundred different diseases were recognized. Many centuries later there were 404. Eastern medicine has a fundamental principle, the Yin-Yang principle, which is used for both diagnosis and treatment. With it, the basic nature of disease can be understood, and everything becomes very simple. Medicine without such a tradition is forced continually to ask "How?" and "Why?" about symptoms; everything then becomes very complicated.

The Eastern way is to treat the patient, not the disease. Thus, two people with the same disease may be given different teas. For this reason we have listed seven different teas for the common cold, and many others would have been possible. The possibilities vary since each tea is supposed to treat the general condition of the entire body, as well as the specific ailment. On the other hand, two people with different problems might be advised to take the same tea. The reasoning is the same. Hachimigan Tea, for example, is recommended for high blood pressure, cataracts, and diabetes. Big Saikoto can benefit the eyes, nose, throat, scalp,

heart, liver, stomach, intestines, gall bladder, bladder, kidneys and sexual organs. The former serves to draw out water from the body; the latter reduces excess energy. Each of these teas, like nearly all the teas recommended in this chapter, treats the general condition of the entire body. Thus it is difficult—and sometimes confusing—to assign them places in a long list of diseases determined by symptoms.

In the following treatments, a simple principle has been followed. From the diagnosis we know the disease to be of either a Yang or a Yin type. The treatment recommended attempts to balance the existing conditions. Thus, for Yang symptoms a predominance of Yin is given, just as the remedy for Yin symptoms is largely Yang. It is preferable to restore balance by reducing Yin or Yang rather than by adding it. Experience has shown that administering strong Yin or Yang can often do harm by causing imbalance. Since everyone is vulnerable to mistakes in diagnosing his own or someone else's condition, it is safer to use the method of lessening Yin or Yang. Although this last method may be slower, it will avert dangerous consequences.

Eventually, after experience and study, the reader will be able to utilize various other methods of cure.

Common Diseases

Information about the herbs and teas mentioned in this chapter, as well as complete instructions for their preparation and use, is to be found in the chapter "Using Herbs and Teas." Recipes for the special food dishes recommended in this chapter are to be found in the chapter "Food Is Best Medicine." Information regarding food in general can be found in "Keeping Ourselves Healthy With Food." Plasters and compresses are discussed in "External Treatments."

ACIDOSIS

Acidosis is not in itself a specific disease; it is a general condition of the blood and is thus the root of many different diseases such as diabetes, high blood pressure and arthritis. Many people today have this blood condition without realizing it.

Causes: acid-forming foods, especially meat, eggs and sugar; anger, worry, fear; shallow breathing (insufficient oxygen); too much physical exertion (rare)

Symptoms: enlarged pupils; crossed eyes

Cure: elimination of meat, eggs and sugar from the diet, and, preferably, other strongly acid-forming foods;[1] increased consumption of alkaline foods[1] (eat plenty of vegetables and some fruit); proper breathing[2]

See also *Blood Stagnation.*

ALKALOSIS

Not as common today as acidosis. Also indicates an unbalanced condition of the blood. Can result in hyperacidity and ulcers (see *Stomach Trouble*).

Symptoms: over-reaction; lack of emotion; contracted pupils; walleyes

Cure: increased proportion of whole grains in diet; proper chewing[2]

ALLERGY

The various allergies are children of modern times. Many other diseases appeared simultaneously with the emergence of industrialized civilization. These include polio, tuberculosis and syphilis. The high incidence of heart disease, mental illness and cancer is also a modern development.

Allergies result from a poor body quality brought about by chemicalized food, especially milk and eggs as found on the market today. The only true cure, which will not result in the emergence of a new and different allergy, is to eliminate those foods and change to a more natural and balanced diet. Brown rice is one recommended food for people with allergies.

AMOEBIC DYSENTERY
(see Dysentery)

ANEMIA

There are several causes of common anemia, or iron deficiency anemia. The name indicates the most common cause, lack of iron in the blood. Many people are anemic

---

[1] See section on grains in "Keeping Ourselves Healthy With Food."

[2] An important step on the road to better health, no matter what the problem.

because they consume too few vegetables, especially green vegetables, and thus their blood cannot retain enough oxygen. Another type of anemia is caused by a lack of protein. Finally, worms and parasites are usually present in the intestines; these are often a cause of anemia (see also section on leukemia).

Western medicine usually prescribes iron pills. Oriental medicine gives iron also, using rust as an ingredient in an herb tea. While this type of iron provides iron quickly, it is not retained very long and the condition recurs rapidly. A more long-lasting treatment is the ingestion of organic iron, found in some vegetables. Radish tops are among the richest sources of iron. Foods such as whole grains, which are rich in manganese, are also recommended, for the body can change manganese into iron by the process of biological transmutation (see *Good News*).

* *

An increase of iron in the blood can bring about a rapid improvement in blood quality, but this effect is only temporary, and continual supplements are necessary. We usually don't need iron, for our body can manufacture it from our daily food by the process of transmutation. All herbivorous animals possess the ability to transmute the magnesium from their food into iron. They produce their blood solely from vegetal foods. They can even produce milk—a transformation of blood—from foods of vegetal origin.

* *

Someone who is easily fatigued and prone to dizziness may very well be anemic. Likewise, shortness of breath, headache, stiffness in the shoulders, and buzzing in the ears are signs of anemia. So is disconnected, "spaced out" thinking.

A severe condition is accompanied by fainting, collapsing, cold feet and hands or increased urination. At this stage curative measures must be taken.

Here is a very popular and effective way to treat anemia:

MUGWORT (WORMWOOD)

Boil mugwort, dry, and pound with mochi.[3] Fry in oil or bake. (Mugwort tea is highly effective in purging the body of worms. Mugwort is often eaten by Orientals; it improves blood quality rapidly. American mugwort is very bitter, much more so than the better-tasting Japanese variety.)

Sautéed radish leaves, chiso leaves and miso soup[3] are also good for improving blood quality. For a severe anemic condition brought about by lack of protein, koi-koku (carp) soup[3] should be eaten once a month.

For cases of anemia involving parasites, Sanmishakosaito or Renju-in Tea is recommended.

See also section on worms.

ANGINA PECTORIS
(*see Heart Trouble*)

APOPLEXY
(*see Heart Trouble*)

APPENDICITIS

This disease is caused by infection and inflammation of the appendix. There is a bacterial increase and the appendix bursts. A sudden, large consumption of animal food may be the cause of the disease.

When pain is first felt, stop eating for one or two days until the pain is gone. Then begin eating soft rice (rice cooked with more water than usual) together with potatoes, in proportions of 2 parts rice, 1 part potatoes.

Symptomatic remedy: either albi plaster (*without* ginger compress first) or chlorophyll plaster can be applied. The area should be made cold. This is an exception; it is nearly always appropriate to keep the area warm in time of illness. Also drink burdock juice (obtained by grating the burdock root), 1 ounce per day, for two or three days; chickweed can be used instead (squeeze the chickweed and take 1 cup of juice for two or three days).

The same treatment should be applied for chronic cases of appendicitis (for diagnosis, see *Stomach Trouble*).

For the best and quickest results, take either of these treatments before eating.

It is interesting to note that Western medicine considers some organs, such as the appendix, useless, whereas Oriental medicine considers no organ of the body useless. In truth, the appendix is the nest for useful bacteria such as colibacilli and lactibacilli. Poor diet may bring about an increase in harmful bacteria, but this does not make the appendix any less necessary.

ARTERIOSCLEROSIS
(*see Heart Trouble*)

ARTHRITIS

This disease of the blood and muscles is caused by excessive consumption of extremely unbalanced foods, such as meat and sugar, over a long period of time. There is a lack of good quality fats and a chronic acid condition in the blood. The most important thing is to stop eating "extreme" kinds of food. Citrus fruits should be avoided (see also *Acidosis*). Diseases such as arthritis, cancer, etc. which develop over a long period of time, may also take a long time to cure. We have no right to expect otherwise.

Symptomatic remedies: ginger compress; ginger bath; albi plaster; old miso (take 1 teaspoon of miso that has aged more than 10 years; dilute in ½ cup of water, and drink); nob of cypress tree (boil 5 grams in 3 cups of water until liquid has diminished by half; drink ½ cup three times a day); radish drink (¼ cup of grated radish, 1 teaspoon of soya sauce; add 1 tablespoon of boiling sesame oil; mix and take once a day). An unusual but effective treatment is carbonized cow's teeth (grind and make powder; take ½ teaspoon with water 3 times a day). Available at Oriental pharmacies.

---

[3] See "Food Is Best Medicine."

Teas: The ginger bath and compress are helpful, but the arthritis will always return if these alone are used. Daio-Bushi tea (Daiobushito) is very effective. It is recommended also for gout. Daio is considered an extremely Yin type of plant, while bushi is very Yang. The combination of these two plants causes the body to "swing" from Yin to Yang. This results in the expulsion of the poisons which have been introduced by the eating of extreme Yin and Yang (see "Using Herbs and Teas" for more information on daio and bushi).

A tea which contains both daio and bushi and is considered highly effective for arthritis—and also rheumatism and gout, which are similar—is Shakkanoshinbuto. It is made with the same ingredients as Daiobushito, plus licorice and peony root, both of which are noted pain relievers. Wild barley tea (Hatomugito or Yokuininto) may also be used.

ASTHMA
(see Respiratory Ailments)

ATONY
(see Stomach Trouble)

BEDWETTING

This is caused by an excessive intake of Yin-type food and drink. It should be noted, however, that in many cases the body condition is Yang. Children who are extremely Yang will be attracted to extremely Yin (sweet, sugared) drinks, which produce large volumes of urine, thin in appearance.

There are also cases of bedwetting caused by an excessive intake of Yang. In such cases one's intake of strong Yang food should be decreased (less salt, for example). Old men who often urinate in the middle of the night have an overly contracted (Yang) bladder which is unable to retain liquid.

A child who goes to bed at ten and wets at eleven or twelve, suffers from Yin (sugar and fruit should be eliminated from his diet), but if he wets at three or four or five in the morning, his condition is overly Yang (Yang food and salt should be avoided). The latter case is not the same as that of the old man who needs to urinate in the middle of the night. The old man has a contracted bladder, whereas the child has a generally Yang condition.

It is important to drink less liquid, which means that much less or no animal food should be eaten. When we take animal food, our body needs much water.

Symptomatic remedies: for the Yang type of bedwetting, Small Kenchuto; for the Yin type, Hachimigan Tea

BERIBERI
(see Vitamin B Deficiency)

BLADDER TROUBLE
(stones, etc.)

This defect is nearly always the result of a Yang-type condition. It is usually related to kidney problems.

Symptoms: pain down the middle of the back of the leg (bladder meridian); painful urination (see also *Gonorrhea*); frequent urination; deficient urination (see also *Bedwetting*)

Cure: vegetables, raw and cooked; Chorei Tea (Hachimigan Tea may also be used)

BLOOD DISEASE

Blood disease is described in detail in the chapter "On Understanding Disease." Bad blood is the underlying cause of many different diseases whose names are familiar—see also *Acidosis, Alkalosis, Anemia, Cancer, Hemophilia, Hemorrhoids, Leukemia, Pyorrhea, Sinus Trouble, Rheumatism,* etc.

The only true cure for blood disease is in changing the bad quality blood into good blood. This can be done only by adopting a balanced, healthy diet. Cures that treat symptoms, while helpful in relieving pain and discomfort, are only temporarily effective; the cause of those symptoms still remains.

The fundamental tea remedy for blood disease is Tokaku Jokito.

BLOOD STAGNATION

This is a disease caused by improper circulation and the presence of old blood in the body. Oriental medicine states that blood stagnation occurs at the lowest part of the abdomen. Many different diseases arise from blood stagnation—for example, hemorrhoids, appendicitis, pyorrhea, uterine tumors and venereal disease.

Symptoms: black under the eyes; broken red vessels in nose and face; abnormally dark lips; black or purple gums; red hands; skin ulcers; uterine tumor; constipation; stomachache; headache

Treatment: Blood stagnation is a Yang type of disease. Those afflicted with it should eat more raw vegetables and increase their intake of sea salt bit by bit. If the person finds his condition changing to Yin too quickly, he should eat more cooked, and less raw vegetables; he should also eat buckwheat.

Tokaku Jokito is an excellent herbal tea treatment for blood stagnation. It helps to break up clots, restore good circulation, eliminate old blood, and remove old feces from the large intestine. It will clean out the uterus completely (see *Uterine Tumor*). Of course, a healthy diet—including whole grains and plenty of vegetables—is the best blood purifier. It does not work as quickly as herbs, teas or any other type of treatment, but it provides the most lasting cure.

See also *Acidosis.*

BRONCHITIS
(see Respiratory Ailments)

CANCER

This disease is caused mainly by the consumption of bad quality, chemicalized food over a long period of time. Just as food makes our body, so food makes cancer, a disease of modern civilization.

When we eat industrialized food, the blood that the body forms does not contain all the elements necessary to bring proper nourishment to every part of the organism. When the balance is thus upset, due to a lack of essential nutrients in the diet, cancer may develop. In order for the cancer cell to become normal again, these missing elements must be restored to the blood.

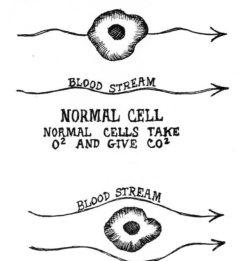

BLOOD STREAM

NORMAL CELL
NORMAL CELLS TAKE
O_2 AND GIVE CO_2

BLOOD STREAM

CANCEROUS CELL

The condition of the cancer cell is such that it is unable to attract sufficient oxygen. Normal cells have the innate ability to attract oxygen and avert cancer. This ability can be restored only by a return to a natural way of eating. When meat and sugar are eaten, the cancer cells increase quickly. Green vegetables should be included regularly in the diet, for they are a good supply of chlorophyll, which is ultimately transmuted into hemoglobin in the body. Iron is the most important component of our red blood globules; it is iron which holds oxygen in the blood cell. Hemoglobin is FeO_2 (iron + oxygen). If cancer cells can get enough oxygen, they will change into regular cells (see also *Leukemia* for more on this process).

Organic green vegetables and seashore wild spinach are good sources of chlorophyll.

Recently Japanese doctors, specialists in herbal medicine, made discoveries concerning the value of plants containing *germanium*. Germanium is the component which is needed by the blood, for it gives the malignant cell the ability to attract oxygen and thus become a normal cell. There are two kinds of germanium, organic and inorganic. Organic germanium comes from plant life, whereas inorganic germanium is a mineral used mostly in the manufacturing of transistors. Sources of organic germanium are ginseng (the best source), nob of wisteria, garlic, wild barley, and certain herbs such as kashi, sanzukon and hishi (see herb list, page 106). Korean soil, where the best ginseng grows, has been found to be very high in germanium.

A cancer patient who is strong enough to chew very well should be given buckwheat and brown rice. These foods effect a more rapid change in the quality of the blood. Those patients who are unable to chew well can have buckwheat soup and cereal creams (especially those made from brown rice). People with cancer of the intestine (colon) have a great deal of difficulty in digesting. For them, rice milk is best. Intestinal cancer is extremely difficult to cure. As a rule, however, cancer in the upper parts of the body—the nose, throat, ears, etc.—is more difficult to cure than other types. The attempt to help cancer patients often means many a sleepless night for the would-be healer!

It is advisable that cancer patients not be given too much nourishment. Their tendency to lose weight is actually beneficial. Reduced eating allows the liver to discharge waste. Fats and bad quality proteins are released from the body.

Many authorities relate lung cancer to smoking and polluted air, whereas it should rather be connected to bad eating habits. A man who eats bad food and smokes is likely to get cancer, while a man who eats well and smokes moderately probably will not get the disease.

Abortions are a possible cause of breast cancer! (See page 133.)

Symptomatic remedy: This is very important. A cancer patient always needs external treatment in addition to special diet. Cancer tumors can be treated with a ginger compress followed by an albi plaster, which should be changed every two hours. For a breast tumor, apply compress and plaster to the side of the breast (for complete details, see "External Remedies").

Other remedies: organic germanium tea; garlic, preferably baked, fried or raw (if eaten raw, garlic should be soaked in soya sauce for a long time). [It is interesting to note that Korean and Yeminite people, who eat red pepper and garlic in large quantities, have the lowest cancer rate in the world.]

One of the following may also be used to help accelerate the cure: Ginseng Herb Tea, Nob of Wisteria Tea, Kashi Tea, Sanzukon Tea, and Yokuinin (wild barley) or Hato Tea.

CEREBRAL HEMORRHAGE
(see *High Blood Pressure* and section on tofu plaster, page 110)

COLDS

Ultimately, a cold does not come from "outside" in the form of an ugly virus. We ourselves are responsible for contracting a cold. Many doctors now recognize that we do not necessarily "catch cold" from being exposed to bad weather. After all, not everyone exposed to the same conditions necessarily develops a cold. Cold and humid weather will only trigger it; it is our poor condition that makes us susceptible. Most people cover themselves with extra clothes because they're afraid of becoming chilled; this belief in their vulnerability is actually a major part of the reason they "catch cold."

When a cold strikes, take radish drink. That will usually check its development. But if that doesn't work, there is an herb remedy: people with a strong constitution (Yang-type people, heavy meat eaters) should take Mao Tea. People with a delicate constitution (Yin-type people) should take Cinnamon Herb Tea. Those somewhere in the middle may take Kuzu Root Tea.

After taking the tea, wait thirty minutes. Then eat soft rice (rice cooked with more than the usual amount of water). The soft rice will intensify the effect of the tea. Meat, fish, eggs, milk, cheese, spices, garlic, onions, fruit, etc. (all strong-smelling food) should be avoided. Keep warm and sleep.

Oriental medicine has many other teas for treating colds, since a cold is considered a general condition of the whole body rather than a particular infection identical for every person. All of these teas are considered treatments for the whole body. The ones listed above are all excellent; there is also Kososan, Soshikokito,[4] Small Saikoto, and Hachimi-gan.

COLITIS

This is a disease of the intestines, the final organ in the digestive process. Sometimes the condition is brought about by parasites, but usually colitis is the result of excessive and improper eating. Alcohol, spices, oil, spoiled food, and foods with a tough texture, or too much roughage, such as meat, raw vegetables and fruit, should be avoided. These are especially harmful when consumed along with much water or liquid. All of these put too much strain on the small intestine, which is already weak in the case of someone susceptible to colitis.

The best cure consists of eating healthy food and avoiding the foods mentioned above, along with sugar, which weakens the intestines. It is most important to chew the food very well to make it easier for the weakened intestines to extract nourishment. Grains and vegetables should be eaten primarily, for they, as contrasted to protein foods, are digested mainly by the saliva in the mouth. If there is an inability to chew well, soft cereals made from whole grains should be eaten, especially rice and buckwheat creams. Miso soup is recommended in any case. Also, kuzu drink should be taken every morning as early as possible and a few hours before anything else is eaten. (For recipes for rice and buckwheat cream, miso soup and kuzu drink, see "Food Is Best Medicine.")

The possibility of parasites should be checked (see *Worms*).

CONSTIPATION

A long history of bad diet causes feces to collect. This is the underlying cause of all disease.

Usually, constipation comes from refined food and strong Yang food, in which case the liquid in the feces is drawn out through the intestinal wall, causing the feces to become smaller, hard and dry, like rabbit stools. It is easy to determine the kind of constipation present. With Yang constipation, the feces are dark brown, round and shiny. Too much salt as well as too much meat can cause Yang constipation.

Yin constipation is caused by a swollen large intestine which lacks the power to eliminate the feces. In this case the feces tend to remain in the intestines for a long time. With Yin constipation, the feces are dark and round, but not shiny.

The Yang type of constipation can be cured with a diet which includes a major percentage of raw and cooked vegetables. Aduki beans, pumpkin seeds, squash seeds, etc. are effective also. They make good roughage, but it is most important to chew them very well. Whole grain is quite effective, but this too must be chewed carefully. Grated radish (2 tablespoons) mixed with 1 tablespoon of raw sesame oil is excellent for Yang constipation. Bancha tea may also be taken. People with a strong constitution may try the appropriate Jokito tea. These teas contain daio, a strong laxative which will soften the feces. It can be taken for a month or so. After that, the intestines will function naturally, without the tea's assistance. People with a weak constitution should try a milder cure. They should try to eat and drink less, following a diet that consists mainly of *rice milk,*[5] rice cream, buckwheat cream, and moderate amounts of vegetable soup. Yin people should not take a laxative. They may take Bushi or Ginseng Herb Tea. These teas give energy to the intestines, causing the bowels to move.

See also "Getting Rid of Waste."

CONVULSIONS
(see Epilepsy)

COUGH
(see Respiratory Ailments)

CROOKED SPINE

This condition, in which the spinal bones themselves may be untouched but where the cushion between the vertebrae has become too thin, is usually due to an excessive intake of meat and sugar. In most cases the cushions become thin on one side, thereby causing a curvature. The location of the curve can reflect organ problems in that same area. For example, when the curve is in the lower back, there are usually problems with the sexual organs, resulting in loss of sexual appetite. Young people who have lost their sexual appetite may be suffering simply because a pinched nerve is causing a bad connection between the brain and the sexual organs.

Remedy: ginger compress on the curved area. After that, massage somewhat firmly for thirty minutes every day, for several days. For the massage, use a mixture of oil and juice from squeezed ginger. Try this for one week; if the case persists, stop for one or two weeks and then try again. Sometimes the body does not respond to this treatment. It then becomes necessary for the patient to change his diet in order to effect the cure.

If after two or three attempts there is still no positive result, try *moshio* (carbonized kombu and salt, available in natural food stores). Add lukewarm water to the moshio and massage into the affected area. Moshio can also be taken as a drink or sprinkled on food in powdered form (¼ teaspoon, twice a day). It is a very effective medicine for people with weak (Yin) constitutions; however, few Americans would fall into that category.

If the spine still does not heal, apply a *jinenjo* plaster, albi plaster, or chlorophyll plaster (see "External Treatments"). If all of these prove unsuccessful, the diet must change.

---

[4] The recipes for these two teas are not included in this book.
[5] See "Food Is Best Medicine."

DIABETES AND HYPOGLYCEMIA

Diabetes is one of the oldest known diseases. Doctors have been wrestling with it for almost 4,000 years without much success.

Most doctors know that the methods now being used to treat diabetes are not effective. Just after the war an international congress of doctors declared insulin injections to be improper and dangerous. But because there is no alternative, insulin is still being advised by most doctors.

The injected insulin is supposed to supply the body with what the pancreas is failing to provide. When it was discovered that diabetes is related to a deficiency in the pancreas, doctors proceeded to struggle with that particular organ alone, instead of finding the true cause.

This disease results from the organism's inability to maintain a constant and proper blood-sugar level. Strong, sweet food such as cane sugar and honey makes the percentage of sugar in the blood rise suddenly, but soon thereafter the sugar level of the blood goes down and does not return to normal for a long time. During this period of low blood-sugar, the person will again crave strong, sweet food. If he satisfies that craving with sugar, he will feel very good for a while, for his blood-sugar content will rise again. Nevertheless, it is likely to decrease dangerously once again. If this cycle is repeated often enough the blood-sugar level will always be low, lacking vital glucose.

At this stage the color of the palms changes to yellow, the forehead becomes especially bright. The body is unable to retain sugar in any form, and sugar is always present in the urine.

In this case there is not only spleen (pancreas) trouble, but also kidney trouble. Thus there is often a loss of sexual appetite (kidneys and sex organs are related—see "The Organs").

When this low blood-sugar condition is produced by a deficiency in the insulin secretion of the pancreas, it is called diabetes. When, on the other hand, the pancreas is too active in secreting insulin, the result is hypoglycemia. There is a simple remedy.

Carbohydrates are the best source of glucose for the blood stream, especially in the case of diabetic people. For a person whose pancreas cannot secrete insulin, sugar—both white and brown—must be eliminated from the diet at all costs. The same is true for a person whose pancreas tends to secrete too much insulin. Sugar is far too stimulating for him. It is interesting to note that Western doctors have begun recently to recommend carbohydrates to people suffering from diabetes. This is the ancient Oriental cure. Whole grains are the best balanced source of carbohydrates.

The patient can have brown rice every day. He must chew it thoroughly, not swallowing it until it is liquid. Naturally sweet foods, such as grains, onions, carrots, sweet squash, etc., are good for the spleen. They are also effective in helping maintain a proper blood-sugar level.

The best food for this disease is aduki beans cooked with sweet squash (butternut, buttercup, acorn, etc.) and deep-fried scallion roots. Take one rice-bowl of aduki-squash and two or three scallion roots every day for three weeks. Kombu seaweed may also be included.

For example, in the morning a diabetic person might have miso soup and a cereal cream. For lunch or dinner, some brown rice, aduki beans and squash, kombu seaweed, and occasionally a salt pickle, lotus root-hijiki seaweed, or grated radish. Once or twice a week he should have mochi and aduki bean soup. Rice may sometimes be substituted with buckwheat. Of course, sugar and sweet drinks must not be taken; otherwise the diet won't give the expected results. For liquid, bancha tea is appropriate.

Hachimigan Tea is a recommended medicinal tea for diabetes. For extremely Yang people, Daiosaikoto is good.

See also *Acidosis*.

DIARRHEA

Diarrhea is caused by an expansion of the large intestine and stomach, overeating, excess liquid, over-acidity, spoiled food, too much roughage, etc.; so it is obviously a very Yin disorder. It is a symptom present in many Yin-type diseases. A proper balanced diet with more grain food (brown rice, whole wheat bread, etc.) is needed to cure the real source of the problem. Take kuzu paste for one or two meals. Salted plum-soya-kuzu-bancha tea drink is an effective remedy.

Symptomatic tea remedy: Shigyakuto

Black Warrior, Ginseng, and Bushi Tea are also effective.

DUODENUM ULCER
(see Stomach Trouble)

DYSENTERY

Usually after about five days' latent period, high fever, stomachache and diarrhea will develop. Sometimes, though, there will be no high fever. The feces become almost liquid and contain blood.

Amoebic and bacillic dysentery are said to be caused by the consumption of unclean food. While it is true that such food will produce dysentery, a healthy body should be able to repel the bacteria or amoebas without any problem, for such a condition is anathema to the causes of disease. In actuality dysentery is a disease of the digestive organs.

Symptomatic cure: ginger compress on abdomen; enema (use lukewarm water with a pinch of salt); fasting

Teas: Kuzu Root Herb Tea (also Kuzu Drink—see "Food Is Best Medicine"); Big Saikoto; Daiobotanpito; Black Warrior

In unsanitary surroundings, eat one salt plum a day to prevent dysentery. For this disease, prevention is most important.

See also *Diarrhea*.

EARACHE AND DEAFNESS

Ear and hearing troubles are related to a malfunctioning of the kidneys. Children can be cured much faster than adults. It suffices to adopt a good diet involving no meat (animal protein) or sugar.

For an earache, albi plaster, chlorophyll plaster or ginger oil may be used externally.

ECZEMA
(see Skin Disease)

ENCARDIUM
(see Heart Trouble)

EPILEPSY AND CONVULSIONS

There are two types of convulsions. A convulsion caused by Yang is contracting: the patient's eyes go down, showing the whites on top. His hands are clenched and his feet warm. There is too much blood in the head. This is usually the case with epilepsy.

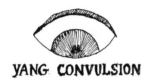

YANG CONVULSION

YIN CONVULSION

A convulsion caused by Yin is expanding: the eyes go up, showing the whites at the bottom; the hands are open and the feet cold.

Sometimes there is a "criss-cross" where one hand is open and one closed. This means that feces are trapped in some specific place. Softly massage the patient's abdomen with your right hand, keeping your left hand on the nape of his neck. When the feces move, the convulsion will subside.

A blockage of the feces in the descending colon makes the right hand clenched and the left hand open. A blockage in the ascending colon makes the left hand clenched and the right hand open.

In the case of a Yang convulsion an enema may be used, although this will clear out only the lower part of the intestinal tract.

Remedy for the constricting type of convulsion (hands clenched): give the patient fresh homemade apple juice or another fruit juice (e.g. orange juice) followed by a vegetable soup if he is hungry. Sanoshashinto may also be given.

Remedy for the expanding type of convulsion (hands open): give Ranshio or salt plum drink (a mixture of salted plum, ginger, soya sauce and bancha tea). Convulsions of the Yin type are rather rare.

Important: if the patient is unconscious, do not put anything into his mouth.

Remedy for epilepsy: in the Bible, "fasting and prayer" are recommended. This is very good; epilepsy stems usually from overeating. An excellent tea remedy is Saikokaryukotsuboreito (Day Lily Tea). For a case history on how this tea has cured epilepsy, see page 97. Sanoshashinto has also proved effective.

EYE TROUBLE

To the question "Do people get bad eyesight from reading a great deal?" I can answer with certainty that reading is not harmful to the eyes. It is bad food, especially an exaggerated intake of sugar, which is responsible for eye trouble. In Oriental medicine, eye trouble is known to be closely related to liver problems. Alcohol, vinegar, chemicals and drugs must be avoided in all cases.

Astigmatism is caused by too much fruit. Stop eating fruit and you will obtain good results.

Cataracts are caused by excess sugar. For the cure, stop taking sugar in any form and make a special tea to hasten the healing. Dry the yellow chrysanthemum flower and make a tea with it. Drink twice a day in place of your usual tea. The yellow flower is of a more Yang quality than the purple one. Hachimigan Tea may also be used.

Colorblindness is caused by raw food such as meat, fruit and vegetables. It can be corrected by properly cooked, good quality food.

Nearsightedness has both a Yin and a Yang form. Most Americans have the Yang type, in which the area of the cornea is too thick. In Yin nearsightedness, the eyeball itself is too big as a result of excess sugar intake.

Farsightedness derives from a Yang condition. The eyeball is too small. A baby is usually farsighted, but when he takes his mother's milk his eyeballs grow to normal size. If the mother's milk is too Yang, however, the condition will take a long time to correct itself. Farsightedness can quickly become "old man's eye" (presbyopia), which requires bifocal glasses in order to be corrected.

For nearsightedness and farsightedness, apply salt-bancha compress (1%) and albi plaster for a week (see "External Treatments"). Ryokeijutsukanto can also be taken. This tea is effective for astigmatism as well.

FEVER

A fever is a strong, burning fire. The body may need a high temperature at certain times, but an extended fever is dangerous. Fever is an almost certain indication of trouble in the lungs or liver.

Oriental medicine considers high fever to be Yang. Fever almost always starts from Yang; however, a person who has weakened his constitution over a period of years and has passed the early stages of disease can begin only a low fever from his present state of health (small Yin). A healthy person starts fever from Yang. A person who does not eat animal food will not develop a fever.

In the beginning stages of a disease induced by Yang, there is a high fever (103°–104°), a cold feeling, a strong superficial pulse, forehead pressure, stiff shoulders, coughing, occasional body pain and possibly sweating.

Symptoms and body quality must be considered in deciding which tea is necessary.

A person who sweats during fever should take Cinnamon Tea. If a patient does not sweat, he should take Mao Tea. For a strong body condition (in which the body does not retain too much water), take Mao Tea once. If there is no effect, try it again in two or three hours.

When there is fever and the pulse is strong, the disease is Yang. When there is fever and sweating, the body condition is Yin. Absence of sweating is a better sign than sweating, for then the disease is from Yang, which means that the disease is at an early stage [6] and the patient is still strong.

If you feel cold while your body temperature is high, this simply means that the environment is colder than your body. The difference makes you feel cold.

The more Yang one becomes, the more the fever causes one to feel better. A tea such as White Tiger will bring down the temperature.

For the common cold and typhoid fever, these same teas can be used.

The first Radish Drink is recommended for a fever.

A high fever accompanying a Yin disease is very rare.

FOOD POISONING

Speaking in a broad sense, all diseases are cases of food poisoning—expecially today, when the bulk of the available food contains so many kinds of chemicals, preservatives, coloring agents, artificial sweeteners, chemical spices, etc. If these materials are taken over a long period of time, chronic food poisoning may result. Alcoholic beverages can also lead to this.

Therefore, it seems that we should always eat natural food. This is easy to say, but not very easy to arrange. So, we will speak here about food poisoning in a narrower sense, referring only to acute troubles. Copper, lead, mercury, etc. sometimes cause problems. These elements are poisonous for us, so we should be careful about our sources of food.

Most cases of food poisoning come from spoiled food, especially spoiled animal food—meat, fish, chicken, eggs, etc. Cereals and vegetables rarely produce such cases. Certain mushrooms, some types of fish (e.g. globefish), and the sprouts of the Irish potato contain poisons.

Usually, one becomes aware of food poisoning 2–20 hours after eating bad food. The later it becomes evident, the worse. Therefore, if you think you may have eaten poisonous food, you should try to vomit it up as quickly as possible. Put your fingers into your mouth as far as you can. If this does not work, take 1 teacup full of salt plum-soy-ginger-bancha (pickled-plum juice with warm water may be used as a substitute), and try again. This may cause vomiting.

After that, you need to eliminate food from the intestines. Take castor oil. Of course, if you already have diarrhea you won't need this. In any case, one or two days of fasting is advisable.

For food poisoning caused by spoiled fish, grated radish is effective.

For mushroom poisoning, make tea with calyx of the eggplant plus water.

For egg poisoning, vinegar is good.

For tobacco poisoning, take miso soup.

A good general remedy for food poisoning is chiso (beefteak) leaves, which come packed with salted plums and are available in natural food stores. Make tea with the leaves (raw or dried) and water. Raw leaves may simply be eaten plain.

Inchinkoto (Gardenia Herb Tea) is also excellent. Big Jokito can be useful in halting any diarrhea that results.

FRIGIDITY
(see Sexual Problems)

GALL BLADDER STONES

The gall bladder is the most Yang of all the Yin organs. In many cases, a gall stone is the result of Yang and rich food. Bread and grains are slightly acid, but not "rich." Meat and sugar are extremely acid and rich.

Fruit in large quantities contributes to the formation of gall stones. It creates a Yin blood condition which in turn causes calcium to be broken down in the teeth and bones and eventually deposited in the gall bladder. Tomatoes and spinach contain oxalic acid, which also breaks down the body's calcium.

Such cases have been cured successfully with a diet of roasted brown rice, which causes the stones to be ejected.

In the case of gall bladder stones, meat and sugar must not be eaten. In general, overeating interferes with the gall bladder's function of secreting bile; thus, reduced eating is important.

Big Saikoto and Inchinkoto are effective in discharging stones. A ginger compress followed by an albi plaster is an excellent pain reliever.

GONORRHEA
(see Venereal Disease)

GOUT

The causes of gout are: an excess of extreme food, especially meat and sugar, consumed over a long period of time; lack of exercise; uric acid deposits resulting from over-consumption of meat.

Cure: vegetables (both raw and cooked vegetables are always advisable in cases of stiffness or sore joints); Daio-Bushi Tea or Shakkanoshinbuto

See also *Arthritis.*

HAIR LOSS

Loss of hair is connected to liver problems. Hair can fall from either excess Yin or excess Yang. When there is no fat under the skin of the skull, more hair will grow; but if there is fat present, not only will hair growth cease, but the rest of the hair will begin to fall out. When there is excess fat, the skin pores are loose and unable to hold the hair. On the other hand, skin that is too tight pushes the hair

---

[6] See *six stages of disease* pages 52–53.

out. The latter is a Yang condition. Excess sex resulting from excess Yang-quality food causes the nourishment that would normally be received by the hair to go out with the semen.

Remedy: avoid alcohol, vinegar, chemicals, drugs, sugar and large amounts of meat or oil. Eat seaweed (kombu, wakame, hijiki). Take these seaweeds at lunch and dinner. Wakame and hijiki are especially recommended.

If you should eat beans, white beans (lima, navy, great northern, etc.) are preferable. They are good for the liver since they contain less oil. Restrict intake of fried foods. Nuts should be roasted before being eaten; this will reduce their oil content.

Tea: Saikokaryukotsuboreito (Day Lily Tea)

See also the section on hair in "The Diagnosis."

HEADACHE

This can be considered as primarily a Ki disease;[7] a headache always indicates a disturbance in the Ki flow. A water disease,[8] however, can be its initial cause. And in the case of a woman, headache can be a blood disease occurring at menstruation time. Headache can also represent a blood disease in both males and females as a result of blood stagnation caused by excess animal food.

Sharp headache pain is Yang, dull pain is Yin. Often there is pain in only one part of the head. This usually means that the source of the headache is Yang. When the entire head is painful, the cause is generally Yin. However, this does not hold true in every case.

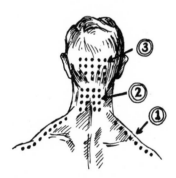

External remedies: try any of these—tofu plaster or chlorophyll plaster on the forehead; apple and radish compress; ginger oil on the head (hair); green leaves on the forehead and back of the neck.

Internal remedies: soy-bancha is quite effective for Yin headaches and migraines. For a Yang headache, take juice from fresh, grated apple or fresh orange juice mixed with hot water. For a headache due to blood stagnation, take Tokaku Jokito. For headache accompanied by stomach ache, see section on stomach trouble.

If there is pain on only one side of the head or in only one place, take Goshuyuto or Tokishigyakukakoshu-yushokyuto (Heavenly Root Tea).

If the headache is accompanied by thirst and decreased urination, take Goreisan Tea.

Sanoshashinto may be taken when the blood goes to the head causing red face, hotness, dizziness and ringing in ears.

When the headache is accompanied by fever (see section on the common cold), take Mao Tea or Kuzu Root Tea.

For dull pain, take Small Kenchuto or Cinnamon Herb Tea.

MASSAGE FOR HEADACHE

Massage for Headache

Here is a fast way to get rid of a headache, or at least to ease the pain. The patient should first take a light soy-bancha drink to improve the circulation. Then massage the shoulder blades. Do not pinch with the fingers, but press hard with the fleshy part of the thumbs. When you have massaged the shoulder blades with the thumbs for three minutes, proceed to pinch lightly with all the fingers. This should not take more than another three minutes.

Next massage the back of the neck. For best results, place yourself at the patient's side, the right hand massaging the neck, and the fingers of the left hand lying on the forehead to control the pressure. Press the head. If this is too painful for the patient, press lightly, increasing the pressure if the patient can take the pain. Massage this area in an orderly manner, line by line, starting from the top and working down. The neck massage can take between three and six minutes. Afterwards, do the back of the head. Now massage the temples, using much less pressure. Start from the forehead and work to the back of the ear (two minutes). Then press the top of the head, and finish by scratching the entire head with the fingertips—or even with the nails, if necessary—as if you were shampooing the head (one to two minutes).

HEART TROUBLE

Overly Strong Heart

Heart disease is very common today, especially in the United States. Everywhere you can see red faces, indicative of overactive hearts. When the tip of the nose is swollen, as it usually is in such cases, a dangerously expanded heart is indicated. The main cause of this condition is an over-consumption of animal food, especially meat and eggs. An excess of these foods brings about kidney trouble and eventually high blood pressure.

---

[7] For explanation of Ki, see "On Understanding Disease."
[8] See "On Understanding Disease."

Today it is popular to blame salt for the prevalence of heart trouble, but to see salt alone as the culprit is erroneous. People have been eating salt for thousands of years, but the large incidence of heart disease is as recent as the acceptance of meat as the mainstay of the diet. Of course, people with a too strong, overly Yang condition should cut down on salt, but still, excess salt is much more likely to cause stomach trouble (e.g. duodenum ulcers) than heart disease. It is the retention of large amounts of protein and animal salts which causes pressure to be put on the heart (see sections on meat and salt in "Keeping Ourselves Healthy With Food").

The first manifestation of trouble from an overly strong heart is high blood pressure. Actually, there are three related contributing factors: the heart is too strong; the blood vessels are too tight; the kidneys are too Yang. High blood pressure can be a necessity: the heart may have to beat strongly in order to push the blood through constricted organs and vessels. When organs and vessels become too constricted, it is necessary for the heart to beat faster so that the blood can circulate properly in these organs. An injection given to lower the blood pressure will only make things worse, for various troubles will develop subsequently. When the pressure is caused to drop suddenly, the hands and feet become cold, the circulation, especially in the brain, is impeded, and often the kidneys —which are too Yang—are unable to pass urine. It is their contraction which necessitates the increase in pressure in order to push through the blood.

A high cholesterol level is another result of an overly Yang kidney condition caused by a long history of meat consumption. The cholesterol collects in the vessels and restricts the passage of blood. The blood itself becomes too thick from excess meat eating.

For further information on high blood pressure, see sections on kidney disease and acidosis.

High blood pressure is a dangerous condition. There are many possible consequences—cerebral hemorrhage, apoplectic stroke, arteriosclerosis (hardening of the arteries), etc.

THE CURE

Increase the amount of Yin-quality food in the diet. This does not include foods such as sugar, alcohol, and large amounts of fruit; definitely not, these are too extreme. Raw and cooked vegetables and seaweed are recommended. Extreme Yang-quality food should be avoided. Meat and eggs should not be eaten at all, and salt intake should be limited.

High Blood Pressure

Teas: Sanoshashinto, Big Saikoto, Bofutsushosan (Sage's Path Tea)

Heart Attack—Stroke

No food should be given as long as the patient is faint. Enemas are not recommended and should not be attempted more than once or twice. Karo Tea can be helpful.

Fatty Heart

Teas: Big Saikoto or Saikokaryultsuboreito (Day Lily)

Asthma Caused by Bad Heart

Mokuboi Tea

Angina Pectoris

The fundamental cure for this disease is a diet of approximately 60% grains (brown rice, millet, barley, wheat in the form of bulghur or fresh, steamed cracked wheat), 30% vegetables, 10% soup. No meat and sugar, of course.

Symptomatic remedies: drink composed of ½ *salt plum*, 1 teaspoon *soya sauce*, 5 drops *ginger juice* and 1 cup *bancha tea;* Karokijitsuto; Mugwort Tea; spiderwart (to be cooked and eaten—a delicious taste)

A person's heart may stop beating because he is too weak or too tight. If the heart stops because of weakness (Yin), then something highly stimulating and contracting (Yang) is needed. Ranshio [9] (extreme Yang) is often given in such cases, but it should not be given to a person whose heart has stopped from constriction (excess Yang), for such a person needs Yin-type (quick, expanding) stimulation.

In emergency situations it is not always clear whether the problem stems from an overly strong or an overly weak heart. What is more, immediate action is required. The judgment must be quick as well as accurate.

A woman collapsed, and her heartbeat could barely be detected. Most people who have a heart attack are large and fat; they require a Yin treatment. However, this petite woman seemed just the opposite. Perhaps Ranshio (very Yang) should be given. But it was the middle of the summer, the weather was hot, and it was known that she had just traveled a long distance, had been working very hard, and had been eating very little. All of these factors are extremely contracting (Yang). So she was given a bit of fruit (Yin). Almost immediately she began to breathe normally. What a relief! Yin and Yang are powerful tools, but they are not always easy to wield. Knowledge and confidence are not always enough. A healer often needs intuition.

Overly Weak Heart

Yin food speeds up the heartbeat but slows the stomach. Yang food does exactly the opposite.

For a person with a weak heart and a weak constitution, Ranshio [10] may be advisable. Great care must be taken in such cases, however, as in the story above.

If the treatment can be extended over a long period of time, egg oil [11] may be considered.

Regular physical exercise is also important. Anemia may be a factor.

Excellent tea treatments include: Black Warrior (Shinbuto); Bushito; Ginseng Herb.

Low Blood Pressure

Black Warrior Tea

---

[9] One egg mixed with soya sauce in proportions of 4:1.
[10] See footnote #9.
[11] See "Food Is Best Medicine."

Encardium (expanded heart)

Symptoms: enlarged fingertips and nose tip
Treatment: egg oil
Tea remedy: Kuzu Root-Safflower Tea

HEMOPHILIA

This is a disease in which the blood fails to clot when it comes in contact with the air. Obviously, this is the result of a very Yin condition producing very Yin-quality blood. To cure this disease, expansive (Yin) foods must be eliminated from the diet so that the binding force can be restored to the body and blood. Avoid sugar, vinegar, alcohol, chemicals, and even fruit. Take less liquid and more salt. With a healthy diet the quality of the blood will improve naturally.

The opposite condition, in which the blood is too thick (Yang), can produce cerebral hemorrhage and apoplectic stroke (see *Heart Trouble*).

HEMORRHOIDS

Hemorrhoids is a blood disease—stagnation of the blood—which is why it is almost always accompanied by a gum problem (pyorrhea) caused by bad circulation.

Bleeding at the lowest portion of the torso indicates a problem resulting from strong foods (meat, cheese, red pepper, etc.).

Remedy: albi plaster in anus. To stop pain and bleeding, eat fresh raw ginger (a piece as big as your thumb).

Tea: Otsujito or Kyukikyogaito
See also *Blood Stagnation.*

HEPATITIS

This is a disease of the liver. It results from overeating in general and from over-consumption of foods bad for the liver (such as alcohol, oil, vinegar, sugar, chemicals, drugs, meat) in particular. Blood transfusions often cause hepatitis. We know that a healthy diet can bring about a rapid improvement in blood quality (see "The Blood"). A healthy diet and a reduction in eating are very important for healing the condition that produces this disease. An albi plaster may be applied directly over the liver. The tea remedy is Inchinkoto (Gardenia Herb Tea), which is very effective for all problems stemming from the area of the liver, spleen, pancreas, gall bladder. Inchinko, the main ingredient, is a species of mugwort.

HERNIA

This is a Yin disorder.
Remedy: proper diet; albi plaster; Small Kenchuto or Saikokeishito

HICCUPS

When hiccups are not serious, they can be cured in various ways—with water, sugar, salt, etc. When serious and stubborn, they can be treated with a tea made from the calyx (stem) of the persimmon.

HIGH BLOOD PRESSURE
(see Heart Trouble)

HYPERACIDITY
(see Stomach Trouble)

HYPOGLYCEMIA
(see Diabetes)

HYSTERIA
(see Mental Disorders)

IMPOTENCY
(see Sexual Problems)

INDIGESTION
(in small intestine)

This trouble is due to the presence of excess food in the small intestine, making it unable to receive and assimilate nourishment.

Remedy: rice milk (see "Food Is Best Medicine"). Drink only the liquid. Vegetable soup is good also.

See also section on stomach trouble.

* *

A Type of Mugwort for Jaundice

Once a woman suffering from jaundice came to me for advice; a long period of treatment by Western medicine had failed to help her. I gave her Inchinkoto (Gardenia Herb Tea), which is composed of inchinko, a special type of mugwort, daio (the root of the Chinese rhubarb) and gardenia seeds. In no more than five days she was cured. Just after that she went to the hospital for a checkup. The doctor was amazed when he discovered that her blood contained no bile at all.

A young man from San Francisco brought me his baby who also had jaundice. I gave the baby this same tea, but only one teaspoon three times a day. After several days the yellow color disappeared. An acute case is almost always cured more quickly and easily than a chronic case.

In Vancouver, Canada, I saw an even younger baby (four months old). Many babies develop jaundice after they are born, but usually they get well naturally. However, this baby had a yellow color which had persisted for three months.

Since she was taking her mother's milk, I gave the mother Inchinkoto. Through the mother's milk, the tea worked for the baby.

* *

JAUNDICE

A yellow body color is the sign of jaundice. The feces usually become white.

Jaundice is caused by a malfunctioning gall bladder which releases bile into the blood rather than releasing it, as usual, through the duodenum. The passageway is swollen or blocked by a stone. When the blood stream receives bile, the skin appears greenish-yellow from the contamination.

Remedy: vegetable soup containing lots of greens; rice cream; Inchinko Tea (see case history, page 127)

KI DISEASE

"Ki" or "Chi" is the life force contained in the body. Acupuncture is based on an understanding and manipulating of the Ki flow in our bodies. A disturbance in the flow of Ki underlies all diseases.

The nature of Ki disease is discussed in detail in the chapter "On Understanding Disease." Many mental and emotional disturbances are said to be forms of Ki disease (see *Mental Disorders*). Strong-smelling foods are often able to cure Ki diseases. The fundamental tea for treating Ki disease is Hangekobokuto. Koboku (magnolia bark), one of the main ingredients, is said to have a very beneficial effect on mental attitude.

KIDNEY TROUBLE

A moist hand is a sure sign that the kidneys are overworked due to excess consumption of animal food. When the system becomes clogged with excess animal food, our body needs a great deal of water. The kidneys are unable to handle all the liquid, and some of the excess is passed through the pores of the skin. The hands should be dry to the touch.

There are two kinds of kidney trouble, Yin and Yang.

Yang Kidneys

In this case, the other organs are most likely Yang too.
Symptoms: reduced urination; dark brown urine resulting from the presence of excess waste products; high blood pressure resulting from the need for increased pressure to push liquid through the contracted kidneys

Consumption of meat and excess salt makes the kidneys hard. The glomerulus of the kidney has tiny holes too small for protein and blood globules to pass through; only water can pass. Animal food can block these holes. Salt forces the entire vessel network to contract, making it difficult for water (urine) to pass out. As a result of this overly Yang condition, the kidneys are unable to filter the blood effectively. The toxins return to the body instead of passing out in the urine. The urine—and the skin—become dark brown. The skin is dark and dirty-looking because the waste is trying to get past it. The body's overall condition, being excessively Yang, causes heart trouble, circulatory problems, and general organ disease due to poisoning and overwork.

Remedy: Shitake mushroom helps induce urination. It may be taken with rice milk. Radish Drink #1, watermelon tea and corn silk tea are also excellent (see recipes in "Food Is Best Medicine"). Also good are eggplant (boiled, baked or sautéed) and plantain seeds. Aduki beans are highly recommended. For serious trouble, take only aduki beans for two or three days; this is usually quite effective. Aduki bean juice is also an excellent remedy.

The fundamental tea treatment for Yang kidney ailments is Goreisan. Hachimigan, Big Jokito, and Sage's Path Tea are also effective. Remember, a tea treats the entire body. See also the tea recommendations for high blood pressure and skin disease.

Yin Kidneys

Symptoms: excessive urination; thin, clear urine; moist hands; swollen body; pale color.

In this case the kidneys are not cleaning the blood properly; they are so expanded that they cannot filter waste. In this condition, some salt is needed. Aduki beans are also good. In the worst cases, the liquid will pass through much more easily, but so will other things besides water and waste products. Important minerals and hormones are lost with frequent urination.

A kidney in such an expanded condition will, with time, reach a final stage of Yin. At that time the patient will be pale and probably will urinate abundantly, as the liquid of the entire body—unable to be circulated or contained by the overall Yin condition of the organs—passes out as urine. This is the most dangerous stage of disease, when the body cannot retain its liquid.

Ranshio or Shigyakuto may help rapidly at this point. It is also recommended that aduki beans be included as a regular part of the diet over an extended period of time. Plantain seed tea is also good.

The kidneys control all body liquid, so water disease, skin diseases and skin eruptions come from kidney trouble.

Kidney trouble sometimes causes a swelling of the calves; this may be from either Yin or Yang. In this case take rice milk with shitake mushrooms (see "Food Is Best Medicine") for two days. The excess water will leave the body. Swelling in any part of the body may be due to the same problem. Aduki beans are good for both Yin and Yang kidney conditions, for they have both strong Yin and strong Yang characteristics.

LEUCORRHEA
(see Venereal Disease)

LEUKEMIA

Western medicine believes leukemia to be incurable. This is not necessarily so, except in the most advanced cases, but certainly leukemia is one of the most difficult diseases to cure.

According to K. Morishita, M.D., blood is made in the intestines. Therefore it is when the intestines are unable to manufacture new blood, that leukemia develops. According to Dr. Morishita, malignant anemia is the result of severe damage to the intestinal villi, which causes the intestine to cease its function of blood formation. Due to his experiments with people affected by radioactivity after the atomic bomb explosion, Dr. Morishita became an expert concerning cancer, leukemia and anemia. He demonstrated that in the case of leukemia, the stomach and intestines and all body cells have been damaged to a great extent. The red blood cells are thus unable to transform themselves into body cells. When the body cells have been damaged by radiation, they are no longer able to guide themselves properly. What happens then is that red blood cells remain in the intermediate stage, which is that of the white blood cell. Cancer cells are red blood cells that have not completed properly the transformation into body cells. This is a strongly Yin disease.

People with leukemia should drink very little. They should eat mugwort mochi, which has proved excellent in building new blood globules. It makes good quality blood and arrests internal bleeding. The patient should chew his food well and be careful not to indulge in any extremes. He should of course stop eating meat, sugar and dairy food of any kind. The very worst foods for a leukemia patient are sugar, vinegar and alcohol. Cereals and sautéed or baked vegetables will be his main food. Ginseng Herb Tea may be taken regularly for an extended period of time.

LOSS OF HAIR
(see Hair Loss)

LOW BLOOD PRESSURE
(see Heart Trouble)

MEASLES

It does not seem a wise idea to be vaccinated against measles, for measles is a common and natural disease which everyone should have early in life. This natural disease can be more or less serious depending on constitution and diet, but it is certainly much more dangerous for adults than for small children.

For this disease, the wisest thing to do is to keep warm. A cold draft could prove very harmful. Do not use ice bags to reduce the fever. Kuzu root tea may help the rash to develop quickly and disappear rapidly.

MENSTRUATION
(irregularity and cramps)

Menstrual problems are a form of blood disease, usually blood stagnation. In the past, when life and diet were more natural, a woman's menstrual cycle was always in harmony with the phases of the moon. The suppression of the natural menstrual cycle in favor of the artificial one created by birth control pills can be dangerous.

For failure to menstruate, take vegetables. If that doesn't help, take mugwort mochi or carp soup.

For excessive menstruation, eat less and eat 5 raw aduki beans once a day.

Tea remedies: for cramps, drink Two Peony Tea (as a preventive measure, take one tablespoon of honey diluted in one cup of water once a day; this may be taken for up to one month. Never take straight honey.) For irregular menstruation, take Two Peony Tea or Tokaku Jokito.

Black beans are also effective—for special preparation, see "Food Is Best Medicine."

MENTAL DISORDERS
(hysteria, depression, anxiety, neurosis, mental illness)

These are the primary diseases of modern times, the result of a combination of bad food, bad air, noise pollution, etc. As with all the prominent diseases of our time, a re-turn to simpler, traditional customs and natural food, the rejection of industrialized and chemicalized food, will restore the fundamental basis of health. Don't take drugs, alcohol, meat, sugar or medicine. Move to the country where it is quiet.

Mental disorders often result from Ki disease and may be related to liver problems.

Tea remedies: Hangekobokuto is the most popular; anyone may try it. Day Lily Tea and Heavenly Root Tea are both good for the nervous system. Kambakudaisoto is an excellent tea for hysteria and similar mental problems. Its main ingredient is wheat. The other ingredients are dates and licorice. However, this tea, strangely enough, is effective only for women and children. Adult men may take Sanoshashinto, which is very effective for hysteria, convulsions, etc. It is made of daio, ohgon and ohren (goldthread).

Meditation involving deep breathing is recommended strongly for all persons with mental illness and related problems.

MORNING SICKNESS
(see Pregnancy)

MUMPS

Apply albi plaster to swollen area. Do not eat extreme kinds of food. This includes excess fruit, dairy food, meat products.

NEUROSIS
(see Mental Disorders)

NOSEBLEED

A nosebleed is the result of excess blood and high blood pressure. Women may be prone to it during menstruation. Persons subject to frequent nosebleeds should eat less. (See also *High Blood Pressure*, under *Heart Trouble*.)

Sometimes very Yin people have this problem. Their blood is too thin. People with hemophilia, leukemia and similar conditions are included in this category. Strong Yin food must be avoided.

A novel but effective treatment for a nosebleed is carbonized hair. Put hair from your head in a can. Seal the can so that it is air-tight and put it over a fire. With no air inside the can, the hair will carbonize and turn to powder. Keep this ready for an emergency. When a nosebleed occurs, mix carbonized hair with water and drink. No more nosebleed!

If a nosebleed occurs at a time or place where no aids are available, have the patient sit and tilt back his head. Then tap the nape of his neck lightly with the side of your hand. Or, try taking three hairs from the indentation where the neck joins the skull.

Tea remedy: Sanoshashinto

OBESITY

The problem of obesity should not be made more complicated than it is. There is no doubt that a controlled reduction of eating and drinking is the best way to lose weight.

Most often a problem of overweight is due to kidney disease. Simple eating, avoidance of meat and sugar, and less drinking are usually all that is necessary to remedy this condition.

If you are red or brown in color, take only raw vegetables for one or two days at a time. Repeat a few times.

Here is a way to determine the most appropriate dieting method for you. Eat rice only (brown, organic). If this works, continue with the same regimen and restrict your intake of liquid. If there is no effect, eat raw vegetables. Kanten (a sea vegetable which is a kind of gelatin) is an excellent food for persons who have a problem with overeating. It has no calories, only minerals.

Afterwards, it is advisable to return to a balanced diet. For important information and advice about losing weight, see "Getting Rid of Waste."

A famous tea which promotes weight loss is Bofutsusho-shan (Sage's Path Tea). However, no recipe is included in this book, for this tea is very complicated to prepare. It can be bought ready-made. Big Saikoto is also effective.

PARASITES
(see Worms)

PARKINSON'S DISEASE

Magnolia bark is the main herb used for curing this disease. Koboku (magnolia bark) is the main ingredient in Small Jokito. In the case of Parkinson's Disease, the amount of magnolia bark should be increased from 3 to 10 grams.

PERITONITIS

This acute swelling of the abdominal membrane is clearly a water disease. Buckwheat plaster (flour and hot water) may be applied directly, or an albi plaster may be used. The appropriate herbal tea remedies are Shinbuto (Black Warrior Tea) and Ogikenchuto. If there is an unusually large amount of water present, an albi plaster should be applied directly in the area of the kidneys, and Goreisan Tea may be taken (see case history, page 98).

PHLEBITIS

To relieve swollen veins, one of two teas may be used, Keishibukuryogan (Two Peony) or Daiobotanpito (botanpi is a species of peony which is used in both teas; tonin, or peach seeds, is also common to both).

Carbonized hair is also very good (see section on nosebleeds in this chapter for recipe).

PNEUMONIA
(see Respiratory Ailments)

POLIO

This is a disease found only in advanced civilization. Therefore, preventive medicine is sure to work.

Polio is usually contracted by children; those who are susceptible to it are very weak, and their diet must be watched carefully. They should not eat extremely Yin foods such as sugar, alcohol, drugs, chemicals and out-of-season fruits; they should eat little or no meat, for polio results from an excessive intake of strong Yin or Yang. In the case of Yin polio, when the feet point out, give more Yang, salty food. For Yang polio, in which the feet point in, give less salt and a balanced diet.

Polio always starts out as a common cold. While it is in that initial stage, it is easy to cure (see *Colds*).

Nyoiti Sakurazawa once cured polio by giving cooked soybeans together with the head of a dried, salted salmon.

Some cases of Yin polio have been cured by Juzendai-hoto.[12]

PREGNANCY PROBLEMS
(morning sickness, miscarriage, breast-feeding difficulties, pregnancy poisoning)

Morning Sickness

A famous tea for treating morning sickness is Small Hangebukuryoto. Hange is rich in potassium and calcium. When a woman has morning sickness frequently, she usually has a lack of calcium. Such a woman therefore tends to take sour food such as vinegar or citrus fruits. Sour food melts down calcium from the mother's bones and teeth, sending it into the blood stream to provide minerals for the baby. Thus, either the baby gets his calcium and the mother loses her teeth, or the mother, who does not have a proper diet but nevertheless takes no sour food, will probably keep her teeth and the baby will suffer.

The best answer, of course, is a good diet including foods rich in calcium and calcium-producing elements. For example, seaweed is much higher in calcium than milk, sesame seeds are high in calcium, and the herb *horsetail* is an excellent source of silica.[13] Hange-bukuryo mushroom-ginger tea (Small Hangebukuryoto) is also highly recommended. If the woman is of a very Yin-type condition, 7 grams of *odo* may be added. Odo is the clay from the bottom of a fireplace (strong Yang). If no odo is available, some pulverized clay from an old teapot may be substituted.

See also *Tooth Decay*.

Miscarriage

A pregnant woman who has had several miscarriages in the past should take Two Peony Tea.

Breastfeeding Difficulties

Every baby must be breastfed. There is absolutely no substitute for mother's milk. Mothers who have trouble producing sufficient milk should eat miso soup and mochi, and, if there is still a lack of milk, carp soup (recipes for all three can be found in "Food Is Best Medicine").

Tea treatment: Kuzu Root Herb Tea or Dandelion Herb Tea

---

[12] The recipe for this tea is not included in this book.
[13] Silica changes into calcium in the body by biological transmutation. See *Good News,* page 54.

Pregnancy Poisoning

Symptoms: high blood pressure; swelling in various parts of the body; high protein content in the urine

Remedy: Goreisan Tea or Inchinkoto (Gardenia Herb Tea)

PSORIASIS
(*see Skin Disease*)

PYORRHEA

This disease is caused by stagnation of the blood, especially in the gums. Tooth decay and pyorrhea are opposite types of disorders. When there is tooth decay, there will not be pyorrhea, and vice versa. Of course, over a period of time there can easily be both.

Tooth decay, as everyone knows now, is caused by excess sugar. Pyorrhea is caused generally by excess animal food. Here are a few things you should do if you suffer from pyorrhea:

Because the disease is caused primarily by blood stagnation, you will have to bring blood to circulate properly in your gums. For that you will need a proper diet and some external remedies including massage.

For the appropriate diet, see section on blood stagnation in this chapter. Apply dentie [14] to the gums and massage before going to bed. Leave the dentie on the gums for a while—ten minutes if you can—and then wash it off with hot water. After that, massage the gums with your fingers to improve the circulation. This cure will take time (one or two months), but it is a certain cure.

Carbonized hair is an effective remedy for bleeding gums (see section on nosebleed for recipe).

Tea remedy: Tokaku Jokito

See also *Blood Stagnation.*

RESPIRATORY AILMENTS
(*cough, whooping cough, pneumonia, bronchitis, asthma, tuberculosis*)

Cough

There are two distinct kinds of cough. A Yang type of cough is an explosion of breathing. There is difficulty in exhaling. Both adults and children usually have this type of cough. The Yin type of cough has a different sound; it is long and drawn out, a sort of wheeze. There is difficulty in inhaling. Yang people should avoid Yang food; Yin people should avoid Yin food. Mao Tea is a good remedy for Yang coughing. It should be taken at least one-half hour before each meal, three times a day. Dragon Tea is equally good. For a Yin cough, Mu Tea or Lotus Root Tea are excellent—to be taken at least one-half hour before meals.

Whooping Cough

This disease begins as a common cold and should be treated while it is still in that stage (see *Colds*). Dragon Tea and Kambakudaisoto are effective against whooping cough, as are the teas recommended as cold remedies.

Pneumonia

Pneumonia always starts as a common cold. The best advice is to heal yourself then, while the problem is still simple and non-critical. People who are susceptible to pneumonia are very strong physically and must be careful to avoid eating Yang-quality foods such as meat.

When the high fever that accompanies pneumonia develops, it should be treated with an albi plaster on the forehead and chest. Dragon Tea or Big Saikoto may be taken.

An old folk remedy for pneumonia is the carp plaster (see "External Treatments").

Bronchitis

There is both acute and chronic bronchitis. For the former, try radish drink, ginger compress and albi plaster. The same treatment should be given to those with and without fever. Watch the diet, of course. A good herbal tea for people with chronic bronchitis is Small Saikoto, and in this case a good diet is even more important.

Asthma

Asthma comes in two types, Yin and Yang. Most of the cases occurring in the United States are of the Yang type. In general, fat people who are asthmatic have the Yang type of asthma. Their color is red or dark brown. Many cases of this type of asthma stem from heart trouble.

Remedies for Yang-type asthma: juice from grated radish mixed with Yinnie [15]; Mao Tea. Yang asthmatic people should eat more vegetables.

Remedies for Yin-type asthma: people with this illness are pale. They should cut down on liquids and eat more Yang-quality food such as whole grains, especially brown rice. Root vegetables are good; lotus is especially effective. Lotus root is excellent sautéed; lotus seeds are good too. Powdered lotus root tea is available in natural food stores. Yin asthmatic people should avoid fruit for a while until their condition improves.

Children in most cases have the Yang form of asthma. They should be given Dragon Tea.

For asthma resulting from heart trouble, Mokuboito is recommended. Big Saikoto will also be effective.

Tuberculosis

Almost all cases of tuberculosis arise from Yin causes. With the mass introduction of industrialized sugar into man's diet, T.B. increased dramatically throughout the world (see box).

Usually, people with T.B. are pale and of a generally Yin constitution. Recently, however, even heavy, Yang-type people have been developing this disease.

When the skin of a tubercular person turns dark brown, the kidneys as well as the lungs are diseased.

For Yin T.B., eliminate sugar from the diet.

---

[14] A black toothpowder made from roasted eggplant and salt. Available at natural food stores.

[15] A candy made from fermented barley. Available at natural food stores.

For Yang T.B., neither animal food nor sugar should be eaten. Yang T.B. is caused by both meat and sugar.

Remedies: garlic, cooked or pickled in soya sauce may be taken for several days. This is good for both Yin and Yang T.B. Ginkgo nuts are excellent also. Do not use the fruit itself, only the pit. Pickle the fruit pits in sesame oil for one month. Take 3 or 4 pits a day. The recommended tea remedy is Small Saikoto.

Physical exercise is very important. Inactivity is the worst thing for tubercular patients. Occasionally (once or twice a month) one may take oysters, carp, or striped bass deep-fried in sesame oil.

* *

Three hundred years ago there was a dramatic and widespread increase in deaths from tuberculosis. *This was the time of the Industrial Revolution, one aspect of which was the increased importation and refinement of sugar. It is known that the highest incidence of tuberculosis at that time occurred among workers in sugar factories. Likewise, in Japan there was a heavy increase in cases of tuberculosis 60 years ago. This increase coincided with Japan's acquisition of Formosa, a source of cheap and abundant sugar. (Prior to that time Japan had never imported sugar on a large scale.) Incidents of tuberculosis rose immediately.*

* *

RHEUMATISM

This disease is caused by a heavy intake of Yin and Yang food—for example, excessive amounts of meat and sugar taken regularly. Rheumatism usually requires a long period of cure.

Remedy: one teaspoon of miso (preferably hacho miso, 10 years old or the oldest you can find) diluted in a small cup of hot water. Mix well and drink slowly, in sips. You can also try a mixture of grated radish (2 to 3 tablespoons), boiling sesame oil (one tablespoon), and soya sauce (one teaspoon).

For severe cases (arthritis and gout, for example), try Shakkanoshinbuto.

Drink less liquid, of course. Avoid sugar in all forms, dairy food, and animal food.

SEASICKNESS

Here is an amazing treatment. Tape one umeboshi plum over the navel! No one knows why, but it works. Good for all types of motion sickness. If you are prone to motion sickness, tape it on before you board the ship or plane. The sickness will not develop.

SEXUAL PROBLEMS
(impotency, excessive desire, oversensitivity, sterility, frigidity)

In Men

Oriental medicine believes that the sexual organs are controlled by the kidneys (see section on kidneys in "The Organs").

Excess meat (Yang) and other high-protein foods cause excessive sexual desire. In the U.S. many people have sexual problems. Erection without ejaculation is due to lack of Yin. Ejaculation is controlled by the parasympathetic (Yang) nervous system. One needs both Yin and Yang food to avoid this problem. A balanced diet, including grains (barley, whole wheat in the form of bread, brown rice), vegetables of various kinds, and occasional animal food, is the most likely to bring about a normal condition (see also the section on crooked spine in this chapter).

Balance is necessary for a healthy sexual appetite. A Japanese saying states, "Man who likes carrots likes women." In America there is a belief that parsley increases sexual appetite. Carrots are a Yang-quality vegetable, while parsley is Yin. Most Americans have a very Yang condition; they need Yin to restore the balance that will release sexual appetite and power. Thus red pepper and onions, beer and whiskey are included among American folk remedies for impotency. Orientals, whose problems stem from a Yin-quality condition, need Yang to provide balance.

Now we can see why ginseng enjoys such renown as a rejuvenator of sexual prowess. Ginseng is a very Yang root. But one man's medicine is not necessarily another's. With strong, Yang-type people, ginseng will probably have no effect. One possibility for such people is to take Yin food, as mentioned above. Another is to combine ginseng with Yin herbs. This will actually increase the ginseng's effectiveness. But the best remedy of all is to follow a healthy, balanced diet and to chew the food very well. Chewing strengthens the sexual organs since they are connected with the jaw muscles. Regular exercise, such as walking, strengthens the lower parts of the abdomen.

Yang persons with a weak sexual appetite may take Day Lily Tea. Weak people with a weak sexual appetite may try one of the following teas: Small Saikoto, Black Warrior, Heavenly Root, Ginseng Herb, Hachimigan. The last is especially effective for diabetics, who are prone to losing their Yang force suddenly, and along with that their sexual appetite.

To reduce sexual desire, simply take extremely Yin foods such as mushrooms, sugar, tomatoes, eggplant, fruit, etc. Because they are assimilated so quickly, sugar and alcohol are at first highly stimulating, but their expanding force soon dissipates all desire.

Five ways to overcome the problem of oversensitivity are:
1) circumcision
2) change in position
3) meditation (deep breathing)
4) long walks (5–10 miles) before bedtime; use of legs
5) proper chewing (chewing muscle is connected with sexual organs; chewing will help set a good endurance pattern for all activity throughout life)

Circumcision is very beneficial. It is extremely sanitary, and it lengthens the time before orgasm by reducing surface sensitivity. These days most babies are circumcised in efficient hospitals and so there is no danger involved.

In Women

Sterility in women is the result of an excess of both strong Yang and strong Yin. Take black bean juice every day for a year.

Tea remedy: if hands, feet and hips are always cold, take Mu Tea. If these symptoms are not present, take Two Peony Tea for three to six months. If this is too Yang, take Tokaku Jokito for one week only. Then rest for one or two weeks, and take the tea again for another week. This alternating may be continued for several months.

Ryotanshakanto is another possible tea cure.

Black beans are recommended for women with sexual problems. They will help cure frigidity and irregular menstruation, if prepared correctly (see "Food Is Best Medicine"). Two Peony Tea may also be tried for these problems.

Abortions are a possible source of breast cancer. Even though a woman has had an abortion, the pregnancy process continues. The body started to prepare to produce milk and was stopped abruptly from doing so. This interference can initiate breast cancer which will surface when the woman is forty or fifty.

There is no such problem with a miscarriage. Miscarriage is a natural function for which all parts of the body are prepared.

SINUS TROUBLE

This is another blood disease. Dirty blood is at the root of it. The sinuses are irritated by bacteria from the air which enter during inhalation; the dirty blood provides an ideal environment for the bacteria to proliferate.

Treatment: an albi plaster may be applied directly as a symptomatic remedy, but most important is to purify the blood by eating good food over a long period of time. Kuzu Root Herb Tea may be taken with shin-i added. Shin-i is the flower pod of a certain species of magnolia. The whole pod should be used.

SKIN DISEASES

Skin diseases such as eczema, erysipelas, psoriasis, and athlete's foot are caused by kidney trouble, a result of excess meat. The kidneys become overloaded with waste materials and the skin is forced to share the burden of elimination. Sugar stimulates and hastens the discharge of excess protein, and thus in turn leads to skin eruptions; but still, the excess animal protein which causes kidney damage is the true source of this problem. The skin disease is but a symptom, and the sugar a catalyst. If the kidneys are healed and a good diet restored, the skin problem will disappear automatically.

Symptomatic remedy: albi plaster on the kidney area.

There are certain skin salves which can be effective, but the use of these exclusively will not correct the kidney problem. A better method is to take one of the special teas that help bring about the discharge of the excess animal protein which is interfering with proper kidney functioning.

The fundamental tea for this type of kidney ailment is Goreisan.

For more information on kidney functioning and treatment, see *Kidney Troubles* in this chapter and the section on the kidneys in "The Organs."

Two teas especially suited for healing skin problems are Jyumihaidokuto and Keishibukuryogan. The former is effective in all cases of active discharge through the skin, as in psoriasis and syphilis. This tea has ten ingredients, most of which are very Yin-type foods.

Keishibukuryogan is known as "Two Peony Tea." It is famous as a purifier of the skin and blood. With two grams of baimo added, this tea when taken will effectively drain pus from skin infections. However, for diseases caused by dirty blood, Tokaku Jokito is much more effective. Two Peony Tea can be taken over a period of several months as a "cosmetic" aid; it beautifies the skin.

See "External Treatments" for plasters and oils which may be applied.

Two Case Histories

A boy in Vancouver had a skin ulcer on his arm. He came to me during a lecture. The other people present guessed that his ulcer was the result of a Yin condition, but I could see that it was caused by blood stagnation— old blood failing to circulate. I recommended Tokaku Jokito, the fundamental tea for blood disease, and in three days the boy was healed completely.

This blood disease (Yang) is fairly common today, although very few people seem to recognize it. The concern is always with its symptoms—skin ulcers, blood clots, uterine tumors, headaches, etc. That the real problem lies in the quality of the blood, is rarely discussed.

A student of mine in New York City brought his mother to see me. Her arm was swollen and yellow and contained a large amount of pus. This seemed to be the after-effect of a recent hospital radiation treatment, undergone for a different problem. I recommended Two Peony Tea with 2 grams of baimo added. After seven days, she was much better. It is unusual to be able to heal the after-effects of radiation treatment so quickly. Hospital methods are drastic, while herbs and teas tend to work gradually. But in this case the cure was complete, for the woman has changed her diet completely and is now eating very well.

SNAKEBITE

Apply a tourniquet to stop the poison from spreading and reaching the heart. Try to suck out the poison by the mouth. If you cannot reach the bite with your own mouth, have someone else do it.

A tourniquet, however, cannot be used for long; it cuts off the circulation. Snake poison is strong Yin, so strong Yang is needed. Ranshio (egg and tamari—see "Food Is Best Medicine") is best, but these ingredients are not always going to be available at the critical moment. Tea made from the bark of a cherry tree will work, but this too may be unavailable. An unusual but highly effective remedy is juice from crushed earthworms. Apply locally.

SORE THROAT

This kind of inflammation, like most other localized swellings, results from overburdened, ineffective kidneys. Thus the real cause is excess meat, salt and liquid, and the most thorough cure consists in eliminating the cause.

Symptomatic treatment: ginger compress and albi plaster; Kikyo Tea. Kikyo, the root of the bellflower, draws mucus and animal poisons from the throat. If neither of these teas is effective after a few days, one of the Hange teas may be taken—either Hangekobokuto or Hangebukuryoto.

STAGNATION OF BLOOD
(*see Blood Stagnation*)

STERILITY
(*see Sexual Problems*)

STOMACH TROUBLE
(*ache, pain, hyperacidity and indigestion, ulcers, cramps*)

Stomachache

This trouble accompanies many different diseases, not only in the stomach but also in the intestines, liver, gall bladder, pancreas, spleen, kidneys, bladder, ovaries, uterus, ureter, etc. Sometimes the pain will be slight, sometimes sharp. The area of the abdomen in which the pain is felt, the type of pain, recent diet, the presence or absence of fever, vomiting, or diarrhea, are all factors which help to isolate the basic problem causing the stomachache.

Stomach trouble causes pain in the upper part of the abdomen and sometimes the pain is felt in the chest, back and shoulders. Intestinal trouble causes pain in the lower abdomen in many cases, and often diarrhea.

Round worms (ascarids) can be a cause of stomach or intestinal pain.

With appendicitis, sharp pain is felt intermittently in the right lower abdomen.

Liver and gall bladder ailments cause pain in the upper right part of the abdomen; spleen trouble causes pain on the left side.

The pancreas is back of the stomach, so pain is felt in the upper abdomen.

Ovary, uterus, and bladder trouble results in pain in the lower abdomen.

For any kind of pain, try ginger compress. *Appendicitis is the one exception;* do not apply a ginger compress in this case.

For sharp pain, Shakuyakukanzoto (peony root and licorice) may work.

Stomach Pain, Atony, etc.

Stomach pain is one of the most common complaints. It is caused by excess eating or bad food. You can try to induce vomiting by putting your fingers into your throat; this may succeed in stopping the pain. Or, mix salt plum with warm water or make Plum-Soy-Ginger-Bancha. This may help induce vomiting.

It is good to make the painful area warm. Roast one pound of salt until hot; wrap in cotton and put on your stomach.

Fasting is very important when the stomach is painful, heavy, or in any way uncomfortable. Tea or warm water may be taken (cold water is harmful).

If fasting is too difficult for you, you may take kuzu paste (dilute kuzu in water and cook until it becomes a paste) or rice soup. Plum-soy-ginger-kuzu (see "Food Is Best Medicine") is also good.

Except in the case of appendicitis, the abdomen should be kept warm.

Avoid ice cream and cold drinks. If blood is vomited from the stomach, and if the feces contain blood (in which case they would be black) fast for one or two days and apply ginger compress and albi plaster (chlorophyll plaster may be used as a substitute) on the stomach area. Change plaster every three or four hours, and cover it with roasted salt to create warmth.

After this treatment, you may take kuzu paste or rice soup. Rice cream, soft rice, vegetable soup, may also be taken. Solid food should be increased gradually.

The albi plaster should be continued for four or five days, or as long as it takes for the problem to subside.

In the case of stomach trouble, each mouthful of food (1 tablespoon) should be chewed more than 100 times. Thorough chewing stimulates an abundant saliva flow, and saliva is good medicine.

When pain occurs soon after a meal, there is trouble in the upper area of the stomach. Pain in the cardia area of the stomach results from strong Yin food such as sugar. If it is in the middle part of the stomach, alcoholic beverages may be the cause. Pain in the lower part of the stomach comes from Yang food or excess salt. Pain from excess salt takes longer to develop—it will arise 2–3 hours after meals. Also, there will be pain at the time when hunger arises. Eating at this time may cause the pain to stop, but this is not advisable. It is important to fast until the pain goes away.

For sudden pain in the lower area of the stomach, Big Saikoto is a good remedy (this very Yin tea is suitable only for an overly strong, Yang constitution).

Hyperacidity and Indigestion

Different types of food are responsible for pain in different parts of the stomach at different times. Pain in the duodenum (lower part) when hunger arises indicates that too much salt is being consumed. In general, pain in that area is also caused by an excess of meat. An increased intake of salt can stop the pain temporarily, but when liquid is taken the pain will return. Pain in the middle area of the stomach comes from excess alcohol. Pain in the upper area of the stomach is caused by excess sugar.

Treatment: for excess stomach acidity, keep a salt plum pit in your mouth for a few hours. This will draw saliva (alkaline) into the stomach. Plum-soy-ginger-bancha drink is good for pain in all three areas of the stomach. Shishikanrento (a tea containing gardenia seeds, licorice and goldthread) can also be taken for specific problems in the lower area of the stomach and for most stomach problems in general. Rikakuto (gardenia seeds, hange, monkshood) can be taken for problems in the upper area of the stomach.

The most fundamental cure, again, is a good balanced diet. It is necessary to chew food thoroughly until it becomes liquid; this is an alkalizing process and prevents further acidity arising from poor digestion.

See also *Indigestion In Small Intestine.*

Experience has shown that acid pain in the stomach indicates that cancer is not present. If there are signs of much acidity in the body, and yet there is no acid pain in the stomach, there is a possibility of cancer.

Duodenum Gastric Ulcers

Fundamental cure: thorough chewing of food; avoidance of soft drinks, fruit, etc., which interfere with proper chewing and digestion. If pain occurs 2–3 hours after meals, the cause is Yang. Reduce intake of salt. Excess salt can be a cause of duodenum ulcers.

Symptomatic cure: Soy-ginger-plum-bancha drink. Keep salt plum pit in mouth for 5 hours to produce saliva. The salt plum turns to alkaline in the stomach and neutralizes the excess stomach acid which causes ulcers.

* *

Sodium Bicarbonate Vs the Umeboshi Salt Plum

Stomach troubles are often the result of too much stomach acid. If you take sodium bicarbonate (baking powder), the symptoms disappear very quickly; however, the stomach soon becomes even more acid.

Chew well; this produces an abundance of saliva, which is alkaline and neutralizes the acid. Salt plums help to draw out the saliva. Although the salt plum is sour, which means that it contains much acid, this acid changes to alkaline very quickly in the mouth and stomach.

* *

Shishikanrento and Saikokeishito are two herbal teas which can help cure stomach ulcers. Shishikanrento is, in general, effective for all stomach troubles.

CASE HISTORY

In Japan, a 39-year-old woman with a gastric ulcer came to me after having consulted a hospital doctor. She had been told that her case required surgery, and that she should return in three days for the operation. Reluctant to undergo this drastic treatment, the woman sought my help. Under such circumstances I was ready to try anything, and she was willing to cooperate. I restricted her diet and gave her plum-soy-ginger-bancha drink. The salt plum stimulates the flow of saliva, and saliva is very alkaline. It helps neutralize the excess stomach acid which is the cause of stomach ulcers. I also had her take Shishikanrento three times a day and eat soft rice, seasoned with salt plum, an hour afterwards. This dish is both highly digestible and alkalizing. Shishikanrento has been used since ancient times to treat all kinds of stomach troubles.

The treatment was effective immediately. By the next day, the woman felt much better. She cancelled the operation and in a short time was completely successful in healing herself.

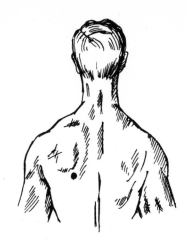

THE STOMACH POINT

Cramps

There are various ways of taking care of a stomach cramp.

Pressure point: to stop the cramp, push many times with the thumb (maintaining the pressure while you count to 2 or 3) at the bottom angle of the left shoulderblade. The patient must lie on his stomach and relax, his arms alongside his body.

External remedy: ginger compress on stomach

Drinks: take either of the following: (1) soy-ginger-salt plum-bancha (see "Using Herbs and Teas"); (2) peony root and licorice tea (boil 4 grams peony root and 6 grams licorice for 30 minutes; drink the juice)

The ideal is a balanced diet, which builds the nervous system. The nervous system needs vitamin B. The best natural supply of this vitamin is whole grains. For vitamin B deficiency, take Kumibinroto, which includes nine herbs. See also section on vitamin B deficiency further on in this chapter.

SYPHILIS
(see Venereal Disease)

TONSILITIS

Oriental medicine asserts that the tonsils have an important function, that of destroying harmful bacteria which enter through the mouth. When the tonsils are unable to fulfill this function, it is not a sign that they should be removed but rather that the body's powers of resistance must be strengthened.

Symptomatic treatment: albi plaster; Mao Tea; Kuzu Root Herb Tea; Cinnamon Herb Tea; Big Saikoto

TOOTHACHE

Dentie[16] or plantain leaves may be applied to the aching tooth. Take raw plantain leaves, rub salt on them, and crush them with your hand. Rikkosan Tea can also help relieve the pain.

---

[16] A black toothpowder made from roasted eggplant and salt. Available at natural food stores.

TOOTH DECAY

Excess drinking of liquids worsens the condition of the teeth.

People in Japan, who eat mainly grains and vegetables and who do not eat meat but consume much salt, are always thirsty and therefore drink excessively. They eat no sugar whatsoever; nevertheless, they have tooth decay. That is because excess water removes minerals from the teeth.

Dandelion, chickweed, spiderwort, mugwort, plantain and seaweed are all organic sources of calcium. Calcium pills, which are inorganic, are very dangerous for they cause swollen joints. Small dried fish, which can be purchased at Japanese stores and added to soups, are also a good source of calcium.

Other elements, such as silica and potassium, can be transmuted into calcium by the body. See *Good News*, page 54.

TUBERCULOSIS
(see Respiratory Ailments)

TYPHOID FEVER

For this disease there is usually an incubation period of several days. Dullness throughout the body, loss of appetite and heaviness in the head are symptoms.

Initially one feels cold, and day by day the fever rises. At this stage the disease is something like the common cold. (See section on the six stages of disease in "On Understanding Disease.") The fever may rise to 104° or 105°, but the pulse will not be so rapid. (With a common cold, if the fever is high the pulse is rapid.)

Pink rashes will emerge on the chest or abdomen, back, face, hands, and soles of the feet. Often the liver and spleen will be swollen.

If the disease has already reached this stage, you must go to the hospital; the law requires this, because typhoid fever is infectious.

However, if the disease is in the first stages, you may try the suitable treatment and the disease will be arrested (see *Colds* and *Fever*).

If you follow a proper diet, you will not be susceptible to typhoid fever. The salt plum is a good preventive medicine.

ULCERS
(see Stomach Trouble)

UNDERWEIGHT CONDITION

Most people who are underweight are too tight (Yang). Eating a large amount of food is not the answer, for this will only serve to overstimulate the eliminatory system, which is already far too active. The problem is not quantity of food, but ability to retain it. Small regular meals should be taken, and the food should be of a smooth, soothing quality. Brown rice is good, but recommended are the more Yin-quality grains and their products, such as sweet rice, mochi, wheat, wheat noodles, barley cream, oatmeal and corn. Also recommended are winter squash, pumpkin, yams, potatoes, black beans, and small amounts of nuts and seeds.

If the problem is due to a weak, Yin-type condition, carp soup is highly recommended.

UTERINE TUMOR

Western medicine usually recommends surgery for a uterine tumor. It is a grave mistake to assume that a tumor indicates a disease curable only by surgery. One should be careful to diagnose correctly before committing a serious error that could make future pregnancy impossible.

In Oriental medicine it is believed simply that tumors are often nothing but blood clots, the result of blood stagnation. Tokaku Jokito is a tea that is highly effective in purifying the blood, breaking up blood clots, improving circulation, and cleaning out the uterus. (In the case of an afterbirth which does not come out naturally, Tokaku Jokito is sure to work.)

See also *Blood Stagnation*.

CASE HISTORY

A couple who had been married for about three years came to me, wanting to know why they could not have a baby. The wife was very obese. Diagnosis revealed a problem of blood stagnation. I advised her to lose some weight. She began eating properly, following a diet consisting mainly of grains and vegetables, with no animal food. After no more than a week, a clot of blood measuring 3 by 9 inches was expelled from her uterus. It was almost black, which means that the blood was very old. When a clot of this sort is expelled, one's condition improves instantly. In this case, the woman conceived less than six months later. When this happens, there need be no more fear of a uterine tumor, especially for someone following a good diet.

VENEREAL DISEASE
(syphilis, gonorrhea, leucorrhea)

Syphilis and gonorrhea constitute a serious problem in America today. Syphilis is a relatively new disease, while gonorrhea has been a problem since ancient times. Both are Yang-type diseases, and are connected to blood stagnation. With good quality blood and circulation, there is a natural immunity to venereal disease.

Treatment: improve blood quality by including many vegetables in diet and avoiding animal food (meat, dairy food, eggs).

Teas: Jyumihaidokuto and Ryutanshakanto. The former is appropriate for cases where there is an actual flowing emission, while the latter is for cases in which the problem remains internal. A tea which is effective specifically for syphilis is Kagawagedokuto, while Choreito and Goreisan Tea (with 4 grams of inchinko added to it) are both effective against gonorrhea. These two teas contain several types of mushrooms and aquatic plants and are known to be very beneficial for the bladder and kidneys. For more about these teas, see "Using Herbs and Teas."

Leucorrhea

This woman's disease involves a white or yellow discharge from the vagina. Recommended is Ryotanshakanto or Two Peony Tea.

* *

The Woman With The Red Face

A woman visited me in Seattle while I was lecturing there. Her face was very red. When I inquired what was wrong with her, she replied that she had itching in the interior of her sex membrane (this is very common among Japanese women). It was the first time I had heard of an American woman having this problem. I advised her to take Ryutanshakanto, a tea famous for the curing of internal problems of the sexual organs. In three days she was cured. This problem is very easily taken care of, compared to cases of gonorrhea and syphilis.

Ryukan is the Japanese name for gentian, a violet autumn bellflower. But gentian root comprises only ⅕ of the entire tea. The tea also includes 8 other herbs.

* *

VITAMIN B DEFICIENCY AND BERIBERI

A large number of people in America today suffer from vitamin B deficiency, and many of them don't know it. If you wish to check yourself, see how this deficiency is diagnosed on page 35.

Symptoms: At first there is a dullness in the legs, and sometimes a slight numbness in the feet, legs, fingers or lips. Often there may be a rapid heartbeat, shortness of breath or shallow breathing, fatigue, difficulty in walking. Swollen calves are also a frequent symptom, and it may well be that vitamin B deficiency is a water disease.

Sometimes there are pains in various parts of the body, and there may be other troubles with the eyes, nose, memory, etc.

All these troubles result from vitamin B deficiency.

Beriberi is caused mainly by refined foods, which lack vitamin B. A hundred years ago, cases of beriberi arose in Japan, coinciding with the advent of polished rice. Fifty years ago the vitamin pill was invented as a result, and beriberi decreased. However, vitamin B in pill form as a supplement to white rice and white bread is not the final answer.

Nowadays we have many vitamin B complex pills and injections. At first, the injections work very quickly; however, we must take vitamin B every day since our body consumes it daily. Thus, if we take vitamin B only in injection form, we will come to need daily injections. It is much better to take vitamin B every day in the form of food.

Vitamin B is found in natural form in the outer layers of whole grains. However, many people are incapable of digesting the vitamin B found in grains. Their intestines lack the beneficial flora which make digestion of vitamin B possible. Antibiotics destroy these intestinal flora, as do drugs, chemical food additives, alcohol and sugar.

Antibiotics especially—as the word implies—are dangerous for people suffering from a deficiency of intestinal flora. While they may be effective in combating bacterial infection, they also destroy several different kinds of bacterial flora which are vitally needed by the small intestine.

In the case of one who eats sugar, even if the body can digest vitamin B the vitamin B reserve will always be depleted.

* *

The Cure For Vitamin B Deficiency Has No Vitamin B!

Kumibinroto, or "Nine Taste Tea," cures vitamin B deficiency, and yet it contains virtually no vitamin B. It works by stimulating the growth of intestinal flora.

I was once approached by a woman whose jaw was so sore she couldn't move it. She was unable to chew, and her diet was restricted to milk and fruit juice. My diagnosis was vitamin B deficiency; I advised her to take Nine Taste Tea for 30 days. After 3 days she was experiencing much less pain, and toward the end of the first week she began to eat. By the end of the 30 days she was chewing grains and gaining weight. Accurate diagnosis and Nine Taste Tea had restored her health.

In many cases patients have come to me complaining that they have seen doctors and had extensive tests yet the cause of their pain could not be determined. Nevertheless, the strange pain persisted. This is usually a sign that vitamin B deficiency is the problem. Usually in such a case I recommend Kumibinroto. The pain usually disappears.

* *

Pills taken to supply the body with missing vitamin B seem to work, but actually they are only effective superficially. Since they flood the body with the missing element, they seem highly effective; however, the body cannot completely assimilate or retain vitamins from pills, for it has never been equipped to do so. The body is designed to break down whole food to obtain the elements it needs. The best supply of vitamin B, then, is whole grains. However, when people begin eating grains such as brown rice, they often find that their stripped intestinal wall is incapable of assimilating the vitamin as it should. In this case it is advisable to eat any of the following: miso soup, whole wheat (sourdough) bread, rice bran pickles. These will help strengthen the intestines and provide bacterial flora, as well as supplying the missing vitamin B. Rice bran, in fact, is the "Oriental vitamin B pill." Rice bran is that nutritious outer part of the grain, which is thrown away in order to reduce brown rice to white rice. Rice bran pickles can be kept well for ten years or more (see "Food Is Best Medicine").

A herbal remedy specifically for vitamin B deficiency is Kumibinroto, or Nine Taste Tea. Another is Keimeisan Tea. It also helps to walk barefoot in the grass in the morning—when there is dew—for 10 to 30 minutes. This last treatment may seem strange, but it has been effective in many cases. And it is very easy to do.

WATER DISEASE

This problem is discussed in detail in the chapter "On Understanding Disease." Abnormal swelling in some parts of the body—often the legs—and excessive mucus are two common problems attributable to water disease. Water disease is associated with the kidneys. Goreisan is the fundamental herbal tea remedy.

WHOOPING COUGH
(see Respiratory Ailments)

WORMS AND PARASITES

This is a big problem in America today. Many people are losing vitality to worms and parasites without even knowing it. Such persons have a good appetite and eat well, but are underweight and lack a glowing complexion.

The following are symptoms of parasites: bluish color in the whites of the eyes; hard, brittle fingernails that curve outwards; itching in the anal area.

When these symptoms are present, parasites must be eliminated. For those people who have a relatively strong constitution, a breakfast consisting of one handful of raw brown rice is recommended for a week or so. This is digestible if it is chewed very well. Parasites, on the other hand, can derive nothing from it. At lunch and dinner regular meals can be taken, but meat and sugar must be avoided. Fasting is not desirable, for it can lead later to overeating, a major hindrance in getting rid of worms.

Mugwort tea is also highly effective in expelling worms and parasites. The mugwort may also be eaten in the form of mochi (see "Food Is Best Medicine"). Buckwheat, prepared in any of the usual ways, is effective as well. Spiderwort and pumpkin seeds are good foods to take during this time.

A very effective tea for the elimination of worms is Sanmishakosaito, known as Three Taste Tea. Its ingredients are shakosai, licorice and daio. This tea should be taken three times a day, at least half an hour before meals. If after one week the parasites still linger, try Jewel's Tea (Renju-in) or Ryokubangan. [17]

---

[17] The recipe for this tea is not in this book.

THE DAILY BREAD

THIS BOOK would not be complete were it not crowned with a chapter on bread. We, here in Binghamton, have bread on the table almost daily. We may not eat it every day, but it is always available to everyone. It is necessary that we share with you what we treasure so much.

Most of us, perhaps because of the lack of quality in present-day bread, like to imagine what the bread of our ancestors was like. The reasons for its superior quality are many, one of them being the serious attention the women gave to the grinding of the flour, the kneading and baking. Bread was the staff of life that gave life; therefore, its preparation was a sacred act which women took pleasure in performing.

Bread gathered the family around the table. A table without bread was no table at all! Bread appeased hunger; it was enough then, when man was less demanding. Now, man's descendant has surrounded himself with material wealth and is reluctant to place brown bread over the light blue napkin in the pink dining room. It seems that modern man does not make value judgments according to true worth, but rather according to form and color, unconsciously rejecting a dark-colored bread because it does not blend with the fine décor. What meets his standard of living is what has been chosen for him as being the fastest, most pleasant, and easiest food to eat. Today's food is produced to please the busy housewife who "has no time" to cook and bake. It is a bouquet for the lazy cook and a banquet for the ignorant one.

The "accordion" bread in today's supermarkets is no bread at all. Foreigners who first see it have to read the word "Bread" to believe what it is. Bread in the U.S. has more looks than nourishment, more vitamin additives than flour. Press it and it releases a pound of air; let it sit a few weeks and it turns into an orange powder, making you wonder if it was made with any flour at all. Its consequences are heavier than its weight in flour. No one has ever chewed it. Some people like to use it when they shave—to stop the bleeding. Some eat it!

A loaf of white, pre-sliced bread has nothing to offer but division. It stimulates one to eat fast, leaving no room for appreciation. Homemade bread has the opposite effect, bringing warmth and unity to the table and inspiring gratitude. The breaking and partaking of homemade bread actualizes the desire to share with others what one possesses.

There are countries in which the main food still is bread, with a little something on the side. Moroccans eat it with olives—that makes their meal. It is a complete food which, when prepared properly, has a familiar taste, texture and aroma that many of us "remember" to be the best.

Good bread is capable by itself of keeping away the psychiatrist, so much warmth and togetherness does it bring to the home.

Bread often proves excellent for anemia, increasing stamina and building good quality cells. Bread made with fresh, unrefined flour is naturally rich in vitamins, particularly B vitamins, and in proteins and minerals—in short, rich enough to satisfy all the nutritional requirements of the average man.

To ensure that your bread is of the best quality, either grind the flour yourself or buy it fresh at your local natural food store. Flour should be used within 48 hours of being ground. Fresh whole wheat flour is an excellent base for bread; the finer it is ground, the easier it is to digest. To obtain the most from bread, chew it well. You will then have made it one of the best of foods.

There are various kinds of bread, each one ideally suited to a specific climate and individual temperament. It takes little to vary the quality of bread—with the lessening or increasing of any one of the ingredients (flour, water, yeast), the bread becomes either hard, spongy, or moist. The elimination of yeast makes it hard; the addition of yeast makes it spongy; an increase in water makes it moist—depending, of course, on the baking time. The different kinds of flour produce totally different tastes. A mixture of flours produces a rich taste and a special texture. To get the best out of the dough, you will sometimes have to knead it longer than at other times. The determining factors are the quality of the flour and yeast, the room temperature, or simply the method of kneading. Batter bread is not kneaded at all, but simply stirred (with a wooden spoon, preferably, to avoid a sour taste).

Sourdough bread is the healthiest because it contains enzymes which aid in the digestion of starch. Yeast contains sugar; thus, yeasted bread is difficult for many people to digest.

Here is some advice which will help you succeed in making good bread:

Always mix the flour with the *starter* (see below) and sprinkle on the necessary amount of salt *before* pouring in the water. Add the water slowly. The warmer the climate, the cooler the water should be.

To obtain a good rising, knead the dough, pressing out from the center. The more you knead, the better the bread will be, especially when wheat flour is being used. Kneading brings out the gluten.

A preheated pan needs less oil; oil spreads faster on a heated surface. This is a helpful hint for people who prefer to restrict their oil intake. Oil makes bread tastier and keeps it from drying out too fast, but a teaspoon or so is sufficient.

The most important ingredient in bread is the attitude with which it is made. If you knead the dough with anger, your feelings will show up in the finished product. Care and care alone—along with some flour, water and salt—can make the best of breads.

The Starter

Using a starter is an easy and most valuable practice. The starter substitutes for yeast. While it makes the bread rise, it does not contain sugar and therefore produces bread that is much more digestible than yeasted bread.

The basic starter recipe is:

> 3 heaping tablespoons unbleached white flour
> 5 tablespoons water

Mix with a spoon to form a paste. Cover the bowl with a paper towel (to absorb excess humidity) and then with a plate (to keep the mixture warm). Let sit at room temperature for two to three days. When the starter bubbles and has a more liquid consistency, it is ready and should be used right away.

Set aside one tablespoon of the starter; add the remainder to the bread you are preparing. The remaining tablespoon may be used as a basis for your next starter. Follow the same procedure, but do not allow subsequent starters to sit as long as the first one. They should be ready within one or two days. The starter should be used and replaced regularly, or it will turn sour.

Here are some other possible starter combinations:

1. whole wheat flour, water, and a pinch of salt

2. whole wheat flour, noodle water, salt, and cooked rice

3. whole wheat flour, salt, and chickpea water (water from boiled chickpeas)

4. miso and water combined with equal proportions of whole wheat flour and rye flour

A very common practice is to simply take a portion of already-risen dough, set aside in a covered bowl, and use it as the starter for the next day's batch of bread. Some people use this same process for years at a time. Since they never break the chain, every loaf of bread is an extension of the last; it is all the same bread.

The Flour

You may try any flour combinations you wish. Be careful only that you don't use too many different kinds of flour at the same time—three is the maximum. Whole wheat flour, which is high in gluten and the richest in vitamins, minerals and protein, is the usual basic ingredient. A little whole wheat pastry or unbleached white flour is often used to make the bread smoother in texture and easier to digest.

Here are some possible flour combinations:

1. 50% whole wheat flour
   25% cooked rice (or rice flour, or any soft-shelled grain)
   25% corn flour (not too coarse)

2. ⅔ whole wheat flour
   ⅓ whole wheat pastry or unbleached white flour

3. 50% whole wheat flour
   25% corn flour (or rye, barley or oat flour)
   25% whole wheat pastry or unbleached white flour

Do not eat the bread until it has cooled.

CHEW WELL!

FOOD STORE DIRECTORY

ALABAMA

Huntsville: Foods For Life Inc.
Montgomery: Aldridge Natural Foods
Tuscaloosa: The Health Food Store
Wilmer: Southern Organic Inc.

ALASKA

Anchorage: The Carob Tree
   Super Natural Foods Store

ARIZONA

Casa Grande: Natural Health Foods
Flagstaff: Cedar Pines Vitality Health
Kingman: Sones Health Foods
Phoenix: Guru's Grainery
Tempe: Gentile Strength Co-Op
Tucson: Aquarian Farmary
   The Granary
   New Age Health Foods
   The Sacred Road

ARKANSAS

Fayetteville: Fayetteville Co-Op
Hot Springs: Reader's Health Food
   Center
Little Rock: Health Unlimited

CALIFORNIA

Antioch: Chuck's Whole Foods
Arcata: Whole Earth Natural Foods
Auburn: Down to Earth
Berkeley: Co-Op Natural Foods
   Food Conspiracy
   Good Natured Foods
   Infinity Foods
   Ma Revolution Natural Foods
   Westbrae Natural Foods
   Wholly Foods
Big Sur: The Grain Man
   Vetana Natural Foods
Boulder Creek: Mr. Natural
Brookdale: Brookdale Grocery and
   Natural Patch
Burlingame: Earthbeam Natural Foods
Calexico: Earthbeam
Calistoga: Iyi Natural Foods
Carmel: General Store
Central Point: Table Rock Natural
   Foods
Chico: Chico-San, Inc.
   Etidorhpa Natural Foods
Cloverdale: Oasis
Corte Madera: Co-Op Basic Food Shop
Costa Mesa: The Granary
Cupertino: Cupertino Natural Foods
Dana Point: Mother Nature's Market
Davis: Natural Food Works
Eldorado County: The Apple Tree
   Astral Pavilion
Elsinore: The Country Store
Encinitas: Fresh Earth
Escondido: Escondido Nutrition Center
   Health Cottage
Eureka: Sun Harvest Natural Foods
Fairfax: Good Earth
Fallbrook: Eden Acres Farm
   Fallbrook Farms Store
Felton: Felton Health Foods
Forest Knolls: House of Richard Natural Foods
Ft. Bragg: Co-Op Natural Foods

Fresno: Ombilical Cord Natural Foods
   The Yoga Center
Garberville: Evergreen Natural Foods
Glen Ellen: Faith and Company
Glendale: Sunset Natural Foods
Guerneville: The Food Store
Laguna Beach: Country Store
   Mother Nature's Market
   Serendip Natural Foods
   Springtime Natural Foods
Larkspur: Boogie Bakery
   Larkspur Natural Foods
Leucadia: Leucadia Health Foods
Long Beach: The Artery
   Tao Natural Foods
   The Umbilical Chord
   The Vegetable Garden
   The Wheat Berry

Los Angeles Area

Hollywood: Back to Eden
   The Store
Los Angeles: Aunt Tillies
   Bergman's
   Erewhon Trading Co.
   Golden Carrot
   H.E.L.P. Unlimited
   My Brother's Keeper
   Patton's
   Purity Natural Grocery Vegetarian
      Market
   The Radiant Radish
   Sunrise Natural Foods
   Vegetable City Organic Food Service
   Cactus Ranch
   The Good Life
   Toluca Lake Natural Foods
   The Food Chakra
   Nature's Health Cove
Venice: Back to Eden
   New Parts

Los Gatos: Good Earth Nutrition
Martinez: Creation
Marysville: Bread of Life
Menlo Park: Earth Sign Natural Foods
Mill Valley: Golden Valley Market
Montara: Orangetree Natural Foods
Monterey: New Family Food
Napa: Hoe-Down Natural Foods

Nevada City: Good Morning Natural
   Foods
Oakland: Cornucopia
   The Food Mill
   The People's Alternative
Ojai: The Natural Spot
Palo Alto: New Age Natural Foods Inc.
Paradise: Paradise Natural Foods
Point Arena: Dandelion Natural Foods
Quincy: People's Natural Food Store
Redding: New Harvest Natural Foods
Sacramento: Country Way Natural Foods
   Sacramento Real Food Co.
San Anselmo: Campo Lindo
   Everybody's Natural Foods
San Diego: Hap and Glenda's Natural
   Foods
   Pleasant House Natural Foods
San Francisco: Ace Hi Foods for Health
   Agape Natural Food Co.
   Arko Natural Foods
   Baptiste Natural Foods
   Bernie's Farmers Market
   Farmer's Market Arcade
   Farmer's Produce
   Golden Road Natural Foods
   Helios Natural Foods
   Hunza
   Integral Yoga Natural Foods
   Naturally High
   Nature's Gifts Natural Foods
   New Age Natural Foods Inc.
   San Francisco Herb and Natural Food
      Co.
   Stanyan Street Natural Foods
   Thom's Natural Foods
   Union Natural Foods
San Jose: Christananda Natural Foods
   The Old Possum
   Sun and Soil Natural Foods
San Luis Obispo: New Morning Foods
San Mateo: Organic Porcupine Natural
   Foods
San Rafael: San Rafael Health Foods

Santa Barbara Area

Isla Vista: Sun and Earth Natural Foods
Santa Barbara: Aloha Natural Foods
   Nature's Prophet
   The Settlement

* *

TEAS

Most of the stores listed here carry the products mentioned in this book, except for the teas, which can be ordered from the following three companies:

West Coast

HERB TEA COMPANY, 440 Judah, San Francisco, Ca. 94122
LONG LIFE, P.O. Box 6581, San Francisco, Ca. 94101

East Coast

THE THREE SHEAVES, 95 Hudson St., N.Y., N.Y. 10013

* *

Santa Cruz: Good Medicine Natural
   Foods
   Santa Cruz Co-Op
   Sun Flower Natural Foods
   Way of Life
   Webb's Organic Farm
Santa Rosa: Organic Groceries
Saratoga: Cereal City Health Foods
   Zach's Natural Foods
Sausalito: Rock Island Line
Sebastopol: Atlantis One
Solana Beach: People's Food
Soquel: Mr. Natural Food Store
South Lake Tahoe: Best In Life Health
   Food Store
Tahoe City: Tahoe City Health Foods
   Tahoe Real Food Co.
Ukiah: The Corner Store

COLORADO

Aspen: Return to Earth Health Bar
Boulder: Green Mountain Grainery
   Lefflers Natural Foods
   New Age Foods
Breckenridge: Amazing Grace Abun-
   dant Life Center
   Joyous Revival Health Foods
Carbondale: R.F. Crystal Co.
Colorado Springs: Colorado Springs
   Natural Foods
   Green Mountain Grainery
Crested Butte: Hara Natural Foods
Denver: Aquarian Age Natural Foods
   The Grainery
   Mustard Seeds Natural Foods
   Village Idiot
   Whole Earth Natural Foods
Durango: Durango Health and Bible
   Center
Fort Collins: The Seed
Gardner: Greenhorn Farm
Grand Junction: Healthway Foods
Paonia: Turtle Health Foods
Pueblo: Sunshine Health Foods
Steamboat Springs: People Feed

CONNECTICUT

Bantam: Prospect Mountain Farm
Bridgeport: Natural Organic Foods
   Nature Food Centers of Connecticut
   Inc.
Danbury: 4 Seasons Health Foods
   Nature's Cupboard
   Whole Earth Health Foods
Danielson: Kenbar Acres Natural Foods
Greenwich: Healthwell Natural Food
   Shop
Groton: Horn of Plenty
Guilford: The Alternative
Hartford: Good Food Store
   Nature Shoppe
Kensington: Nature's Harvest
Killingly: Kenbar Acres
Mansfield: Not by Bread Alone
New Haven: Natural Organic Foods
   Our Food Shop
New London: The 5th Season
Norwalk: Norwalk Natural Foods
Ridgefield: Vital Vittles
Westport: Colonial Healthways Inc.
   Earth's Bounty
   Four Seasons Farm Inc.
   Organic Market
Wilton: Evergreen Good Food Co.
   Natural Living Center

Wilsted: Elmbrook Farm
Woodbury: New Morning Trading Co.

FLORIDA

Clearwater: Alternative Vittles
Daytona Beach: Nutrition Center
Ft. Lauderdale: Coral Ridge Natural
   Foods
   Gateway Natural Foods
   Scarborough's Health Food Store
Fort Pierce: Berry's Health Food Center
Gainesville: Mother Earth
Jacksonville: Nutrition Center

Miami Area

Coconut Grove: Oak Feed Store
Miami: The Come Together Natural
   Food Shopper
   Nature's Own
Miami Beach: Carrot Patch, Inc.
North Miami: Life Natural Foods
Ocala: Reeser Health Foods
Orlando: Chamberlain Natural Foods
Pensacola: Feedbag General Store
Pompano Beach: Dandelions Unlim-
   ited
St. Augustine: Tree of Life Natural
   Foods
St. Petersburg: Tree of Life Natural
   Foods
Tallahassee: Second Story Shop
Tampa: Keepwell Nutrition Center
West Palm Beach: General Nutrition
   Center

GEORGIA

Athens: Ad Infinitum
Atlanta: Aquarian Health Food
   Atlanta Nutrition Center
   The Egg and the Lotus
   The Good Earth
   New Morning Food Co-Op
Columbus: Staff O' Life Food Store
Macon: Valentine's Health Foods
Sandy Springs: The Good Earth

HAWAII

Haleiwa: Haleiwa Natural Foods
Hilo: Fourth World General Store and
   Restaurant
Honolulu: The Good Earth
Lahaina (Maui): Incite
Wailuku (Maui): Jamar Health Foods

IDAHO

Boise: Good Medicine General Store
Fruitland: Foods for Health Store
Idaho Falls: Wilma's Natural Foods
Ketchum: Wood River Natural Foods
Lewiston: Lewiston Health Food Center
Moscow: Pilgrim's Natural Foods
   Seeds of Harmony
Mountain Home: J-F Natural Foods
Pocatello: Cottage Health Foods
   The Organic Grocery
Sandpoint: Dharma
Twin Falls: The Sta-Well

ILLINOIS

Bloomington: Alice's Health Foods
Carbondale: Mr. Natural Foodstore
Chicago: The Family
   Food For Life
   The Growth and Life Store
   Kramers Health Food Store

   New Life
   Sun and Earth Natural Foods
Elmhurst: Food For Life
Lawrenceville: Medlins Natural Foods
McNabb: Halbleib Organic Farm
Rock Island: Vegetable Brothers
South Beloit: Scratching Chicken Nat-
   ural Food Shop
Urbana: Earthworks Earthfoods

INDIANA

Bloomington: The Clear Moment
Chesterfield: A & B Natural Foods
Indianapolis: Good Earth Natural Food
   Store
   Grepke Health Mart
   Moore Natural Foods
Millerburg: Lone Organic Farm

IOWA

Ames: Sunrise Foodstore
Cedar Falls: The Food Trip
Comanche: Aquarian Natural Foods
Davenport: Good Earth Food Store
Des Moines: Campbell Foods
   Earth
   Earth Natural Foods
   Wonder Life Natural Foods
Iowa City: Bowery General
   New Pioneers Co-Op Society

KANSAS

Lawrence: The Mercantile
Leavenworth: Loyd Fight
Salina: Nyles Nutrition Square
Topeka: Health Food Store
   Sunshine House

KENTUCKY

Covington: Dandelions Unlimited
Louisville: General Nutrition Corp.
Owensboro: Natural Food Store

LOUISIANA

New Orleans: Fine Foods
   Something Beautiful
   Sunshine Workshop
Shreveport: Eartherial Trade Co.
   Fresh Earth Foods

MAINE

Bangor: Seven Seas
Brunswick: Hunts Health Foods
Gorham: Feeding Acres Natural
   Organic Food
Lewiston: Axis Natural Foods, Inc.
Portland: Model Food
Rockland: Root Cellar
Wiscasset: Health Food Store

MARYLAND

Annapolis: Sun & Earth Natural Foods
Baltimore: Good Earth
   Miss Fannie L. Harn
   Sunshine Food Restaurant and Co-Op
College Park: Beautiful Day Trading
   Co.
Glen Burnie: Nature's Cupboard of Love
Mt. Rainier: Glut Food Co-Op
Oakland: Eli A. Yoder's Organic Farm
Ocean City: Sundance Brotherhood

MASSACHUSETTS

Amherst: Whole Wheat Trading Co.
Boston: Erewhon Natural Foods

Massachusetts (continued)
Food Conspiracy
The Good Food Store
Brighton: Life Foods
Cambridge: Attar
The Corners of the Mouth
Orson Welles Food and Grain Co-Op
Rising Earth
Walden Organic Market
Whole Earth Resource Co., Inc.
Chatham: Chatham Natural Food
Market
Life Naturganic Food Market
Concord: Concord Spice and Grain
Falmouth: Mother Earth
Fitchburg: Blossom Street Market
Pure & Simple Natural Foods
Framingham: The Life Preserver
Stern's Farm
Hyannis: Wholly Earth Foods
Leominster: The Source Natural Foods
Marblehead: Marblehead Natural Foods
Maynard: The Alchemist
Milford: House of Natural Foods
Montague: Asparagus Valley Co.
New Bedford: Natural Food Market
North Attleboro: Natural Health Foods
Northampton: The Granary
Oak Bluffs: Good Food Club
Osterville: Cape Cod Health Food
Center
Pittsfield: A.E. Hecker Natural Foods
Provincetown: Earth Foods
South Egremont: The Sunflower Co.
Wayland Centre: Wholefoods Trading
Co.
West Newton: New Life Health Foods
Westfield: Red Owl
Whitman: Natural Food Center
Williamstown: Cold Mountain Co-Op
Worcester: Bread Basket
Living Earth
Nature Food Center

MICHIGAN

Ann Arbor: Eden Organic
Organic Food Co-Op
People's Food Co-Op
Battle Creek: Country Acres Bakery and
Natural Food Shop
Birmingham: Joyous Revival

Detroit Area

Berkley: Eartharvest Natural Foods
Detroit: Eden Trading
Incredible Edibles
Highland Park: Sauer's Vita Health
Rochester: Vita Mill
Royal Oak: Nutri-Foods

Grand Rapids: Harvest Health Inc.
Kalamazoo: Sun Traditional Foods
East Lansing: Family of Man, Inc.
Lansing: Randall Health Foods
Livonia: Zerbo's Foods
Orchard Lake: The Carrot Patch
Saginaw: General Nutrition Corp.

MINNESOTA

Minneapolis: Cayol Natural Foods
Foods for Life
North Country Co-Op
Shaktih Organic Foods
Tao Traditional Organic Foods
Whole Foods

St. Paul: Health Food Center
St. Paul Food Co-Op

MISSISSIPPI

Jackson: The Grainary

MISSOURI

Clayton: Clayton Natural Foods
Columbia: Columbia Food Co-Op
Kansas City: Community Food Co-Op
The Granary
Health Food Haven
Prichards Mill
St. Joseph: Holswon Health Food Store
Riverbluff Mill & Grocery
Ferguson: Al Mueller's Organic Farm
St. Louis: Angelo Russo
Chrysalis
Community Collectives
Morning Dew Organic Foods
New-Dawn Natural Foods
Staff of Life
Springfield: Evans Health Studio

MONTANA

Billings: Bonanza Health Foods
Good Earth Foods
Schroeders Health Food Center
Missoula: The Good Food Store
High Mountain General Store and
Restaurant
Mr. Natural

NEBRASKA

Brownsville: Brownsville Mills
Kearney: Specialty Foods
Lincoln: Dirt Cheap
Omaha: Mother Earth

NEVADA

Carson City: DuBois Health Center
Las Vegas: Buddy's Health Food
Food For Thought

NEW HAMPSHIRE

Alstead: New England People's Co-Op
Alstead Center: The Source
Barrington: Calef's Country Store Inc.
Concord: Granite State Natural Foods
Stone Ground Soul Food
Greenville: Brookwood Ecology Center
Keene: Erewhon Farms Store
Laconia: Natural Foods
Lancaster: The Source
Lebanon: Honey Gardens
Manchester: Bonne Sante Natural Foods
Uncle Dave's Growing Team
Milford: Return to Earth
Moultonboro: The Old Country Store
Nashua: Center of Aquarius Health
Foods
Return to Earth
Portsmouth: Up Front Organic Market
Tuftonboro: Pier 19 Natural Foods

NEW JERSEY

Elizabeth: Natro Health Foods
Englishtown: Pumpkin Seed Point
Madison: Food For Thought
Millington: Reed Bridge Organics
Montclair: Montclair Health Food
Centre
New Brunswick: Back to the Garden
Health Food Store
Garden of Eden

Paramus: Basic Health Center
Plainfield: ABC Health Foods
Princeton: Nature's Best
Whole Earth Center of Princeton
Rutherford: Third Day
Teaneck: Aquarius Natural Food Center
Back to Nature
Tenafly: Healthway International
Wildwood: Back to Earth

NEW MEXICO

Albuquerque: Fountain of Health
Osha
Shala-Min Natural Foods Store
Farmington: Bite-O-Life
Las Vegas: Old Town Natural Foods
Santa Fe: Age of the Sun
Riggs

NEW YORK

Albany: Earth Food
The Store
Binghamton: Off Center
Buffalo: Allentown Foods Co-Op
Hildegard's Health Foods
Lexington Real Food Co-Op
North Buffalo Community Coopera-
tive
O'Toole's Health Food Store
Chatham: The Main Street Granary
No. 1
Guilford: Deer Valley Farm & Country
Store
Hudson: Sun Natural Food
Ithaca: Ithaca Food Conspiracy
Johnson City: Belly of the Whale
Dorothy's Natural Food Shop
Lake Grove: Down to Earth
Levittown: Levittown Diet & Health
Foods Center
Margarettville: The Store
Middletown: Unison
Monticello: Movement
New Paltz: Good Food—Natural Home
Cooking
The Real Food Store
Niagara Falls: Niagara Health Food
Center

New York City Area

Bronx: Bio-Organic, Inc.
Brooklyn: Garden of Eden
Nature's Nest
Quite Naturally Health Foods
Manhattan: A-1 Health Foods Corp.
Bountiful Acres
The Brickyard, Ltd.
Brownie's Natural Foods
The Cauldron's Well
Food Liberation
Good Earth Natural Foods
Good Shepherd Cereal Co.
Gramercy Natural Food Center
Greenberg's Natural Foods
Mother Nature and Sons, Ltd.
Natural Foods
Integral Yoga Institute Natural Foods
Kubies
Living Foods Co-Op, Inc.
Mr. Natural Comes to the City
Nature's Cupboard
New Health Foods
Organic Deliveries, Inc.
Panacea
Pete's Spice and Everything Nice

Prince Wooster Health Foods Store
Sunny Health Foods
Super Natural Foods
Tilly's
Whole Earth Provisions
Wild Rice
Winter House (Summer House)
Queens: Forest Gardens Health Foods
Guru Health Foods
Organic Energy Co-Op
Rego Park Health Foods Supermarket
Sumline Health Foods
Spa Health Foods, Inc.
Staten Island: Gericke's Organic Farm

Pelham: Middle Earth Organic Food Co.
Poughkeepsie: Harmony Foods
Rochester: Genesse Co-Op
The Health Food Company
Rome: Staff of Life Natural Foods
Roslyn: Never When, Inc.
Saratoga Springs: Saratoga Traders
Scarsdale: Mother Nature's Nutrition Centers
Schenectady: Eco-Symbio Co-Op
Spring Valley: Threefold Corner
Sugar Loaf: Juniper Farm Whole Wheat Products
Syracuse: Healthful Diet Shoppe, Inc.
Walkill: Good Seed
Woodstock: Rainbow Farms Food Co-Op
Sunflower
Woodstock's Health Foods

NORTH CAROLINA

Asheville: Good Health Food Store
Boone: The Green Revolution
Carrboro: Harmony: The Natural Food Store
Chapel Hill: Earth Inc.
Charlotte: Care Food & Bakery
Durham: Natural Nutrition
Greenville: Sunrise Health Foods
Winston-Salem: Friends of the Earth

NORTH DAKOTA

Fargo: Pioneer Specialty Foods

OHIO

Akron: Alexander Health Foods
Athens: Farmacy
Berea: Back to Eden
Bowling Green: Food For Thought
Cincinnati: Earth's Bounty
Eden Natural Foods
Natural Life Health Foods
Wholesome Earth
Cleveland Heights: The Food Project
Columbus: Morningstar Organic Foods
Dayton: Olympia Nature Foods
Hubbard: Quimby's Organic Gardens and Nutrition Center
Kent: Kent Natural Foods
Lima: General Nutrition Corp.
Marion: Nichols Health Foods
Oberlin: Good Foods Co-Op
Somerville: Wildwood Acres Natural Food Store
Toledo: Dietrich's
Yellow Springs: Real Good Food Co-Op
Youngstown: Natural Health Foods

OKLAHOMA

Norman: The Earth
Oklahoma City: Nutritional Food Center
Skiatook: Great Plains Naurtal Foods Distributors
Tulsa: Earl's Health Store
Nature's Cupboard

OREGON

Albany: Nichol's Garden Nursery
Ashland: Ashland People's Food Co-Op
Friends of the Earth
Twin Oaks Natural Food Store
Bend: Van's Natural Foods
Canyonville: The Burris Bunch Organic Specialty House
Central Point: Rogue Valley Natural Foods
Corvallis: 1st Alternative
Penny's Natural Foods
Scott's Natural Foods
Eugene: Scarborough Faire
Sundance Natural Foods Store
Vital Food Shop
Williamette People's Food Co-Op
Grants Pass: Albertson's Food Center
Field of Merits Natural Foods
Merricks Natural Foods
Klamath Falls: Natural Food Center
Lake Oswego: Miro's Bakery & Health Foods
Medford: Monn's Health Foods
Newport: Good Things Natural Foods & Restaurant
Portland: Food Front Co-Op
Friends & Food
Good Earth Foods, Inc.
King's Harvest Natural Foods
Nature's Table
People's Food Store
Sunshine Natural Foods & Gates of Eden
Roseburg: Roseburg Natural Foods
Salem: Lawson's Natural Foods
Springfield: The Health Food & Pool Store
The Dalles: Mother Earth Trading Co.
Wonder: Wonder Natural Food Store

PENNSYLVANIA

Allentown: Queen's Nutritional Products
Bryn Mawr: Satori
Chaddsford: Pennyfeather Sunshine Natural Foods
Coatesville: Snowhill Farm Natural Foods Market
Erie: General Nutrition Center
Federicksburg: Sangerdale Farms
King of Prussia: Martindale's Health Foods
Lancaster: Natural Foods
Lansdale: North Penn Health Food Center
Penns Creek: Walnut Acres
Philadelphia: Chestnut Hills Natural Foods & Nutrition Center
Concept Natural Foods
Essene
Your Brothers' Natural and Organic Food Center
Good Earth Natural Foods
New Life Natural Foods Co.
Reading: Home of Natural Foods
Natural Foods Store

Richardtown: Buck's County Natural Food Center
Southampton: Bunn's Natural Foods
State College: Dandelion Market
Youngberg's General Store

PUERTO RICO

Santurce: The Trading Post

RHODE ISLAND

Kingston: Alternative Co-Op
Newport: The Good Earth
Providence: Church of the Mediator Food Co-Op
One Clear Grain
Woonsocket: Cass Avenue Health Center

SOUTH CAROLINA

Charleston: Sunshine Health Foods
Greenville: Natural Food Center
Summerville: God's Green Acre

SOUTH DAKOTA

Sioux Falls: Wayne and Mary's Nutritional Center

TENNESSEE

Knoxville: Honeycomb
Honeycomb Natural Foods
Knoxville Community Whole Foods Co-Op
Natural Foods
Natural and Organic Foods
Sunflower Health Store
Memphis: Good Life Natural Health Foods
Whole Foods General Store
Nashville: Mother Nature's Cupboard
New Morning Organic Food Store

TEXAS

Abilene: Natural Food Center
Austin: Eat's Natural Foods
Good Food Store
Good Food Store North
29th Street Food Store
Big Spring: Big Spring Health Food Center
Corpus Christi: Natural Foods & Country Store
Dallas: Health Food Cottage
Roy's Nutrition Centers
Denton: Family Feed Store and Family Village Garden Ice
Shree Gurudev Siddha Yoga Ashram and Kosmic Kitchen
Hereford: Arrowhead Mills Deaf Smith County Grains
Houston: Green Acres Organic Foods
Moveable Feast
Nassau Bay Natural Foods
Staff of Life Natural Foods
Tao Whole Foods
Longview: Health Food Store
New Braunfels: Gardenville
Odessa: Health Food Center
San Angelo: Natural Foods
San Antonio: More Natural Foods
Pure Food & Health Store
Tyler: A-1 Health Foods
Ogden: Goddard's Health Food Mart
Provo: Scheibner's Health Center
Salt Lake City: Gwaltney's Natural Foods

VERMONT

Bennington: Gingerbread House
Brattleboro: The Good Life
   Guilford Country Store
   Natural Universe
Burlington: Solanaceae Natural Foods
Manchester Center: Tree of Life
McIndoe Falls: McIndoe Falls Inn
Middlebury: Om Natural Health Foods
Newport: Green Mountain Natural
   Foods
Plainfield: Earth Artisan Co.
Poultney: Wholemeal
Putney: Bungaree Natural Foods
Ripton: Ripton Country Store, Inc.
Rutland: Cold River Natural Foods
South Burlington: Mother Nature's Natural Foods
St. Johnsbury: Hatch!
Stockbridge: Tweedmeadow
Stowe: The Good Life, Inc.
   Mother Nature's Food Store
Westminster: Bungaree Natural Foods
Weston: Tamarack Farm, Mill and
   Bakery
Wilmington: Natural Foods

VIRGINIA

Alexandria: Nature's Harvest
Arlington: Khanna Enterprises
Charlottesville: Sylvania Organic Foods
Fredericksburg: Good Earth Foods
Hamilton: The Natural Mercantile
   Store
Lexington: Shenandoah Valley Natural
   Foods
Newport News: Garden of Allah
Richmond: The Organic Food Company
Springfield: Kennedy's Natural Foods
Virginia Beach: Cosmo Barbiere
   Earth Food Restaurant
   Natural Foods Store

WASHINGTON

Bellevue: Cook's Nutrition Center
   Nature's Pantry
Bellingham: Community Food Co-Op
Enumclaw: Rainier Institute
Everett: Everett Health Foods
   The Golden Flower
Ferndale: Terri's Bread Farm
Friday Harbor: Gourmet's Galley

Olympia: Health-Way Food Center
Port Angeles: Golden Age Foods
Post Townsend: The Food Co-Op
Seattle: Ballard Natural Foods
   Capitol Hill Co-Op
   Cerealia
   Erewhon Trading Co.
   Genesis Natural Foods
   Growing Family Natural Foods
   Henry & Henry Natural Foods
   Janus Natural Foods Inc.
   New Morning Natural Foods
   Pilgrim's Natural Food Gallery
   Puget Consumer's Co-Op
   Pilgrim's Natural Food Gallery
   Rising Sun
Spokane: The Store
Tacoma: Harvest Natural Foods
   Tacoma Natural Foods Co-Op
Van Zandt: Everybody's Store
Winslow: Soybeans and Such Natural
   Foods
Woodinville: Fertile Earth Foods
Yakima: The Golden Hoard

WASHINGTON, D.C.

Gazang Organic Groceries
Yes!, Inc.

WEST VIRGINIA

Charleston: Foods for Life, Inc.
Morgantown: Natural Foods Store

WISCONSIN

Beloit: Scratching Chicken Natural
   Food Health Shoppery
   Schwartz's Natural Foods
Brookfield: Down to Earth of Brook-
   field Square
Fort Atkinson: Oakland Center Organic
   Store
Green Bay: Bay Natural Foods
Madison: Common Market
   Concordance Natural Foods
   Mifflin Street Co-Op

WYOMING

Casper: Wyoming Natural Foods
Laramie: The Whole Earth Granary &
   Truck Store
Wilson: Eleanor Onyon's Here and Now
   Natural Foods

CANADA

Aberta

Edmonton: Natural Health Centre Ltd.

British Coumbia

Alert Bay: Sun and Seed Natural Foods
Brentwood Bay: Whole Grains and
   Foods
Burnaby: Manna Natural Foods
   The Source of Happiness
Golden: Sundance Natural Foods
Harrogate: Sundance Natural Foods
Vancouver: Lifestream Natural Foods
   The Natural Food Store
   Nature's Path
   Shum Organic Foods
Victoria: Earth Household Natural
   Foods
   Logical Health Foods
   Sunyata Natural Foods
   The Vegetable

Manitoba

Winnipeg: Earth People

Ontario

Hamilton: Nu Vite Nutrition Centre
Ottawa: Globe Health Food Store
   Good Nature Natural Foods, Ltd.
   Pestalozzi Food Co-Op
   Raw Deal Health Foods
Peterboro: Sangsara Natural Foods and
   Crafts
Thunder Bay: The Corner Store
Toronto: Goldberry's Natural Health
   Food Store
   The Golden Ant
   Good Earth Natural Foods
   McMillan Health Center
   Oasis Health Foods
   Tree of Life Food Store
   Whole Earth Natural Foods

Quebec

Montreal: Cooperative D'Ailments
   Naturales et Macrobiotiques
   Macrobiotic Health Food Center of
   Canada
   Natural Food Co-Op

INDEX